# Preface and Acknowledgements

The origins of this book lie in a suggestion by Valerie Rose at Lund Humphries, namely that I might like to write about interesting contemporary theatres. The aim was a book focused on 'architectural practice', which might appeal to people designing or working in theatres, and similar kinds of building, as well as those with an interest in the conception, design, and delivery of contemporary public buildings. At the time, I was coming to the end of a lengthy project (and substantial book) on the history of British theatre architecture between the 1940s and the 1980s. The opportunity to spend time looking at more recent examples of a fascinating building type was too good to miss. As the project developed, we agreed that the research would lead to a book with an extended introduction and a series of case studies, comprising theatres realised or conceived during the last ten years. These case studies would document the original 'vision' for each project, the ways in which the 'vision' was developed, the fundraising process and the experience of construction, as well as the reception of the completed building (for those projects which had been completed at the time of writing).

In researching and writing *Play On*, I have been fortunate to be able to speak at length with many people involved in contemporary British theatre and its architecture. It has been a privilege to be able to have tours of the buildings, and for project documentation to be made available. I am enormously grateful to all the individuals and organisations who have helped. In particular, I would like to thank Anna Anderson, Deborah Aydon, David Beidas, Bill Black, Tom Clarke, Clare Clarkson, Alex Clifton, Paddy Dillon, Phil Eccles, Simon Erridge, Tim Foster, Louise Gittins, Robin Hawkes, Jane Hetherington, Paul Jozefowski, Judith Kilvington, John Langley, Vanessa Lefrancois, Graham Lister, Robert Longthorne, Andy Maddox, Claudia Mayer, Julian Middleton, Jon Morgan, Grahame Morris, James Nelmes, Stuart Parker, Alex Reedijk, Alan Rivett, Nick Starr, Tom Stickland, Graham Sutherland, Kully Thiarai, Ian Timms, Steve Tompkins, Robin Townley, Jatinder Verma, Nicola Walls, Roger Watts, and Gary Young.

At the University of Edinburgh, I am grateful to my colleagues for their encouragement (and for diverting coffee breaks), in particular Miles Glendinning, Ola Uduku, and Diane Watters. Edinburgh College of Art's Research, Knowledge Exchange & Outreach Fund helped with some of the research costs.

For their help in supplying images I am grateful to many people, not least the architects of the case study theatres, who went to considerable effort in locating drawings and photographs, and putting me in touch, where necessary, with photographers. For permission to reproduce images – often with a generous discount or without charge – I would like to thank Aedas Arts Team, Hélène Binet, Mark Carline, the Citizens Theatre, Peter Cook, Hawkins\Brown, Haworth Tompkins, Hufton + Crow, Keith Hunter, Sam Laughlin, LDN Architects, Andrew Lee, Page\Park, RIBA Collections, Richard Murphy Architects, Stanton Williams, John Turner, Philip Vile, Wilton's Music Hall, and Wright and Wright. Barnabas Calder very kindly took several photos of the Everyman, Liverpool, including the image which features on the cover of the book. Robert Proctor also deserves particular thanks for his photographs of Bristol Old Vic, as does Ola Uduku for an image of Home, Manchester.

At Lund Humphries, I would like to thank Valerie Rose for being an encouraging and enthusiastic editor. Pamela Bertram skilfully oversaw the production process, while Jacqui Cornish copyedited the text meticulously and was also responsible for the layout of the book.

Members of my family continue to take a welcome interest in my work, for which I am grateful. In particular, my parents, Mandy and Malcolm Fair, keep me well-supplied with press clippings and web stories about theatre architecture. At home, Anthony Catchpole has tolerated the incursion of yet another book into our life. As always, I am grateful to him for everything.

# List of Abbreviations

| | | | | |
|---|---|---|---|---|
| ACE | Arts Council England | | HLF | Heritage Lottery Fund |
| ACW | Arts Council of Wales | | NPV | (Doncaster) New Performance Venue |
| ATG | Ambassador Theatre Group | | NT | National Theatre |
| BREEAM | Building Research Establishment Environmental Assessment Method | | NTS | National Theatre of Scotland |
| CABE | Commission for Architecture and the Built Environment | | *OJEU* | *Official Journal of the European Union* |
| | | | RFO | Regularly Funded Organisation |
| CDM | Construction Design and Management Regulations | | RIAS | Royal Incorporation of Architects in Scotland |
| CW&C | Cheshire West and Chester Council | | RIBA | Royal Institute of British Architects |
| DMBC | Doncaster Metropolitan Borough Council | | RST | Royal Shakespeare Theatre |
| | | | STV | Scottish Television |

## A Note on Terminology:

During the period covered by this book, the RIBA produced a new 'Plan of Work', replacing the lettered workstages of 2007 with new, numbered workstages in 2013. These numbered workstages should not be confused with the similarly numbered milestones found in Arts Council England funding applications.

# Introduction

'If music be the food of love, play on', wrote William Shakespeare in *Twelfth Night*. 'Play On' is what theatre has done in the ten years since 2008, in spite of a recession and significant cuts in public expenditure. Indeed, not only has theatre 'played on', but the last decade has also seen some extraordinarily creative projects, in spite of (sometimes perhaps because of) the challenges of austerity. Notably, Liverpool's rebuilt Everyman Theatre won the prestigious Royal Institute of British Architects (RIBA) Stirling Prize in 2014, in effect recognising it as the best British building of the year and also, perhaps, making a statement of the value of 'public' architecture after several decades in which the collective and civic values of the post-war consensus have been challenged.

This book documents – and celebrates – Britain's contemporary theatre architecture. It is about the conception, design, and delivery of spaces and buildings for drama between *c.* 2008 and 2018, and will, I hope, be of interest to theatre enthusiasts, to those who design theatres and other complex buildings, and to individuals and organisations contemplating a capital project of their own. It is worth being clear at the outset about what the book is not. It is not a design guide, nor does it offer a list of dos and don'ts. Furthermore, it is not concerned with the specialised subjects of theatre equipment and technologies. *Play On* should be read alongside accounts which take a longer historical perspective,[1] especially those written by people active in theatre and its architecture,[2] as well as studies which examine theatre companies and their work,[3] theatre design guides,[4] and specialist technical literature.[5]

*Play On* is in two parts. The first part consists of three essays, while the second part comprises ten case studies. As far as the essays are concerned, the first briefly presents a history of British theatre architecture during the twentieth and early twenty-first centuries. It is followed by an overview of the financial and organisational context of contemporary British theatre. Finally, there is a narrative of the last decade in theatre architecture as a prelude to the case studies which follow. My approach to the case studies owes something to an earlier study, *Geometry and Atmosphere: Theatre Buildings from Vision to Reality*, published in 2011 and based on research carried out between 2004 and 2008.[6] That book, which I co-wrote with others, discussed five theatres of the late 1990s and early 2000s, drawing on the archive of each project as well as interviews with key members of the design and client teams. *Play On*'s case studies are likewise based on a close reading of project documents and interviews. They similarly explore questions of process and collaboration, and so challenge the often visual basis of contemporary architectural criticism. However, *Play On*'s case studies are shorter, partly because there are more of them and partly in recognition of the single-researcher nature of this project. Furthermore, my aims are slightly different. Whereas *Geometry and Atmosphere* investigated apparent failings in the design and procurement processes, my aim here is to give snapshot views of success, offering what might be called 'contemporary histories' of projects which seem to have something interesting to say. In this respect, there are parallels with the short case studies published between *c.* 2000 and 2010 by the former Commission for Architecture and the Built Environment (CABE), which documented the ideas that informed over 400 exemplary buildings as well as the processes by means of which these buildings were realised.[7]

The case studies are drawn from Britain, and specifically from England and Scotland. This is not to say that there are no interesting examples in Wales; some are discussed in the first part of the book. In addition, within the wider context of the

United Kingdom, major new arts buildings have been built in Northern Ireland, and these are also touched on briefly. Of course, theatre in Britain is rooted in a series of international contexts, too. British architecture is no hermetic thing, while people involved in theatre often work around the world. Nonetheless, despite the attraction of seeing and writing about interesting new theatres overseas, I have chosen to limit my focus. Partly, the reason was one of practicality. In a short time and a short book (and with a limited research budget), it would have been impossible to do justice to global theatre architecture. At the same time, it is my contention that theatre in Britain operates within specific organisational and financial circumstances: for example, the ways in which theatre is funded, often with a degree of public subsidy. (One might nonetheless argue that the use of the term 'Britain' risks skating over administrative and other differences between England, Wales, and Scotland, or, indeed, between the regions of each of these countries.)

In choosing the case studies, I wanted to explore the question: what is contemporary theatre architecture in Britain? The case studies give some idea of the different ways in which that question can be answered. Some of the theatres are large, some much smaller. Some are completely new, while others are refurbishments, an area which has been a significant focus of activity during the last decade. Of course, it is too soon to offer a considered historical analysis of any of these buildings. Indeed, some had not been completed at the time of writing in autumn 2018. Nonetheless, I hope that what follows offers a foundation on which future historians might build, whilst in the meantime giving an insight into the reality of contemporary theatre design.

# 1  Historical Context

At the start of the twentieth century, British theatre architecture was dominated by buildings designed by specialists such as C.J. Phipps (1835–97), W.G.R. Sprague (1863–1933), and especially Frank Matcham (1854–1920; fig. 1.1).[1] Often eclectic in their architectural style, these buildings were skilfully and efficiently planned. Theatres at that time were commercial enterprises which lived and died by the box office, and so it was essential to squeeze in as many seats as possible. The trick was to maximise the amount of the site given over to the auditorium, around which would be wrapped the numerous separate entrances, staircases, and foyers considered essential at a time when patrons who had bought cheap tickets were routinely segregated from their wealthier counterparts. Considerable design skill was also needed in the light of a growing emphasis on safety, evident not least in terms of fire precautions.[2]

1.1  Buxton Opera House, a classic 'Matcham' theatre of 1903, seen here in 1979

1.2 Shakespeare Memorial Theatre, Stratford-upon-Avon, the riverside elevation as originally completed to Elisabeth Scott's designs in 1932

The rise of cinema meant that fewer theatres were built during the 1920s and 1930s, although many cinemas were in fact constructed with sizeable stages and dressing rooms. Indeed, some cinema–theatre hybrids of this period now function as successful theatres: in London, for example, Ernest Wamsley Lewis' New Victoria (1930) is now the Apollo Victoria, a home for major musicals. Among those buildings constructed specifically for live drama, meanwhile, there was occasionally a degree of experimentation when it came to stage design. In 1926, for example, the Cambridge Festival Theatre was created within the shell of an older theatre. Its director, Terence Gray, dispensed with the proscenium arch which was then almost universally found in western theatre auditoria. This arch 'framed' the action on stage, which typically played out in settings designed to be as naturalistic as possible. In Cambridge, by contrast, actors and audience occupied the same 'room'. Not only that, but sets were made up from abstract stepped rostra of a kind which owed much to the contemporaneous experiments of Adolphe Appia and others in Germany. However,

this sort of innovation was rare, at least in Britain. The country's most prominent new theatre of the inter-war years, the Shakespeare Memorial Theatre at Stratford-upon-Avon (1932, fig. 1.2), retained the proscenium arch. Nonetheless, Elisabeth Scott's design could be understood to be 'modern' in other ways. For example, Scott emphasised functional considerations, giving the theatre a fan-shaped auditorium in which all the seats faced the stage essentially straight on, while its unadorned brick elevations were evocative of contemporary Dutch architecture.[3] However, the auditorium quickly became unpopular with many directors and actors, partly because of its proscenium arch and partly because some seats – especially in the gallery – were a long way from the stage. It was remodelled several times before being entirely reconstructed between 2007 and 2010.

After the Second World War, economic austerity and a focus on building for essential purposes only (e.g. housing) meant little theatre-building took place before the late 1950s. In the meantime, however, the context in which British theatre was organised and funded changed significantly. The second half of the 1940s saw the introduction of public subsidy for the performing arts, transforming what had hitherto been a commercial affair into something which could be regarded as the cultural arm of the emerging Welfare State. The foundation of the Arts Council of Great Britain in 1945 provided a means for a limited amount of state funding to be channelled routinely to theatre for the first time. Guided initially by the economist John Maynard Keynes, the Arts Council defined its interest as 'the fine arts exclusively' and sought to encourage professional excellence, rather than amateur groups. In the case of theatre, this interest meant the major London opera and ballet companies plus a growing number of regional repertory theatre companies. The latter had grown up since the start of the twentieth century, notably in Birmingham and Liverpool,[4] and typically presented a mixed programme of classics and new work. For them, the introduction of subsidy was transformative. Although it only ever formed a small part of their income, it supplied a valuable safety net.[5] It encouraged longer rehearsal periods and enabled a move away from so-called 'weekly rep', in which companies would put on a new play each week, performing one play in the evenings while rehearsing the next week's play during the day. Standards gradually increased, as did audience numbers and artistic ambitions, prompting the director Norman Marshall to write in 1963 about a 'renaissance in the provincial theatre'.[6] In 1977, the

critic Michael Billington wrote that 'the subsidised repertory companies are far more exciting than the West End of London'.[7]

At the same time, the Local Government Act of 1948 allowed local authorities to use a small part of their 'rates' income to subsidise the arts. Crucially, however, not only could they offer funding to theatre companies (like the Arts Council), but they were also empowered to take over theatre buildings as civic venues, to fund building refurbishment projects, or to contribute to the costs of constructing new theatres. The years after 1948 thus saw the emergence of the 'civic theatre', owned by the local authority itself. Early examples were typically existing theatre buildings taken into municipal ownership, but in 1958 the Belgrade Theatre, Coventry (fig. 1.3), was Britain's first purpose-built civic theatre as well as the first all-new professional theatre to be built in Britain since 1939. Designed by the City Architect's Office under Donald Gibson and Arthur Ling, it formed one of the first examples in a wave of subsidised theatre construction,[8] which lasted into the 1980s.

A second source of public funding for building projects came into being after Labour's 1964 election victory. The previous Conservative government had increased the Arts Council's budget, but Labour – increasingly interested in questions of 'leisure' – sought to do more. Jennie Lee became Britain's first Minister for the Arts and oversaw the publication in 1965 of a landmark White Paper, 'A Policy for the Arts – the First Steps'.[9] Lee shared Keynes' interest in supporting professional excellence whilst also believing that the arts should be available to all. The Arts Council's budget was significantly increased, and a new programme, 'Housing the Arts', was launched as a way to part-fund capital projects.[10] Although grants were limited, the apparent endorsement of the Arts Council often encouraged others to contribute. Many repertory companies also raised substantial sums from their audiences and the wider community, while Britain's entry into the European Economic Community in 1973 meant that European funding became available for projects deemed to have a role in economic development.

Britain's post-war civic and repertory theatres were not 'planted' from the centre by the Arts Council, but were conceived locally. Nonetheless,

1.3 The expansive foyer at the Belgrade Theatre, Coventry, open all day to visitors: an innovation when the theatre was completed in 1958

1.4    Crucible Theatre, Sheffield (Renton Howard Wood Associates, 1971), the entrance at night

the terms in which many of them were discussed were similar. For example, egalitarianism and a belief that the 'best' should be available to all was important and was genuinely meant, even if the definition of the 'best' was sometimes rather narrow in practice (relating to certain kinds of 'high' culture and professional practice, rather than amateur work or more populist forms).[11] In addition, there was real optimism; the arts were thought to have a central role to play in the development of a modern, culturally literate Britain.[12] Nonetheless, while they thus embodied similar ideas, the actual forms of Britain's new theatres varied. Some were conceived as substantial public buildings, among them the National Theatre (Denys Lasdun and Partners, 1976) as well as major regional venues such as Nottingham Playhouse (Peter Moro, 1963) and the Crucible, Sheffield (Renton Howard Wood Associates, 1971, fig. 1.4). Sometimes theatres were

located in new civic centres in order to represent the idea of the subsidised arts as a public amenity, as was the case at Birmingham Rep (by Graham Winteringham of S.T. Walker, 1971) or Theatr Clwyd, Mold (by the County Architect, 1976). Other theatres, however, formed part of commercial developments. Leicester's Haymarket Theatre, designed by the City Architect and completed in 1973 (fig. 1.5) was, like Derby Playhouse (Roderick Ham, 1975), constructed within a shopping centre, the idea being that it would become part of everyday life rather than being regarded as something rarefied. The Barbican Arts Centre, London (1969–82) was an integral part of the surrounding new housing estate, and was designed by the same architects as the housing, Chamberlin, Powell & Bon. Universities often built theatres and arts centres, too, seeing the performing arts (whether studied by students or experienced by

1.5 Haymarket Theatre, Leicester (Leicester City Architect, 1973), showing the theatre located above street-level shops

them as audience members) as something which could break down traditional subject boundaries and create a sense of community among students, staff, and local people (fig. 1.6).[13]

The contemporary appearance of Britain's new theatres in the 1960s and 1970s not only distinguished them from their pre-war predecessors but was also thought by some literally to embody the new world of subsidised theatre.[14] Internally, too, these buildings were unlike older theatres. Their large foyers were shared by all patrons, with no segregation by ticket price. They were typically open all day and often included a coffee bar, restaurant, and space for exhibitions (fig. 1.7). The likes of the director Hazel Vincent Wallace at the Thorndike Theatre, Leatherhead (Roderick Ham, 1969), stressed the centrality of such facilities to the idea of theatre as a 'community project'.[15] More pragmatically, of course, selling refreshments also generated useful income.

Auditoria, meanwhile, were planned in different ways. In place of the established proscenium-arch format, some theatres featured 'open stage' arrangements, including 'thrust' and 'in-the-round' staging. These 'open' layouts, much debated during the 1950s and 1960s, were often felt to encourage a closer relationship between actors and audiences, and to emphasise the uniquely live, three-dimensional nature of theatre in contrast to film and television. Key thrust stage examples include Chichester Festival Theatre (by Powell and Moya, 1962) and the Crucible, Sheffield, while the open amphitheatre of the Olivier auditorium at the National Theatre derives from similar thinking. 'In-the-round' theatres were created in such places as Scarborough and at Stoke-on-Trent. Other auditoria featured more flexible layouts, in which seating and staging could be reconfigured; examples include the Crescent, Birmingham (Graham Winteringham, 1964) and the Derngate, Northampton (RHWL, 1983). However, flexibility often proved difficult to achieve in large auditoria and so was typically confined to the small new 'studio' spaces which sprang up from the end

1.6 Warwick Arts Centre, designed by Renton Howard Wood Levin and opened in 1974, was one of a growing number of university arts venues built during the 1960s and 1970s

1.7 Café-restaurant at the Mercury Theatre, Colchester (Norman Downie, 1972)

of the 1960s. Meanwhile, new proscenium-arch theatres continued to be built, not least because this form still had its advocates (fig. 1.8). It was seen by some as being inherently flexible and suited to a range of styles of play, while others were simply uninterested in abstract debates about stage layout.[16] A proscenium-arch stage was also essential if a theatre was to take touring shows, given that it was the most common type of staging.

Some architects in this period, notably Peter Moro and Roderick Ham, specialised in theatre architecture, with the latter penning an influential book, *Theatre Planning*, published in 1972 and revised in 1987. The Association of British Theatre Technicians, founded in 1961, served as a key conduit of knowledge, while also important was the long-running magazine *Tabs*, which covered theatre architecture in Britain, continental Europe, and North America. The so-called 'theatre consultant' also became increasingly prominent during this period and often played an important role, especially when an architect was new to theatre. In such cases, the consultant might not only specify technical equipment but could also advise on conceptual matters.

Inflation and recession led to cuts in public expenditure after 1974 which affected 'Housing the Arts' (which was wound up after 1984) as well as local government spending. Some major projects (such as Edinburgh's large Castle Terrace Theatre) were cancelled in the mid-1970s, but others – especially those conceived in modest terms – went ahead, including Pitlochry Festival

1.8   Thorndike Theatre, Leatherhead (Roderick Ham, 1969), a well-received medium-sized repertory theatre of the late 1960s with a single rake of seating and a 'hidden' proscenium arch

Theatre (by Law and Dunbar-Nasmith, 1981) and Dundee Repertory Theatre (Nicoll Russell, 1982).[17] In addition, while some new theatres of the 1970s and early 1980s, such as Plymouth Theatre Royal (Peter Moro Partnership, 1982, fig. 1.9), had an uncompromisingly 'modern' appearance, others took a more contextual approach at a time when the architecture of the 1960s was increasingly being criticised. Among these contextual examples we might count Eden Court, Inverness (Law and Dunbar-Nasmith, 1976, fig. 1.10), the Wolsey Theatre, Ipswich (Roderick Ham, 1979), and the so-called 'Leeds look' of the West Yorkshire Playhouse, completed in 1990 to the designs of the Appleton Partnership as the last major theatre of the 'Housing the Arts' boom.

Eden Court was also significant on account of its auditorium, which features boxes cascading down its sides in a deliberate attempt to 'paper the walls with people'. Although some larger auditoria of the late 1950s and 1960s had included rear galleries, few had traditional side galleries or boxes. Among the exceptions were the Belgrade, Coventry (inspired by the Festival Hall), and Billingham Forum (1968), whose architects, Elder and Lester, were apparently inspired by West German opera houses. The inclusion of boxes at Eden Court was encouraged by the theatre consultant, Iain Mackintosh, an influential enthusiast for the densely packed auditoria of eighteenth-century theatres. Mackintosh also played a key role in the evolution of the so-called 'courtyard' auditorium during the 1970s. Building on the examples of the Young Vic (1970) and the theatre at Christ's Hospital (1974), both by Howell Killick Partridge and Amis, as well as more historic theatres such as Richmond, Yorkshire (1788), the 'courtyard' found definitive form in 1976 in the Cottesloe auditorium at the National Theatre, which was designed by Mackintosh.[18] With a flexible stalls floor area and narrow side/rear galleries, the courtyard rapidly became a popular approach, especially in smaller theatres. Among the best examples was the Tricycle, Kilburn, an effective, concentrated space designed by the architect Tim Foster and built economically in 1979–80 using an off-the-peg scaffolding system within a redundant hall (fig. 1.11).[19]

1.9   Theatre Royal, Plymouth, as completed to the designs of the Peter Moro Partnership in 1982. One of the last major theatres of the 'Housing the Arts' era, by an architect who specialised in theatre design

1.10   Eden Court, Inverness (Law and Dunbar-Nasmith, 1976), detail of exterior

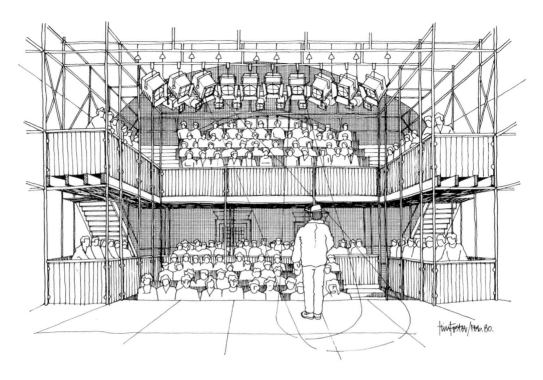

1.11   Tricycle Theatre, Kilburn, courtyard auditorium structure inserted within the former Foresters' Hall (Tim Foster, 1980)

While there evidently remained a place for purpose-built, substantial new theatres, other trends emerged during the 1970s and 1980s. First, under the influence of the internationally prominent director Peter Brook – who reportedly told Denys Lasdun that he would prefer 'a bombed site in Bethnal Green' to a purpose-built National Theatre – and others, a new breed of 'found spaces' came into being, in which redundant buildings were repurposed for performance.[20] Some, such as Brook's Bouffes du Nord in Paris, had been built as theatres; others, however, were abandoned industrial structures.[21] Frequently, these buildings were presented ostensibly 'as found'. Obvious interventions were kept to a minimum in the interests of preserving a sense of their history and enjoying the richness of their often-distressed interiors. Brook's challenge to Lasdun demonstrates the extent to which the 'found space' can be understood as a riposte to the purpose-built

modern theatres of the post-war boom, which all too easily might seem too perfect. (For example, the director Ronald Eyre was reported to have suggested that the National Theatre should close for twenty years, acquire 'its own shabby and disreputable history', and then 'when the corners had been rubbed off' and 'every breath of Art dispersed', be 'reclaimed for theatre'.[22]) Others were concerned about the apparent permanency of new theatres. The director Michael Elliott, thinking particularly of the National Theatre's concrete terraces, queried in 1973 whether building 'for posterity' was the right approach: 'in future, shouldn't we try to retain a certain lightness and sense of improvisation, and sometimes build in materials that do not require a bomb to move them?'[23] Elliott's ideas informed the conception of the Royal Exchange Theatre, Manchester (1976, fig. 1.12), a theatre 'module' of steel and glass designed by Levitt Bernstein and inserted into a redundant

Victorian building at a fraction of the cost of (and with apparently greater flexibility than) an all-new theatre.

Another growing strand of work during the 1970s and 1980s comprised the rehabilitation of the country's surviving Victorian and Edwardian theatres, partly to accommodate a revival in the fortunes of touring theatre and partly as the heritage value of these buildings was increasingly recognised.[24] In this respect, the foundation of The Theatres Trust in 1976 as a statutory consultee in the planning process was intended to stem the tide of demolitions, which had been commonplace during the previous two decades. The Theatre Royal, Nottingham, was transformed by the architects Renton Howard Wood Levin in a £4.6 million project between 1976 and 1978, combining the sympathetic restoration of the auditorium with the reconstruction of the front-of-house, stage, and backstage areas.[25] Northampton Theatre Royal

(1983) was subsequently treated similarly, as were other theatres including Newcastle Theatre Royal (1986–88), the Lyceum, Sheffield (1990–91), and the Empire Theatre, Edinburgh, which, as redesigned by Law and Dunbar-Nasmith, became the Festival Theatre in 1994. In 1987, meanwhile, the Theatres Trust's powers were substantially increased when theatres were deemed to be *sui generis* in planning terms, in effect meaning that they formed their own 'use class' and that almost any change to a theatre, whether listed or not, in use or closed, required planning consent and thus the scrutiny of the Trust.[26]

By the time the Edinburgh Festival Theatre opened, a new wave of theatre-building was beginning, ten years after 'Housing the Arts' had been wound up. As in the 1960s and 1970s, public funding was important, but now it came from a new source. The arts were designated as one of the 'good causes' to be supported from the proceeds

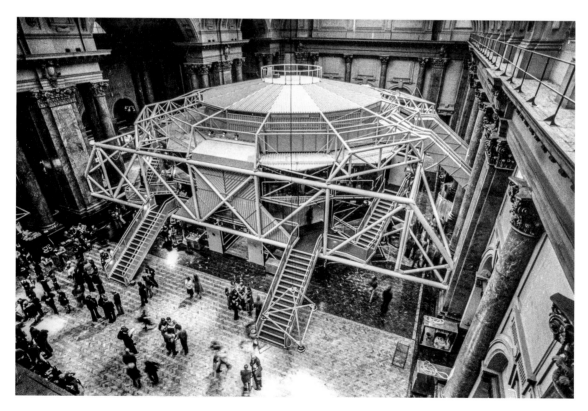

1.12  Royal Exchange Theatre, Manchester, the auditorium 'module' within the former Exchange hall (Levitt Bernstein, 1976)

1.13    The Lowry, Salford (Michael Wilford and Partners, 2000), in which galleries and foyers
wrap around the centre's two main auditoria

of the National Lottery, launched in 1994.[27] The principle on which Lottery funding was made available was one of 'additionality', meaning that it had to complement existing funding streams (that is, revenue subsidy), rather than replace them.[28] The result, as the National Audit Office later reported, was 'a huge and unprecedented increase in the number and scale of capital projects'.[29] Certainly the perception was soon that 'Lottery money was flowing like water';[30] in the early days, money was entering the Lottery's coffers faster than it could be spent.[31] The Arts Council of England (created in 1994 as one of several successors to the Arts Council of Great Britain) launched its first Lottery-supported capital programme in early 1995. By 1998, 2055 grants totalling more than £1 billion had been made.[32] Similar capital programmes were run in Northern Ireland, Scotland, and Wales. In England, Lottery money was put to further uses, including a stabilisation fund for arts organisations

in difficulty.[33] Major projects were also part-funded by the Millennium Commission, while the Heritage Lottery Fund was a further source of money. A second Arts Council England programme of capital projects was launched in 2000, though with a smaller budget of £176 million. It was followed by a third round in 2003–04 before the capital department was wound up in 2007.[34] Funding was subsequently diverted to the 2012 London Olympics, although the intention was also that local authorities would pick up the slack as far as arts capital projects were concerned.[35]

Many of the new arts buildings of the late 1990s and early 2000s were substantial structures. For example, The Lowry, Salford (2000, fig. 1.13), houses several performance spaces as well as a gallery in a landmark building by Michael Wilford and Partners, the successors to James Stirling's internationally famous practice. At times there was a definite pursuit of the 'iconic', something which was a trend more generally in this period's architecture.[36] Not all of the results were welcomed, however. The Lottery's support for some projects, such as the expensive and supposedly 'elitist' reconstruction of the Royal Opera House, was controversial.[37] In addition, some projects went dramatically over budget (for example, Curve, Leicester, 2008, by Rafael Viñoly); it was reported in 2007 that one-quarter of 24,000 projects funded through the Lottery between 1995 and 2006 had been completed late.[38] Some, infamously The Public in West Bromwich (Will Alsop, 2008), also experienced financial difficulties after opening.[39] Arts Council England was keen to rebut criticism, however, pointing to the large number of successful projects.[40] The Lowry, for example, spearheaded a wave of new buildings, including studios for the BBC and ITV, whilst the organisation itself has engaged productively with local communities.[41] Other theatres have been recognised for the quality of their architecture. Alan Short's Contact Theatre, Manchester (1999), for example, has an innovative natural ventilation system which is given tangible form in the tall stacks which rise above the building's roofline (fig. 1.14), while Keith Williams' Unicorn Theatre, London (2005), made it to the penultimate round of the 2006 Stirling Prize.[42]

The extent to which arts capital projects conspicuously benefitted from Lottery funding in the late 1990s nonetheless obscures a broader narrative of 'crisis' which is evident in discussions of the practice and funding of theatre since the early 1980s.[43] In 1984, the Arts Council of Great Britain report 'The Glory of the Garden' made the (positive) case for decentralisation and a greater focus on the arts beyond London but also proposed that several long-standing recipients of subsidy should lose their grants, and that 'Housing the Arts' should close.[44] The report partly reflected the broader re-evaluation of the post-war political consensus which followed the election in 1979 of a Conservative government keen on deregulation,

1.14   Contact Theatre, Manchester (Short Ford and Associates, 1999), with a dramatic skyline of natural ventilation stacks

privatisation, and a reduced role for the state. In the case of the arts, the government sought to encourage 'business-like' practices as well as increased private sponsorship and fundraising. Subsidy levels overall rose only very slightly during the 1980s, and many theatres saw little improvement in their financial position.[45] At the same time, and indicative of government interest in the economic value of the arts, there was much discussion of the extent to which the theatre and music might contribute to the economy and to urban regeneration.[46]

The early 1990s saw several years of standstill funding and then a reduction in the arts budget in 1994–95, at just the same time as a recession was causing audience numbers and commercial sponsorship levels to fall.[47] Local government spending freezes also worked against theatre, especially as the Arts Council sometimes used low levels of local-authority subsidy in order to justify a cut in its own grant to a particular theatre.[48] Between 1979 and 1997, the number of regional producing theatres fell by one quarter.[49] In 1995, three-quarters of 45 major regional theatres in England were thought to be in debt.[50] Lord Gowrie, chairman of the Arts Council of England from 1994–97, likened his role to that of a doctor running a casualty ward.[51] For example, Salisbury Playhouse (built in 1976 to the designs of Norman Downie) was caught in a perfect storm of declining funding, falling audiences, inefficient administrative practices, and the unpopularity of some of its programming: 'everything that could go wrong, went wrong', reported consultants in 1994.[52] Several major venues closed, if only temporarily, while others stopped producing work in house. Things were a little brighter in Scotland and Wales, however, where there was an increase in spending on drama as an art form between 1986–87 and 1997–98.[53]

The election of a New Labour government in 1997 only partly reversed the market-driven ideology which had informed government policy since the early 1980s. However, there were positive developments as far as public funding for the arts was concerned. New – and welcome – priorities emerged, not least relating to inclusion, accessibility, and education.[54] In 2000, Peter Boyden's well-received report *The Roles and Functions of the English Regional Producing Theatres* was followed by a new national strategy for theatre in England and a significant increase in Arts Council England's budget.[55] This and other sources of funding promoted what Elizabeth Tomlin has referred to as a 'golden age of experimentation' in writing and production; by 2010 'the UK ha[d] never […] enjoyed an aesthetically richer mainstream'.[56] A further positive step came in January 2008, when the McMaster review stressed that artistic practice should be liberated from 'burdensome targets'; excellence, innovation, and risk-taking were to be prioritised.[57] However, by now, saving money was once again on the agenda. In 2005, the Department for Culture, Media and Sport announced that funding levels in England would be frozen until 2008.[58] Two years later, Arts Council England (ACE) proposed cuts which were not reversed, despite a slight increase in arts funding following the 2008 Comprehensive Spending Review.[59] Venues such as Derby Playhouse and Bristol Old Vic closed, albeit temporarily,[60] while ACE was required to reduce its staff numbers and administration costs.

Despite these challenges, the critic Lyn Gardner was able to write in 2009 of theatre's renewed 'self-confidence and sense of risk'.[61] Yet Gardner also asked: had the money used for buildings been well-spent? As she put it, 'new buildings take a long time to plan and build: is there a risk that some theatres will be obsolete by the time they open their doors?'[62] This concern was not new. In 1972, at the height of the 'Housing the Arts' boom, Michael Billington had asked whether theatre was suffering from an 'edifice complex',[63] while we have already noted Michael Elliott's contemporaneous views on the wisdom of building for posterity. The timing of Gardner's comments was, however, significant, as the post-2008 economic downturn was beginning. What were its effects on the funding and practice of the arts?

# 2   Theatre in an Age of Austerity

Writing in Arts Council England (ACE)'s 2008–09 Annual Report, the organisation's chief executive, Alan Davey, suggested that 'the key is not to panic', despite the then recent financial crash and gloomy predictions of recession.[1] Dame Liz Forgan, chair of ACE, took up the theme elsewhere in the report, recording that recent months had been 'demanding' and predicting that there were 'tough times ahead'.[2] Two years later, ACE's Annual Report referred to the continuing effects on the arts of 'severe recession'.[3] Although in England the government emphasised the value of public funding for the arts in its 2016 Culture White Paper, the first on the subject since 1965,[4] the document was published following a series of spending cuts which seemed to challenge the relationship between the state and the arts as it had existed since the 1940s. Of course, theatres have faced reductions in their subsidy on several occasions since the 1970s. However, the events of 2008 led to a distinctive and prolonged period of austerity, with the Conservative-led coalition government of 2010–15 and its Conservative successors being especially keen to reduce public spending. Before we turn to some of the buildings of this period, it is worth briefly setting out the financial and organisational context of contemporary British theatre.[5]

## Funding for the Arts

Since the dissolution of the Arts Council of Great Britain in 1994, there have been fully independent bodies in England, Scotland, and Wales: the Arts Council of England (later Arts Council England [ACE]); the Scottish Arts Council, which merged with Screen Scotland in 2010 to form Creative Scotland; and the Arts Council of Wales. (Across the Irish Sea, the Arts Council of Northern Ireland has played a similar role since the 1960s.) These organisations' budgets are made up of funding from government (that is, the devolved administrations in the case of Scotland and Wales) and the National Lottery. As has long been the case, subsidised arts companies derive the largest share of their income not from subsidy but from ticket sales and other 'non-box-office' revenue (such as catering). For example, Creative Scotland reported in 2018 that its funding represented 24 per cent of its supported companies' overall projected budget, with £35 million coming from local authorities, £27.4 million from trusts and foundations, and £178.5 million being earned.[6] Yet although subsidy is thus limited in its extent, it is frequently thought to offer vital security and to enable experiment, and its removal can send companies to the wall.[7]

The cuts which followed the 2008 spending review were noted in the last chapter. More were to come, however. Following the election in 2010 of the Conservative/Liberal Democrat coalition, a further government review aimed for an £81 billion reduction in public expenditure by 2015.[8] In England, the Department for Culture, Media and Sport faced a £61 million reduction in its budget, with a £19 million cut in ACE's funding.[9] Reductions were made in ACE staff numbers and an across-the-board 0.5 per cent funding cut was imposed on Regularly Funded Organisations (RFOs).[10] In November 2011, all RFOs were asked to reapply for their funding, and a new 'National Portfolio' was created.[11] Although a number of new groups joined the portfolio, ninety-seven theatres lost some or all of their funding.[12] The financial challenges continued. In 2014, ACE's chair, Sir Peter Bazalgette, reported a 33 per cent fall in the organisation's grant-in-aid spending since 2010.[13] In addition, by 2015 the balance between Lottery funding and grant-in-aid had shifted, prompting some to question whether Lottery money was being spent on ACE's core activities, despite the 'additionality' principle which had previously meant that Lottery funding was allocated to activities outwith the

Council's core remit.[14] A note of caution also needs to be sounded about reliance on the Lottery, as its ticket sales were falling by 2018.[15]

The story in Wales is similar. The Arts Council of Wales (ACW) reported in 2017 that

> From 2000, there was more than a decade of sustained public and Lottery investment in our cultural life. However, the five years of funding cuts that followed have meant that the value of the growth in Welsh Government funding in the 1990s and 2000s has been eroded. Combined grant-in-aid and National Lottery funding is worth less today than it was 21 years ago.[16]

A major review of ACW's portfolio in 2010 led to thirty-two organisations having their funding cut or significantly reduced.[17] Thereafter the picture remained mixed. Cuts in spending led ACW to warn organisations not to rely on its grants, although there was a 3.5 per cent increase in 2017–18 on the previous year, with £31.2 million of the Welsh government's £31.7 million arts budget going to ACW.[18] The Welsh administration launched an inquiry in August 2017, considering how arts organisations could be helped to increase self-generated income.[19]

In Scotland, Creative Scotland had a long and difficult birth, finally coming into being in 2010. Additional Lottery money was allocated to cancel out reductions in government support, in fact serving to increase the total spending budget, but Creative Scotland's decision in 2012 to remove funding entirely from all forty-nine of its flexibly funded companies caused consternation and much criticism; theatre critic Joyce McMillan led the charge against 'commerce-driven ideology'.[20] Creative Scotland responded with a new ten-year plan, the return of three-year funding contracts, and, in 2014, increases for some organisations,[21] but by now only building-based and national companies were being funded from 'core' spending.[22] Support for independent theatre-making companies was to come from the Lottery in a move which implied that these groups were now seen in terms of 'additionality'.[23] As of 2018, Creative Scotland's Regular Funding Network included 121 organisations, supported by £101.6

million grant-in-aid funding.[24] However, the creation of the 2018 portfolio was once again controversial: some decisions were publicly challenged and later reversed.[25] Of the 102 organisations which previously received regular funding from Creative Scotland, sixty-eight were awarded standstill funding (compared with 2015–18), while twenty-seven saw an increase and seven a reduction. Of course, standstill funding in effect meant a cut in real terms, once inflation was taken into account.

Support for capital projects was maintained in England, Scotland, and Wales after 2008, but at a much reduced level compared with the late 1990s and early 2000s, as ACE's Alan Davey noted in 2011:

> Previous capital programmes have been about big, new, brash buildings. This capital programme won't be about that – it is more about getting the most out of the existing estate.[26]

ACE made £180 million available that year, offering grants of £500,000 to £5 million and emphasising 'renewal and resilience'. ACE's 2015–18 capital programme was similarly focused, while further new rules meant that organisations outside the national portfolio had their access to larger capital grants curtailed.[27] In Scotland, a £30 million Lottery-funded capital programme was announced by Creative Scotland in 2013; this had been exhausted by 2016. £30 million was also offered in Wales in the 2012–17 Capital Strategy, which supported major schemes including Pontio, a new arts centre in Bangor.

## Local Authority Funding

Local government has been able routinely to spend a proportion of its income on the performing arts since 1948, leading, as we have seen, to the creation and construction of civic theatres as well as subsidies for theatre companies and other arts groups. By 2009, local-government support for the arts could be described as a 'billion-pound' concern, helping 1099 theatres, concert halls, arts centres, and museums and galleries, while councils also played a 'facilitation role' in other cases.[28] However, spending was subsequently affected in many cases by cuts in local government budgets.

In May 2010, savings in 'non-front line public services' were announced.[29] £1.165 billion of these savings would be made in local government. The Government also announced the removal of the ring-fences around c. £1.7 billion of grants to local authorities 'to give them greater flexibility to re-shape their budgets'.[30] Reductions in support for the arts followed in some areas. In 2014, the Audience Agency told the Culture, Media and Sport Select Committee that

> Although the Inquiry is focusing on the work of Arts Council England, we ask it to consider carefully the current erosion – and in some cases 100% withdrawal – of local authority support for culture. This presents a potentially fatal threat to the regional cultural infrastructure – and ACE's capacity to work to lobby against and address such swingeing cuts has been decimated.[31]

Newcastle-upon-Tyne, for example, cut its £2.5 million culture budget by 100 per cent in 2013, instead investing £600,000 in a new Culture Fund.[32] A 2016 report suggested that total spending by councils in England on arts and culture development and support, theatres and public entertainment, museums and galleries, and the library service had declined from £1.42 billion to £1.2 billion, a 16.6 per cent reduction.[33] While the total resourcing of Arts Council National Portfolio Organisations increased by 17 per cent between 2010 and 2015 (attributed to better fundraising and increased income from commercial activities), the proportion of funding derived from local government fell from 8 per cent to 5 per cent.[34] A report for Creative Scotland, too, suggested that approximately half of Scottish local authorities had reduced the level of revenue expenditure on the arts.[35] Reflecting on its own survey of the subject in summer 2017, the *ArtsProfessional* website noted that staff were doing more work for less money or were making more use of volunteers; half of survey respondents worked for organisations which had reduced staff numbers.[36] Often cuts particularly affected outreach programmes and educational activities.[37]

One increasingly common strategy is for local authorities to devolve theatres (and libraries, museums, and archives) to other organisations, such as charitable trusts or mutually owned bodies.[38] Such arrangements in England partly reflect a shift in policy since 2010 towards 'localism' and the creation of initiatives intended to facilitate local (often voluntary) action in place of state-directed and funded programmes. New income streams have also been encouraged; the well-established practice of sponsoring a seat or 'buying a brick' can be rebranded as 'crowdfunding'.[39] Charitable trust status opens doors to funding which are not available to local authorities.[40] However, these models are not without their challenges, as The Theatres Trust noted in 2014:

> Over the last few years we have noticed an increase in the number of local authority managed theatres which local authorities are unable to fund, and which have therefore become independent charitable trusts or have found other operators. Our belief is that a significant number of regionally based local authorities will stop managing and funding the theatres that they currently own over the next couple of years, and in addition they will also reduce or significantly cut the funding that they provide to independent theatres within their area. This situation presents particular challenges for ex-local authority funded regional theatres, who will be trying to develop new operational models and ways of working with very limited resources, and there appears to be little support and advice available for them.[41]

In Harrow, for example:

> To access funding, Cultura [the organisation which had taken on the local arts centre] needed the right sort of lease. But the Council wouldn't agree to this until it was satisfied there was enough of the right sort of money in the project to spread the risk. And because it couldn't get the lease, Cultura said it couldn't get more grant funding or public donations, which in turn increased the risk for the Council.[42]

Similar problems were encountered in Dudley, where a local group was granted a five-year lease of the Hippodrome, but with conditions which restricted their availability to raise funds.[43] In Sutton, meanwhile, the local authority sought a commercial rent for two theatres, which placed them out of the reach of community groups.[44]

Yet the picture is not entirely one of doom and gloom. Among the respondents to *ArtsProfessional*'s 2017 survey were several who noted that some local authorities had maintained their commitments to the arts.[45] As we shall see, the case studies in *Play On* include buildings and organisations which have been generously supported by local government, not least in Chester, Doncaster, Glasgow, and Leeds. As has often been the case since the 1980s, such support has frequently been justified in terms of the arts' contribution to the economy. In this respect, it was reported in 2013 that for every £1 invested in the arts, another £4 was generated, with cultural businesses reportedly contributing £28 billion to the economy.[46] When Waltham Forest was announced as the first London Borough of Culture in 2018, its leadership wrote of the way that 'we see culture as a vital component of economic growth'.[47] Flick Rea of the Local Government Association told The Theatres Trust's 2013 conference that 'what matters to councillors is regeneration and growth' and that 'a theatre should highlight its contribution to the visitor economy and talk about how it creates jobs'.[48]

Despite talk of money and jobs, the more intangible benefits of the arts have not been entirely forgotten. In England, The Theatres Trust successfully lobbied to influence the 2012 National Planning Policy Framework (NPPF). After the consultation draft of the document ignored culture entirely, the final version stated that the planning system has a 'social role' in fostering 'a high quality built environment, with accessible local services that reflect the community's needs and support its health, social and cultural well-being'.[49] Similarly, discussions of 'place-making' – a buzzword in contemporary urban discourse – frequently make reference to the potential for the arts to animate the urban scene and to inform local identity. 'Cultural well-being' and 'place-making' are hardly phrases which would have figured in Jennie Lee's vocabulary. However, the idea that the arts can have a central role in contemporary society suggests that her wish for a Britain where the best of the arts was available to all, and which would be 'gayer and more cultivated', has not completely vanished.

# 3  Ten Years of Theatre Architecture

Announced in December 2014 and intended to provide a major new northern English cultural centre, Factory, Manchester, is conceived on a scale to rival the major capital projects of the 1990s National Lottery boom. Designed by a team led by the Dutch architects OMA, Factory has been described by its promoters as 'a new type of venue – one that can commission, produce and present the widest range of opera, dance, theatre, visual arts and popular culture, with an emphasis on new cross-art-form collaborations, for a much wider audience than any traditional venue'.[1] It is planned as a 'catalyst' in the regeneration of the St John's area of central Manchester, where it occupies the site of the former Granada television studios.[2] It is hoped that it will boost the local economy and create 'community pride'.[3] The centre will have two main performance spaces: a theatre with 1600 seats, and a highly flexible space able to accommodate up to 5000 people, both of which will be used by the Manchester International Festival. Space will also be provided for training and education. The complexity of the design as well as its 'epic scale' – 13,500 square metres – to some extent account for Factory's likely cost, which has risen more than once. In late 2018, an increase of £20 million was announced, making the projected final total £130 million, £78 million of which is being provided by central government as a direct grant (an unusual though not unprecedented form of funding which contrasts with the 'arm's length' principle which has long governed arts funding). £40 million is currently planned to come from Manchester City Council, double the amount initially anticipated. The 2018 increase partly reflected the proposal's complex engineering, the cost of which was becoming clearer as the designs became more detailed, as well as changes to improve its functionality, not least in terms of the acoustics.[4] However, questions were asked about project oversight and governance, and the cost of abandoning the scheme was apparently evaluated.[5] Due for completion in 2021, the project is an interesting one. There have been many attempts around the world since the 1950s to design large flexible performance spaces, but few have been thought by practitioners to be entirely successful.[6] Will Factory be the exception?

In its size and cost, Factory represents one end of the spectrum in contemporary British theatre architecture. At the other end we might find groups like the National Theatre of Scotland (NTS) or its Welsh equivalents, Theatr Genedlaethol Cymru and National Theatre Wales, which have eschewed the idea of a substantial building (like the National Theatre in London) for a more fleet-of-foot approach, with the NTS aiming to be a 'theatre without walls'. Its headquarters building in Glasgow, 'Rockvilla', completed in 2016, is a converted warehouse which deliberately does not include a performance space. The Scottish and Welsh national theatres are not alone in avoiding a permanent home venue. Many companies, including Kneehigh, Punchdrunk, and Graeae, similarly specialise in taking shows out on the road, often to buildings and spaces not originally designed as theatres. Working in this way offers the chance to tailor productions to the places in which they are staged and to develop immersive, site-specific responses, something which is also evident in the rise of 'pop up' theatres, such as the King's Cross venue created for *The Railway Children* in 2014–15.

The space between these two poles is occupied by a diverse range of buildings. In what follows, a selection of recent projects is introduced as context for the more detailed case studies of the second part of the book. Some of these buildings were inherited and adapted, perhaps having been designed for other uses; others were newly built.

Some of the theatres which are discussed were bespoke creations which responded closely to the agendas of particular directors or groups. Others were conceived by local government; in such cases, what actually happens on stage may have been only part of the project 'vision', which might also have been framed in terms of other factors, such as economic development. Some of these theatres were the product of new partnerships, between theatre organisations and developers, local authorities, or universities. Several themes emerge. At a time of decreasing subsidy, many managements have been concerned to reduce operating costs and to increase non-box-office income, not least from catering. A further theme is that of accessibility, for staff as well as audiences, especially in refurbishment projects. A small number of wheelchair positions in one part of the auditorium is rarely now considered adequate. Questions of environmental sustainability, too, have become especially significant, not least in the light of ambitious national carbon reduction targets as well as the requirements of the building regulations, with The Theatres Trust as well as organisations like Julie's Bicycle (a London charity) and Creative Carbon Scotland playing important roles in supporting the sector.

There are several architectural practices in Britain whose expertise in theatre design dates back to the 1970s and 1980s, including Aedas Arts Team (formerly RHWL), Foster Wilson Architects, and Burrell Foley Fischer. They have more recently been joined by several firms which have each tackled a number of arts projects, including Page\Park, Bennetts Associates, Keith Williams Architects, and not least Haworth Tompkins, who have been exceptionally prolific since the turn of the century. But, like all buildings, theatres do not simply arise from the drawing board of the architect. They are created by multi-disciplinary teams, often with significant input from the client organisation. Theatre engineering is complex, both in structural terms and with respect to mechanical and electrical services; acoustics, too, are a specialised area of design. Among theatre consultants, whose work is often critical to the success of a project and can range from technical advice to concept design, successful new practices such as Charcoalblue have joined stalwarts such as Theatre Projects

Consultants and Theatreplan. Such consultancies work internationally. Increasingly, clients also appoint a dedicated project manager or adviser, sometimes internally, sometimes drawing on external expertise, in order to navigate successfully the sometimes fraught relationship between the impermanence of performance and the fixity of architecture. At a national level, The Theatres Trust offers strategic direction. It remains a statutory consultee for planning applications affecting existing theatres (as well as proposals for new theatres in Wales); it also advocates generally for the sector. Finally, the Association of British Theatre Technicians remains a key forum for professionals. Its long-established Theatre Planning Committee, chaired by Tim Foster, offers a peer-review service, to avoid technical mistakes and to improve the quality of proposals.

## New Buildings

Although the rate at which new theatres have opened since 2008 has hardly matched the booms of the 1960s or late 1990s, this period has nonetheless seen the completion of a steady stream of all-new theatres. The following narrative – inevitably highly selective – introduces some of these projects.

A first group of projects comprises those conceived by local government. Their decidedly 'civic' conception is not new. As was discussed in the first chapter, Britain's first civic-run theatres date from the late 1940s, while newly built civic theatres sprang up from the end of the 1950s. They were often substantial buildings intended to demonstrate the local authority's interest in the arts. Some recent theatres are very much in this mould, but they also demonstrate how the idea of the 'civic' venue has been developed, not least through partnerships. 'Place-making' is an oft-cited goal. This contemporary term refers to the idea that places should be attractive and interesting to use and experience, with a definite identity and character. 'Place-making' can also have an economic element. In Taunton in 2013–14, for example, the local authority was keen to encourage the re-opening of the Brewhouse Arts Centre, seeing the arts as something which could contribute to a 'vibrant' town centre and which would make Taunton – designated for expansion as a 'garden town' – an attractive place for new residents and businesses.[7] At the time of writing, a feasibility study for the expansion of the Brewhouse has been produced by Foster Wilson Architects, and plans for redevelopment are being drawn up.

One obviously 'civic' project of the last ten years is Corby Cube, which opened in 2010 (fig. 3.1). This £47.5 million building, designed by Hawkins\Brown, includes two auditoria. One has 450 seats, arranged in raked stalls and two horseshoe-shaped galleries; the smaller space is a 150-seat studio. The Borough Council had initially sought a pair of buildings, one an arts centre, the other a civic centre, but the final design brought everything together in a single structure. As well as the theatre auditoria, it includes the Borough Council's assembly chamber and offices, the local Registry Office, and a public library, all connected by a 'promenade' which rises from the ground-floor entrance to a roof terrace.[8] It demonstrates how the arts can still find a place

3.1   Corby Cube (Architect: Hawkins\Brown, 2010)

3.2   Marlowe Theatre, Canterbury (Keith Williams Architects, 2010), calmly 'civic' with its slender columns

3.3   Cast, Doncaster (RHWL Arts Team, 2013), faces a new public square and is adjacent to the local authority's new office building

within the 'municipal project', echoing the inclusion of theatres in some 1960s and 1970s civic centres, but at the same time the project has a strongly contemporary slant, being intended to contribute to the regeneration of Corby. It was built amid £2 billion of public and private investment in the town, including a new railway station, civic quarter, and shopping centre. The idea that a range of functions might be efficiently combined in a single building has been developed elsewhere, notably in Chester at Storyhouse (2017).

In Canterbury, Keith Williams Architects oversaw the reconstruction between 2008 and 2010 of the city council-owned Marlowe Theatre, originally designed as a cinema and adapted for theatre use in 1984.[9] There were various problems with the old building, not least its capacity: 950 seats was slightly too small to be economically attractive to major touring shows. A feasibility study by Burrell Foley Fischer showed that the auditorium could be altered to increase its capacity, but in the event Keith Williams Architects – fresh from the well-received Unicorn Theatre in London – went further, demolishing everything but the stagehouse. Alongside the reconstructed auditorium, a 150-seat studio was built, while extensive foyers were created behind a screen of tall, slim columns (fig. 3.2). Foley, reviewing the completed building, thought it 'slightly austere', but Williams noted that his aim had been to give the building a dignified form of architecture appropriate to its status as a major theatre in a cathedral city, in contrast to the 'jazzy' appearance of the former cinema.[10]

Cast in Doncaster (2013) presents a similarly sober image, at least externally (fig. 3.3). The theatre forms part of a strategy to regenerate Doncaster's Waterside area in which a development partner company, Muse, played a significant role. The creation here of a new 'Civic and Cultural Quarter' was intended as a device to channel investment into Doncaster, creating jobs and enhancing the local economy. Designed by RHWL Arts Team, Cast is located on one side of a new public square, alongside offices for the local authority. The theatre's main elevation is made of full-height glazing, pushed back within a deep 'frame' which looks a little like a portico. Rectilinear, its formality subverted by an asymmetrically positioned, copper-clad volume which pushes

3.4   Waterside Theatre, Aylesbury (RHWL Arts Team, 2010), evocative of the Chilterns in its organic form and timber

forwards and upwards, the overall impression is one of calm order, and here Cast – which is discussed in more detail in the case study section – contrasts with the more playful, poetic forms of another recent Arts Team project, Aylesbury's Waterside Theatre (2010, fig. 3.4). A standalone building which occupies a prominent site near a major town-centre junction, the Waterside's sinuous roofline, timber fins and pebble cladding strike an organic note, reportedly inspired by the nearby Chiltern Hills.[11] A slender clocktower also evokes the inter-war Dutch modernism of W.M. Dudok and the many public buildings in Britain which it inspired. The theatre contains two auditoria, one with 1200 seats (which can accommodate 1800 standing) and the other with 225 seats. It was designed for a mix of rock and pop concerts, theatre, opera, and ballet, and replaced the previous Assembly Hall in a town which is earmarked for significant expansion; it also forms part of wider plans for the redevelopment of its immediate surroundings. The theatre is managed on behalf of the local authority by the commercial operator, Ambassador Theatre Group.

In addition to these 'civic' schemes are theatre projects where the 'vision' is that of a resident

3.5 Everyman Theatre, Liverpool (Haworth Tompkins, 2014)

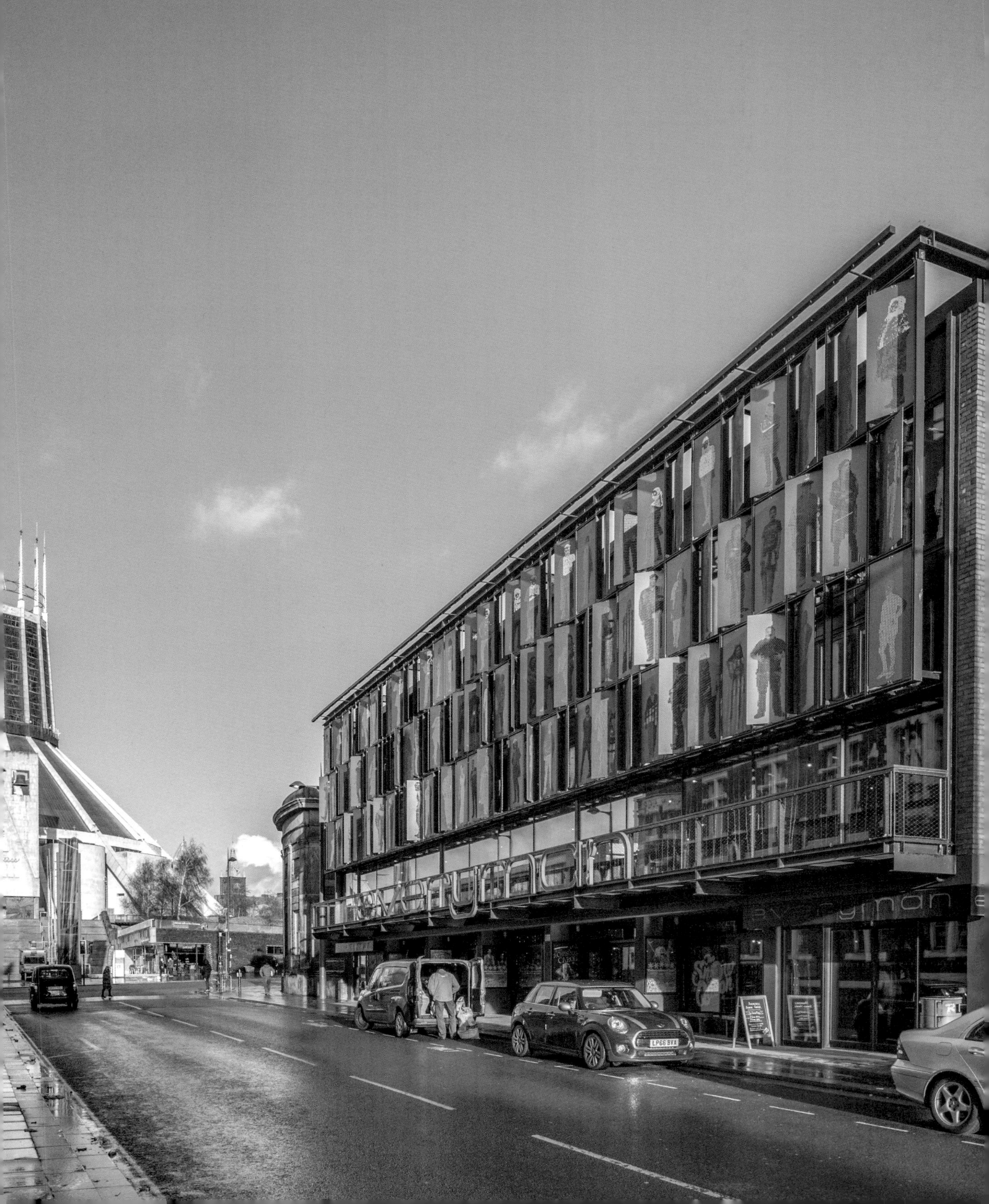

arts organisation. In Liverpool, for example, the Everyman (2014) replaced a much-loved theatre which had been created in a converted chapel in the 1960s and which quickly developed a strong reputation for the quality of its work. After financial difficulties in the 1990s and subsequent administrative retrenchment, Haworth Tompkins was appointed to redesign the theatre on a slightly expanded site. As is discussed in more detail in the Everyman case study, the team sought to preserve the essentials of the theatre's wide-thrust auditorium as well as its reputation for informality and accessibility, whilst improving the experience of audiences and staff. Externally, the theatre signals its ambitions with an elevation featuring images of ordinary Liverpudlians (fig. 3.5). Internally, the building has an unpretentious and robust character, with exposed brickwork (recycled from the old theatre) being juxtaposed with board-marked concrete, while lighting has also been effectively used to generate atmosphere. There is a sense of the provisionality which Haworth Tompkins is known for. The building has a strong character of its own, but also invites occupation and use.

Environmental sustainability was a central part of the brief at the Everyman, which is crowned by the four massive stacks ('John, Paul, George, and Ringo') of its natural ventilation system. Hull Truck Theatre, too, is an exemplary piece of sustainable design. Here the aim was a building which would relate to Hull's industrial heritage; client John Godber wanted something 'rooted in Hull'.[12] Wright and Wright's design, completed in 2009, is a modest, unpretentious and welcoming building whose dark brick echoes the city's historic warehouses (see colour plates).[13] Large windows give views into the foyer bars and café. Brick dominates these areas: the floor is finished in it and so are the walls, the lower parts of which feature hardwearing black glazed bricks – a practical but perhaps also theatrical gesture which lifts the building. Ceilings are exposed concrete, with the industrial theme also being evident in the use of perforated metal screens. The two auditoria, meanwhile, seat 450 (in a wide thrust arrangement) and 150. A passive ventilation strategy, devised with the mechanical and electrical engineers Max Fordham and Partners, reduces energy use and running costs.[14] The building has an exposed,

heavyweight concrete structure which aids its thermal performance by storing heat and coolth. Air enters the building at roof level, high above the noise and pollution of the adjacent busy road. It passes along two shafts, each with a substantial free cross-section area of 5 square metres. The shafts' size means that fans are not needed to drive the air, as would be the case with smaller ducts (which would offer greater resistance). In addition, the shafts' concrete construction means that incoming air is tempered as is passes along them, while their length, plus the use of acoustic attenuation, also means that outside noise is not audible during performances.

Air enters the auditorium at low level. It passes over the audience and so collects heat and rises, with theatre lighting adding to this effect. Once more, no fan is needed to draw it through. Extra provision for summer cooling has been made; there was a concern that summer matinees might use up the coolth stored in the structure before the evening performance. A borehole therefore draws water from an underlying aquifer and passes it over a heat exchanger. Finally, the stage is also naturally ventilated, with there being a 20-metre-long plenum built around the roof structure. Air is exhausted through a roof cowl, the form of which prevents rain from entering. A fan is built into the cowl for use on hot, still days. The result is a building which, when completed, was one of the best-performing theatres in Britain in environmental terms.

In Greenock, the Beacon Arts Centre replaced the old Arts Guild building in 2013 (see colour plates). The 'client' organisation was the Arts Guild, whose wish for a new building resonated with Inverclyde Council's plans for the regeneration of Greenock town centre and waterfront in the face of a declining population. Through the construction of new schools and by encouraging housing and leisure developments, Inverclyde has sought to make the area more attractive to families.[15] The Beacon's riverside site was acquired by the Arts Guild through a land swap with a development company, Peel Holdings. Designed by LDN Architects (formerly Law and Dunbar-Nasmith, a firm with much theatre experience) and completed at a cost of £8.5 million, its major funders were Creative Scotland and Inverclyde Council.

Externally, the building reads as a collection of cuboids, faced in opaque and clear glass. It has a strongly horizontal emphasis, appropriately enough on this open riverside site. The centre contains two auditoria as well as a rehearsal/function suite and waterfront café. The larger auditorium seats 500 in an end-stage arrangement. With three tiers and small boxes stepping down the side walls, it feels a little like a miniature, updated version of Law and Dunbar-Nasmith's acclaimed Eden Court Theatre, Inverness, of 1976. The stage itself is one of the largest in Scotland and is intended to accommodate major productions which previously would not have travelled west of Glasgow. Both auditoria are equipped for broadcasts, with the cables leading to special points in the secure theatre yard where outside broadcast vehicles can be stationed. The centre secured a prestigious Royal Incorporation of Architects in Scotland (RIAS) Award in 2013, with the judges deeming it 'elegantly contemporary in its materials and form, both open and welcoming'.[16]

Although not in 'Great Britain' as such, two new theatres in Northern Ireland are worth noting. The Lyric Theatre, Belfast, by O'Donnell + Tuomey (2011) contains two auditoria in a carefully considered, tactile structure.[17] The main auditorium (390 seats), studio theatre (110–150 seats), and rehearsal room are each located in their own red-brick box, around which are wrapped the foyers and staircases. Meanwhile, elsewhere in Belfast the MAC (Metropolitan Arts Centre) was rehoused in a new building by Hackett Hall McKnight in 2012.[18] Occupying one side of a new public square, its architecture contrasts with that of its neighbours. Whereas the other three sides of the square are regular, symmetrical, dominated by giant classical columns and pilasters, and finished in a cream render, the MAC presents an asymmetric elevation of brick and basalt, with a glazed tower rising above the roofline. Inside, the way that this part of central Belfast is dominated by narrow streets and tall buildings is echoed in the foyer, a full-height, top-lit space which cuts through the building and features a rich mix of brick and concrete textures.

Like the MAC, 'Home' in Manchester is located within a larger city-centre redevelopment project. Designed by Mecanoo (fresh from the new Library of Birmingham) and opened in 2015, this £25 million building, led by Manchester City Council,

3.6 Home, Manchester (Mecanoo, 2015), with a statue of Friedrich Engels in front of the theatre

sits alongside bars, student accommodation, a hotel and offices. It provides a new home for the city's Library Theatre as well as Cornerhouse, an arts centre and bar originally established in the 1980s. Home contains two auditoria, the larger seating 500 in a compact space with stalls and two narrow curved galleries; the smaller is a 150-seat black-box studio. There are also several cinemas and extensive foyers, including a restaurant, which are clearly visible after dark through the building's tinted glass façade (fig. 3.6). The brief was to avoid a 'precious' building, with the director Dave Moutrey wanting 'a nice cosy place to hang around with your friends'.[19] There is an appropriately unpretentious feel to the building's exposed concrete and plywood surfaces. Writing in *The Guardian*, however, Oliver Wainwright was unimpressed with its 'dour' architecture, 'clumsy' finishes, and 'compromised' location.[20] Early plans had reportedly given Home a street-facing location, but as built it sits at the centre of the development, having given up its street frontage to more lucrative buildings. Wainwright concluded that the result represented a missed opportunity in a city known for its high quality Victorian civic buildings.

In Bangor, north Wales, 'Pontio' replaced the 1970s Theatr Gwynedd. Designed by Grimshaw and opened in 2016, it is a stone-clad building which seems to grow out of the hillside below Bangor University's main building, housing a 480-seat theatre, studio auditorium, and cinema, as well as space for technology-led teaching. Pontio is one of several new university-run arts centres, with universities such as Derby and Sussex reopening theatres which had closed. Schools, too, have been important patrons of theatre since 2008. Some newly built state schools included a theatre, especially those planned before the sudden termination of the 'Building Schools for the Future' programme in 2010. Private schools have long built arts centres, sometimes of architectural significance: one thinks of the flexible courtyard theatre by HKPA at Christ's Hospital, Horsham (1974). Recent examples include Foster Wilson's Parabola Arts Centre at Cheltenham Ladies' College (2009). This award-winning £6 million scheme, designed by a practice with much experience of theatre design, comprised the conversion of a Grade II* listed Regency villa to provide public space and teaching accommodation, plus the construction of a new, galleried 325-seat auditorium (see colour plates). Similar in scale, and similarly award-winning, is Foster Wilson's Quarry Theatre at Bedford School, in which a redundant church has been converted into a flexible 300-seat auditorium. A new steel structure was inserted into the church, creating a performance space with a flat floor and slender side galleries.

Whereas the theatres discussed thus far occupy standalone buildings, others form part of bigger multi-functional complexes. Such venues can present significant logistical and engineering challenges, not least in terms of preventing sound transfer, especially where residential use is involved. The means of bringing materials and people into venues located above or below street level also requires careful consideration. In addition, it can be tricky to signify the presence of this sort of theatre to the world at large. In practical terms, the theatre may have only a limited frontage. Symbolically, meanwhile, how easy is it to create 'theatrical' architecture when the designer's job may be limited to fitting out an already-existing shell?

The Other Palace in central London is located at street and lower-ground levels below several floors of apartments.[21] Opened in 2012 as the St James Theatre and designed by Foster Wilson Architects, it was renamed in 2017 after being acquired by Andrew Lloyd Webber's Really Useful Group, for which it serves as a home for new musicals (fig. 3.7). The theatre is a purely commercial venture, and so

3.7  The Other Palace, London (Foster Wilson Architects, 2012)

the building has to work hard. Its signage proclaims that it is a 'Theatre/Studio/Bar' in equal measure, the bars and restaurant are generously sized relative to the two auditoria, while the theatre was designed with an eye to significant conference and events use. It has two auditoria, the larger of which seats 312 while the smaller space is a flat-floor cabaret venue for c. 100.

The Other Palace occupies the site of the former Westminster Theatre, which closed in 1990 and was destroyed by fire in 2002. The provision of a new theatre here was the result of a 'Section 106' planning agreement (that is, a set of conditions attached to a planning permission to make acceptable a development which would otherwise be refused consent), with the developers of the site being required to reserve space for a theatre. Several theatres have been built in London in recent years as a result of such arrangements, including the New Diorama, King's Cross (2010). In the case of the St James' Theatre, it was initially proposed that the space would be occupied by the Talawa Theatre Company as Britain's first permanent black theatre centre. These plans collapsed, however, and so the shell of the theatre remained empty while an alternative use was sought. In 2009, Foster Wilson Architects was appointed to fit out the space. They had to contend with the fact that the structure had been designed for a subsidised theatre producing its own work, rather than a commercial operation. Fitting in as many seats as possible therefore became important. For the larger auditorium, a courtyard arrangement like Tim

3.8  Southampton's new mixed-use cultural development, including NST City (CZWG/Glenn Howells, 2015–18)

Foster's earlier Tricycle Theatre was considered, but the executed steep single rake yielded a higher number of seats and also created space below the seating for ancillary facilities. Echoing the same architects' reconfiguration of the Whitehall Theatre as Trafalgar Studios, the seating wraps around a flexible forestage area. It is possible to create a small apron stage, or to have proscenium-arch or open end-stage arrangements.

A more recent example is Southampton's new theatre, NST City (fig. 3.8), which opened in 2018.[22] It is located within a £30 million mixed-use development, which includes restaurants, housing, and an art gallery, and represents a partnership between the city council, Grosvenor Developments, Southampton University, and Arts Council England. It is operated by the same management as the city's established Nuffield Theatre (now re-named 'NST Campus'), which was built as part of Southampton University in the 1960s and has been an independent theatre since 1982. Whereas NST Campus is now run largely as a 'receiving' or 'presenting' house which stages touring work, NST City is a producing theatre putting on its own shows, but the late announcement that it would be used in this way means that the building lacks some of the facilities one might expect, such as a scenic workshop.

Getting the theatre (and adjacent art gallery) built was a long process, with successive developers and masterplans falling victim to financial difficulties, while the final scheme, designed externally by CZWG, is a truncated version of what was originally intended.[23] Interiors, meanwhile, were by Glenn Howells Architects. One of the CZWG team reflected that 'we didn't know what was happening on the inside while we were designing the outside [...] it was almost like a refurbishment project, with us working for Grosvenor, while they were doing the fit-out for the council'.[24] With commercial uses being prioritised at street level, the theatre is located upstairs, connected to the street by means of stairs and a 5-tonne goods lift. There is a 133-seat studio and a 450-seat auditorium. The latter features a mixture of permanent and flexible seating/staging units (devised with specialist manufacturer Plann), and so can be set up in end-stage, in-the-round, thrust, and transverse configurations. Cables for live broadcasts are embedded throughout, while projection facilities will allow screenings of National Theatre productions.

Reviewing NST City in *The Stage*, Tim Bano found much to like, but thought that its presence was slightly lost: 'there's something unassuming, slightly corporate' about it, he wrote, suggesting that it would 'easy to mistake the new building for an office block or luxury flats'.[25] Oliver Wainwright in *The Guardian* was even less convinced, commenting that 'commercial interests have overshadowed a bold cultural vision':

Where you might expect to find this publicly funded arts beacon celebrating its presence on its frontage on Guildhall Square, instead you are greeted with a Nando's, Costa and Gourmet Burger Kitchen. The theatre is up four flights of stairs, while the listed Victorian park behind, meanwhile, is treated to a parade of service entrances and ventilation grilles.[26]

And yet, after several abandoned schemes, is it not better that Southampton has a new theatre in some shape or form, rather than nothing? It is surely remarkable that the city authorities kept faith in the idea of a new arts complex. Early signs, too, are encouraging. The well-received opening production, Howard Brenton's *The Shadow Factory*, confirmed the theatre's ambition to be a major regional presence.[27]

The way in which the likes of NST City and The Other Palace are embedded in bigger developments is not new. Earlier examples include the Royalty/Peacock Theatre in London of 1960, which was located below an office block and replaced the Stoll Theatre, the demolition of which was made conditional on the provision of a new theatre.[28] The Haymarket in Leicester (1973) was built on the upper floors of a shopping centre (not unlike NST City, in fact). However, one wonders whether this kind of theatre might become increasingly common if subsidy levels continue to decline and developers are encouraged by the planning system to make space for 'cultural' or community uses. Such spaces offer opportunities. For example, the Bridge Theatre, London (2017) was conceived as a 'start-up', occupying a 'cultural' space provided at the bottom of a residential block. Like the Park, Finsbury Park (2013) – part-funded by the sale of flats – the Bridge, which is considered in more detail in the case study section, suggests the emergence of a renewed entrepreneurialism in contemporary theatre-building.

## Refurbishment and Transformation

In November 2007, Eden Court Theatre, Inverness, reopened after the completion of a £19 million extension and refurbishment project, designed by Page\Park. The aim was to make space for a broader range of cultural activities and to create expanded conference facilities. As a result, the theatre gained a studio auditorium, two cinemas, two studios, and new dressing rooms. The extension was planned as an exemplary piece of low-energy design: its rooftop ventilation stacks give it a memorable image and also echo the gables of the historic Bishop's Palace on the other side of the original theatre building. The original building, meanwhile, was sympathetically repaired and refurbished, with a particular focus on the foyers. These spaces were stripped back in order to celebrate their hexagonal geometries. A new café and restaurant was created, whilst accessibility throughout the theatre was also improved. The result of all these changes is that the proportion of Eden Court's turnover made up by subsidy fell from 50 per cent to 21 per cent, while the work has reportedly saved 30,000 tonnes of carbon *per annum*.[29]

Projects involving the restoration, refurbishment, and often also the extension of existing theatre buildings have been numerous during the last ten years. Partly this trend is because recession and austerity have prompted managements to make the best of what they already have, partly because ACE and Creative Scotland have targeted funding to these projects (in response to their own limited budgets), and partly because, after sixty years of investment, few places lack a major arts centre or theatre.[30] In October 2018, The Theatres Trust reported that 148 theatres which had responded to a call for information had collectively spent £312 million on maintenance and upgrades during the previous five years.[31] As well as necessary repairs, these projects often also address broader themes. As is the case in new theatres, there is often a wish to create more space for education, to ensure accessibility, to reduce energy use, and to maximise non-box-office revenue through the provision of new facilities or by achieving efficiencies, as many of the following projects show.

### Pre-1939 theatres in London and beyond

In 2003, The Theatres Trust estimated that London's West End theatres – mostly built before 1939 – would need £250 million spending on them during the next fifteen years.[32] Falling plaster in the Apollo Theatre's auditorium in 2013 served as a reminder of the problem. In addition to repairs and the technical upgrades that are needed to serve the latest generation of major blockbuster shows, audience expectations are increasing in terms of comfort and sightlines, the availability of toilets, and accessibility.[33] Auditoria are reasonably easily (if not cheaply) dealt with: the position of seating can, for example, often be adjusted. Major interventions in front-of-house and backstage areas, however, are more difficult. Many West End theatres are listed as structures of architectural significance, while central London sites are typically cramped and theatre owners are reluctant to let venues go 'dark' for prolonged periods. Nonetheless, money has been spent by all the major West End owners, including the Really Useful Group, Nimax, and especially Delfont Mackintosh.[34]

In east London, meanwhile, Wilton's Music Hall has been brought back to life. Originally opened in 1859 and rebuilt in 1878, it is a rare survivor of the Victorian 'pub hall', in which entertainment was combined with refreshments. The building had fallen into disrepair by the 1990s and was placed on the World Monuments Fund's endangered sites watchlist in 2007. By this date, a new team led by Frances Mayhew had taken charge of the building. A specialist design and construction team, including the architect Tim Ronalds, was appointed in 2006. Ronalds, who had previously overseen the extension and refurbishment of the Hackney Empire, was keen to maintain its as-found ambience: 'we took a new approach to conservation, by not "restoring" the building in the usual sense but by doing only what was essential to make it secure, safe, and useable, aiming to preserve the very special atmosphere Wilton's has of a derelict theatre rediscovered'.[35] By September 2015, £4 million had been spent. The building was made structurally secure, the auditorium was conserved, and new front-of-house areas were created, including space for educational activities (fig. 3.9).

3.9   Wilton's Music Hall, auditorium in 2013

3.10   Bristol Old Vic, after the completion of the new foyer by Haworth Tompkins, 2018

Across the rest of the country, too, older theatres have been sensitively upgraded and restored, including Hull New Theatre, Newcastle Theatre Royal, and the Everyman, Cheltenham. At Bristol Old Vic, the eighteenth-century auditorium was sympathetically refurbished by Andrzej Blonski Architects in 2011 while the front-of-house areas were reorganised by Haworth Tompkins in 2016–18. As part of this work, the theatre's 1970s extension (designed by Peter Moro) was swept away. Moro's building contained the theatre studio and so presented a virtually windowless wall of brown brick to the street. In its place has come a new foyer (fig. 3.10), with the studio being relocated elsewhere on the site. The new building has a glazed elevation, with cheerful bright-red signage and perforated screens. Light and airy, with exposed timber beams, the foyer is dominated by the newly exposed brick wall of the historic auditorium. Bearing the scars of previous alterations, this wall has a strong character and suggests something of the theatre's age and history.

In Chester, the city's 1930s Odeon cinema was reconfigured and extended between 2014 and 2017 to become Storyhouse, a combined library/theatre/cinema. As is discussed in the case study section, Storyhouse offers a large, flexible auditorium, a theatre studio, a cinema, library, and café. The local authority maintained its support for the project even after the local Conservatives (who initially championed it) lost power to Labour, with both parties ultimately seeing an arts building as something which could add to the vitality and attractiveness of Chester. Collaboration and partnership were the project's keynotes: between politicians and officials; between different funders; between the library service and the arts organisation which was to take on the building. An experienced project manager and a non-partisan chair provided expert direction. What could have become an exercise in penny-pinching – locating the library alongside the theatre – has in fact yielded a creative, well-used, and popular building which offers a compelling organisational and architectural model for new civic buildings.

Three of the other case studies comprise historic theatres which have been substantially altered, namely Glasgow Theatre Royal (2010–14), Perth Theatre (2010–17), and the Citizens Theatre, Glasgow (2014–20). However, as was the case at Wilton's Music Hall, dramatic change is not always wanted. 'Character' can assume real significance. For example, Ash Sakula's refurbishment of Chapter Arts, Cardiff, was praised in 2010 for maintaining the 'homegrown, organic aesthetic' of this former school, used as an arts centre since the 1970s.[36] Similarly, Aedas Arts Team's reconstruction of Tara Theatre, London (2015–17) drew strongly on the company's ethos as an Asian-led theatre company, presenting plays from around the world in London, working in a Victorian building in the twenty-first century. It, too, is considered in more detail in the case study section of this book.

## Major national venues

Three major national venues have been re-worked since 2008, namely the Royal Shakespeare Theatre (RST) in Stratford-upon-Avon, the Royal Opera House in London, and the National Theatre. The first to be completed was the RST. Designed by Elisabeth Scott and opened in 1932, the theatre was, as was discussed in Chapter 1, never much liked by actors and audiences. It was transformed between 2007 and 2010 by a team led by Bennetts Associates after earlier proposals for an all-new theatre (designed by Erick van Egeraat) had been abandoned. There was much discussion with English Heritage and the Twentieth Century Society of the approach to be taken, and a detailed study of the existing building was made by conservation specialists Alan Baxter and Associates. Historically significant areas such as the foyers were carefully restored, but otherwise major changes were made (fig. 3.11). The building was extended (acquiring a tower in the process), a new glazed promenade was built linking the RST foyer with the Swan Theatre to the rear, and the RST auditorium itself was gutted.

3.11  Royal Shakespeare Theatre, Stratford-upon-Avon (Elisabeth Scott, 1932; Bennetts Associates, 2010)

The design of the new RST auditorium drew on that of the temporary Courtyard Theatre, designed for the Royal Shakespeare Company (RSC) by Ian Ritchie Architects with input from consultants including Charcoalblue. This 1000-seat space opened in 2006 and demonstrated the potential of a courtyard auditorium of this size, serving as a kind of working prototype for what might be built in the RST. The aim was to locate actors and audiences in the same space, unlike the 'two rooms' of Scott's proscenium-arch RST, and for audiences to be as close to the stage as possible. The concept for the Courtyard Theatre was developed in close collaboration with members of the RSC's technical teams, who went on to play an important role in the design of the 'new' RST auditorium (see colour plates). As reconstructed, the original proscenium arch and stage survive, but a new, galleried thrust-stage auditorium has been created in the space previously occupied by the audience. It has been felt by many to be a marked improvement on its predecessor, offering the proximity and actor–audience contact long felt lacking at the RST.[37]

In London, Stanton Williams was responsible for the £51 million Royal Opera House (ROH) 'Open Up' project.[38] In addition to improved public facilities and the reconstruction of the venue's smaller auditorium, the aim was to bring something of the life of the surrounding area into the building during the day by providing daytime public access to the foyers for the first time. Working almost entirely within the ROH's 1990s extension, originally designed by Dixon Jones/BDP, Stanton Williams carved a new public route through the building, connecting the historic Bow Street entrances with Covent Garden piazza to the west and making space for a new shop and café/bar as well as educational activities. The aesthetic is calm and restrained: cream walls, textured plaster, and Spanish marble sit alongside walnut panelling in an antidote to the ornament of the historic auditorium. The new Linbury Theatre, created within the shell of the ROH's old black-box studio and devised with the theatre consultant, Charcoalblue, is a compact and deliberately 'characterful' auditorium, with curving galleries richly finished with walnut fronts (fig. 3.12) and the possibility of adjusting the stalls rake to suit the varying needs of opera and ballet. The work was entirely funded by private donations

3.12   Linbury Theatre, Royal Opera House, London (Stanton Williams, 2018)

and carried out whilst the ROH remained open – no mean feat in either logistical or engineering terms.

On the other side of the Thames, the National Theatre was transformed through a series of interventions in its foyers and backstage areas, overseen by Haworth Tompkins. Under the banner 'NT Future', the work (discussed in full in the case studies) included the extension of Denys Lasdun's 1976 building to create new workshops and the reconfiguration of other backstage areas, not least to make room for on-site facilities for education. Within the foyers, alterations made in the 1990s were reversed, notably at the main entrance, where something of the sequence of spaces originally provided by Lasdun was reinstated, while a new bookshop and expanded café were created, the latter being one of several measures intended to improve the theatre's relationship with the adjacent riverside walk. Elsewhere, the accretions of forty years were stripped back, with the design, construction, and client teams displaying a real understanding of (and respect for) the building's significance. A full Conservation Management Plan was produced at an early stage. Following the completion of the work, the NT's foyers now buzz with activity during the day. They have become a well-used workspace as well as a popular meeting place, showing how contemporary theatres can be more than playhouses alone.

### Re-working post-war theatres

The National is not the only theatre of the 1960s/70s boom to have been refurbished since 2008. Many regional venues of this era have also been transformed, in what has emerged as a distinct group of projects. Some work is relatively routine, and perhaps little-noticed. Upgrades to building fabric and services are frequently needed in buildings which are now entering their fifth or sixth decade, and which were designed in an era of cheap energy, before questions of thermal performance or environmental sustainability became significant. Many projects have, however, gone further. Amid enthusiasm for what has become known as 'mid-century modern style', a core aim when these buildings are refurbished is often to remove unsympathetic alterations and to celebrate their original architectural quality. Indeed, post-war theatres are increasingly recognised as being of heritage value. As of 2018, fourteen post-1945 theatres in England, one in Wales, and one in Scotland are 'listed' for their special architectural or historical interest.[39]

Although not a theatre, the re-working of the Royal Festival Hall (1951) by Allies and Morrison between 2005 and 2007 forms an important example in which sympathetic restoration was combined with extensions and technical improvements. Many theatres have followed in its wake. Coventry's Belgrade Theatre (1958) was restored and extended by Stanton Williams between 2005 and 2007, ridding the foyers of the dark colours and panelling that had been introduced in the 1980s and 1990s. A substantial extension provided a second auditorium, hospitality space, a new bar, and much-needed rehearsal room. In Sheffield, the Crucible Theatre (1971) was restored and extended between 2007

and 2009; the architects were Burrell Foley Fischer. In a £15 million project, new function rooms and expanded foyers were provided while the box office was moved closer to the main entrance. The auditoria and backstage areas were refurbished, and access was improved throughout the building. The work gave the theatre a bold new frontage onto Tudor Square, but at the same time care was taken to respect the integrity of the original design. For example, the boldly patterned foyer carpets are very much in the spirit of the 1971 originals. In Birmingham, meanwhile, a major capital project took place at the Repertory Theatre (1971) between 2011 and 2013. The theatre was connected to the adjacent, newly built Library of Birmingham while the front-of-house and technical areas were refurbished. The result of all this work was that the 'Rep' gained a new 300-seat studio auditorium (replacing a previous studio), an extended foyer, a refurbished bar/restaurant, upgrades to its glazing and lighting, as well as new backstage facilities.[40] The theatre's executive director, Stuart Rogers, highlighted the extent to which the team had sought to recover the spirit of the original design: 'we feel it's true to the 1970s architecture but also includes the best technology of the twenty-first century.'[41] A different approach was taken in Cardiff, where Sherman Cymru's rather bland early-1970s façade was entirely hidden during 2010–11 by a street-facing extension intended not only to provide additional space but also to give the theatre a stronger presence and clearer identity.[42] It had previously blended into the adjacent Student Union building, having been built as a university college venue.

Other major projects include Rick Mather's £20 million extension to the Lyric Hammersmith (2010–15), which provided the theatre – located within a 1970s shopping centre – with new spaces for training and education, and significantly improved its environmental performance.[43] The location of the theatre's extension on the shopping centre roof made it challenging to deliver. In Chichester, Haworth Tompkins oversaw the restoration of the Grade II*-listed Festival Theatre (1962) between 2010 and 2014, demolishing the ad hoc additions to Powell and Moya's original building, creating a new backstage block, improving the thrust-stage auditorium, and sensitively restoring the foyers

3.13 Chichester Festival Theatre: Powell and Moya's design of 1962 following restoration and the construction of new backstage extensions by Haworth Tompkins

(fig. 3.13).[44] In Plymouth, the Theatre Royal (1982) was extended in 2013. Conceived by Andrzej Blonski, who had served as the project architect for the Peter Moro Partnership when the theatre was built, the work included new cladding and glazing, a foyer extension, a new function area with a balcony, a new café, and an additional performance space dedicated to community and outreach work.

At Sussex University, the Gardner Arts Centre was re-born as the Attenborough Centre for the Creative Arts. Closed in 2007, the building – designed by Basil Spence – was reconfigured by RH Partnership in 2014–15, combining sensitive restoration with improvements to the auditorium. York's Theatre Royal, meanwhile, was reworked by De Matos Ryan in 2015–16.[45] Previously owned by the city council, during the course of the work the theatre was sold to York Conservation Trust for £1. Its Victorian auditorium gained a new flat stage and new seating, floor levels in parts of the building were tweaked in the name of accessibility, while the foyers – largely located in a stylish extension of 1968, designed by Patrick Gwynne – were decluttered, re-roofed, and restored as a place to meet, eat, and drink, with new lighting highlighting their hexagonal concrete columns and mushroom-like vaults (fig. 3.14). The scope

3.14    Theatre Royal, York, following refurbishment and restoration by De Matos Ryan, 2016

of works was reviewed using a system of 'lenses', with potential interventions being tested against criteria such as their potential to generate income or reduce energy use.

In Eastbourne, the façades of the Congress Theatre (1963) were restored after falling masonry caused concern, while work between 2017 and 2019 saw the restoration of the listed theatre's interiors (recapturing the spirit of their crisp 1960s modernism) and the renewal of its mechanical services. In Leicester, the Haymarket Theatre (1973) reopened in 2018 after having been dark for ten years, while Warwick Arts Centre (1974) is, at the time of writing, in the middle of a major reconstruction scheme which will provide new auditoria and a new gallery. In Bolton, large sections of the Octagon Theatre (1967) have been demolished as of late 2018, with the theatre being rebuilt around the retained core of the

auditorium to designs by Feilden Clegg Bradley. When completed, it will not only have a stronger presence in the streetscape, but also will include new studios for community and youth work as well as a larger café. In Leeds, builders are on site at the Playhouse, opened in 1990 as the last theatre of the 'Housing the Arts' boom. Its new entrance, extended foyers and reconfigured auditorium are discussed in the case studies. Looking ahead, Liverpool Playhouse – built in the nineteenth century and extended in 1968 – is to be restored and reconfigured by Haworth Tompkins, following on from the same architects' work at the nearby Everyman Theatre. In Scotland, finally, plans for the £26 million refurbishment and extension of Pitlochry Festival Theatre (1981) have been announced, including the provision of a purpose-built studio auditorium to designs by Nicoll Russell Studio. The project took a step forward in

November 2018 when the theatre received news of a £10 million grant courtesy of the Tay Cities Region Deal.[46]

### A new process?

One final example challenges the idea that a capital project involves a linear journey from original 'vision' to built reality. At Battersea Arts Centre, a nineteenth-century town hall used as an arts centre since 1974, Haworth Tompkins worked with artistic director David Jubb and his team in a more experimental fashion (fig. 3.15) over the course of nearly a decade. What Jubb called a 'uniquely iterative' design process, dubbed 'play grounding', allowed ideas to be tested before final decisions were made.[47] Steve Tompkins commented that the team worked in 'accretive, empirical' ways akin to the methods of a producing theatre,[48] with initial, experimental interventions in the building being related to the needs of specific productions. As he explained in 2011:

BAC asked us to invent the future of the theatre with them. To transform the Town Hall for improvisation and experiment by theatre artists, but also to work like theatre artists ourselves. Artists-in-residence, in fact. So, on the one hand, we've begun to take the listed building back towards a more authentic incarnation as a town hall, removing generic arts centre overlays and remapping technical infrastructure so that the whole building can operate as a found space once again. On the other hand, we've been adding to the building, with production-specific interventions. Redecorations, refittings, demolitions, new theatrical layers of production for shows.[49]

The feasibility and design process was thus iterative and exploratory. Ideas and solutions emerged as the process unfolded, before a more definitive brief was drawn up. The final result, Tompkins concluded, thus came about following a long period of 'managed instability', which allowed the

3.15   Battersea Arts Centre, Grand Hall, following reconstruction by Haworth Tompkins, 2018

creative team to continue working in (and working with) a building that they loved, and delivered their ambitions at a lower cost than would have been the case for a more conventional capital project.[50]

As of 2018, virtually the whole building has been repurposed as performance space, with technical infrastructure available throughout. Offices have been moved to create more space for performances and events. Writing in the *Architects' Journal*, Merlin Fulcher was enthusiastic: 'it feels like a school where the teachers have run away and anything is possible but everyone has consensually agreed to respect the historic building and its trendy contemporary light fittings'.[51] However, the final part of the journey was not easy. There was a major fire in the Grand Hall in 2015, just as the rebuilding project was drawing to a close, and for a moment everything seemed to be in doubt. As it turned out, however, the catastrophe allowed the architects a freer hand. The rebuilt hall preserves the memory of its original form: for example, the vault was reinterpreted in perforated timber panels. There are also allusions to the fire in, for example, the distressed wall surfaces. New technical infrastructure has been installed and the stage has been lowered. As one might expect of Haworth Tompkins' work, the result is open-ended.[52] That is to say, the theatre wears its history on its sleeve but also invites its users to make their own contributions. For Tompkins, the experience was a revelation. In 2018, he commented that 'working alongside Battersea Arts Centre for twelve years has taught us to listen harder, to care less about sole authorship or frozen architectural perfection and more about open communication, creative risk-taking and social engagement'.[53]

## Conclusions

In 2007, Kully Thiarai asked of new theatre architecture, 'should we play safe and repeat old models?'[54] Thiarai was then the artistic director at Leicester's soon to be opened Curve, the design of which sought to 'turn theatre inside out' by placing two substantial auditoria at the centre of the building with the possibility of views onto the stage from the foyers. Has British theatre architecture 'played safe' since then? At the

beginning of this book, we noted that it is too early to offer a detailed analysis. Nonetheless, some themes have emerged from the account thus far and are developed further in the case studies which follow, not least accessibility, sustainability, place-making, education, engagement with diverse communities, the value of non-box-office income, and an ever-increasing emphasis on theatres' role in encouraging economic development and cultural 'well-being'. Many of these themes are not entirely new, as we saw in Chapter 1. The economic role of the arts, for example, has been discussed since the 1980s, while the daytime use of foyers for meeting, eating, and drinking can be traced to the late 1950s and theatres like the Belgrade, Coventry. As for the performance spaces themselves, many of the contemporary theatres discussed here include walls 'papered with people' in auditoria whose tiered arrangement and side galleries develop the historic courtyard principles first revived during the 1970s. Though a degree of flexibility is often desired in contemporary theatre, it is frequently balanced by a desire for character rather than architectural neutrality.

What is significant about the period covered by *Play On* is the extent to which theatre organisations have navigated a challenging funding context, the product of a prolonged period of recession as well as sustained spending cuts. Capital projects have frequently been more modest than those of the late 1990s, space has to work hard, and refurbishment projects have been numerous as organisations make the best of their buildings. There are parallels with the late 1970s and 1980s, a period with its own economic and political challenges whose theatre architecture was dominated by modestly conceived new theatres as well as a notable number of refurbishment projects. However, at the same time, there are differences. New partnerships and new emphases have emerged since 2008, as have often-entrepreneurial approaches (the Bridge, for example) and a willingness to think creatively about what an arts building might offer or how it should be run (as at Storyhouse). Some decisions have been made out of necessity rather than choice. For those whose ideal is the subsidised theatre of the 1960s and 1970s or the often high levels of architectural specification of that era, the results may be disappointing at times. One thinks of – and

3.16   Bristol Old Vic, the foyer during the day

sympathises with – Oliver Wainwright's description of Southampton, where the 1930s civic centre is now a privately run concert venue, where council services have been outsourced, and where the new theatre and art gallery are 'wrapped with a money-making skin of restaurants and apartments' in a 'diagram of public funds being swallowed by private interests'.[55]

Yet despite all the challenges, a key theme of the post-war boom, namely the theatre as a 'public' place, has survived intact. Indeed, the advent of wi-fi, the growth of freelance/flexible working, and increasing student numbers have all generated new users for the spaces within theatre buildings (fig. 3.16). Community groups, too, often meet in theatres, and in some cases have also taken an active role in saving these buildings. Theatres may be valued as venues for entertainment, but they can also offer welcoming, even non-commercial oases to meet and to 'be' at a time when public services are often being cut back. In Chester, for example, 48 per cent of visitors to Storyhouse come to spend time in the building.[56] One hundred and fifty groups meet there; others come to see friends, have lunch, or to pass the time. Furthermore, theatre-going remains popular. Despite the advent of on-demand streaming services, which bring a cornucopia of entertainment into the home, and despite economic recession, audience numbers have held up. In 2017, 500- to 1000-seat presenting houses and smaller producing houses enjoyed a record-breaking year in terms of sales and box office income.[57] Although smaller theatres saw their income fall, the reduction was largely attributed to a reduction in the number of performances; larger producing theatres and concert halls sold fewer tickets but saw a modest growth in income. In real terms (taking account of inflation) the overall average price paid for a ticket rose by 2 per cent after 2013, and has fallen by 2 per cent since 2016.[58] Theatres which saw the biggest rises in audience numbers (producing houses of all scales) also reported the greatest rises in average price paid during the previous five years. Some productions, like the National Theatre's staging of Michael Morpurgo's *War Horse*, have been phenomenally successful in Britain and internationally. One might speculate that the 'authentic', live quality of

theatre and the experience of theatre-going itself are both prized in an increasingly digital, even virtual world. Nonetheless, new technology has also reshaped theatre-going, not only opening up new possibilities on stage but also allowing the major national companies to extend their reach like never before. The National Theatre's 'NT Live' programme of filmed productions has, for example, been seen by 5.5 million people in over 2,000 venues around the world, including more than 650 venues in the UK.[59]

What do the next ten years hold? Arts Council England's draft ten-year strategy for the 2020s calls for both public and private funding levels to be increased, for arts organisations to connect to a greater degree with Britain's diverse communities, and for the arts to engage fully with the digital revolution. There are clearly challenges ahead, not least those which may follow Brexit; there are likely to be further funding cuts. However, theatre-makers seem to have an innate ability to weather storms, and, indeed, sometimes to thrive on them: 'the show must go on'. If those who run, design and fund theatres can rise to the challenges of the next ten years as they have those of the last ten, 'the show' should be an exciting one.

(right)
Plate 1 Hull Truck Theatre (Wright and Wright, 2009)

(below)
Plate 2 Beacon Arts Centre, Greenock (LDN Architects, 2013): the auditorium, a miniature reprise of themes the architects had first explored at Eden Court, Inverness, in the 1970s

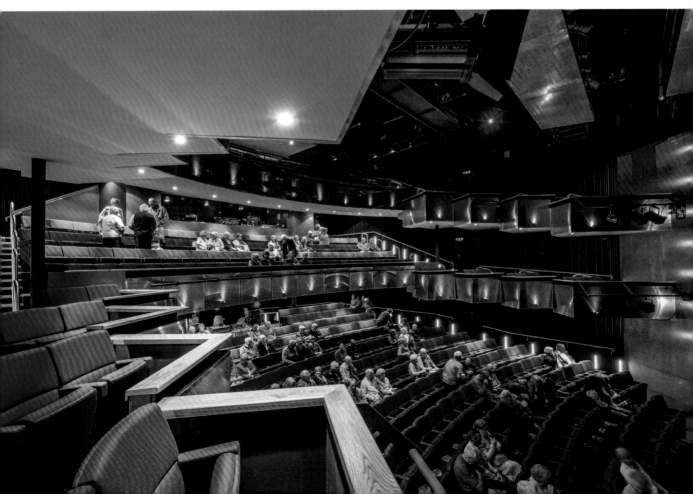

Plate 3   Parabola Arts Centre, Cheltenham, auditorium (Foster Wilson Architects, 2009)

Plate 4   The new Royal Shakespeare Theatre auditorium (Bennetts Associates, 2010)

Plate 5    Everyman Theatre, Liverpool (Haworth Tompkins, 2014)

Plate 6   Everyman Theatre, Liverpool: detail of façade

(*left*)
Plate 7 Everyman
Theatre box office,
with the sliding shutter
of the multi-purpose
performance/function
space above

Plate 8 Cast (RHWL Arts Team, 2013), with the brightly illuminated ribs of the largest auditorium billowing into the foyer and clearly on view through the glazed elevation. Above the entrance is the copper-clad volume containing the studios and education space

Plate 9  Café at Cast, a well-used meeting place during the day

Plate 10    Storyhouse, Chester (Bennetts Associates, 2017), looking back from the location of the original cinema screen towards the café, cinema, and library

Plate 11    The auditorium at Storyhouse in thrust-stage mode

Plate 12    Automated ticket machines at Storyhouse, set into a patterned brick wall

Plate 13    Tara Theatre, London (Aedas Arts Team, 2016)

Plate 14   National Theatre at night following the completion of NT Future, with Jake Tilson's illuminated signage

Plate 15   The Pigott Atrium at the National Theatre, looking out towards the riverside walk and Somerset House

Plate 16    Dorfman Theatre foyer, National Theatre

Plate 17   Within the National Theatre foyers, new lighting has been installed
to celebrate the texture of Denys Lasdun's board-marked concrete

Plate 18    Theatre Royal, Glasgow, as reworked by Page\Park (2014)

Plate 19 The new foyers and stairs at Glasgow Theatre Royal

Plate 20   Perth Theatre foyer (Richard Murphy Architects, 2017)

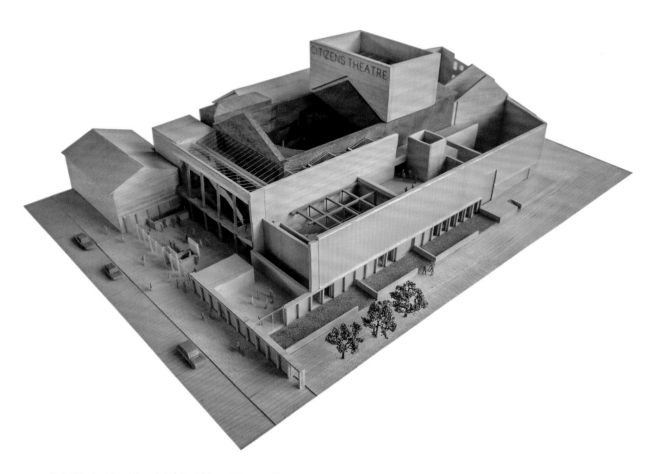

Plate 21 Architects' model of the Citizens Theatre, Glasgow

Plate 22   Bridge Theatre (Haworth Tompkins, 2017), detail of auditorium seating with fabric and leather

# Case Studies

Everyman Theatre, Liverpool

Cast, Doncaster

Storyhouse, Chester

Tara Theatre, London

National Theatre, London: NT Future

Theatre Royal, Glasgow

Perth Theatre

Citizens Theatre, Glasgow

Leeds Playhouse

Bridge Theatre, London

C1.1 Everyman Theatre, Liverpool, the Hope Street elevation with shutters featuring images by Dan Kenyon and lettering by Jake Tilson

# Everyman Theatre, Liverpool

Architect: Haworth Tompkins

Client: Liverpool and Merseyside Theatres Trust

Contractor: Gilbert Ash

Structural engineer: Alan Baxter and Associates

M&E: Watermans Building Services

Project manager: GVA Acuity

CDM co-ordinator: Turner and Townsend

Acoustic engineer: Gillieron Scott Acoustic Design

Theatre consultant: Charcoalblue

Access consultant: Earnscliffe Davies Associates

Stage engineering: Stage Technologies

Artists: Antoni Malinowski, Dan Kenyon, Jake Tilson

'An everyman for everyone' was the strapline attached to the £28 million reconstruction of Liverpool's Everyman Theatre, completed in 2014. The slogan reflected the Everyman's well-established tradition of accessible informality and the extent to which the theatre inspired fierce devotion among its audiences. The architect Steve Tompkins later recalled that 'many people expressed the view that, if we messed this up, we needn't bother coming back to the city'.[1] As he put it:

> People were anxious that it would become too posh, that the soul of the building would be lost. One taxi driver actually stopped the cab and said: "You fuck that up, you're fucking fucked." That was pretty much the text for the project.[2]

The idea of 'an everyman for everyone' is made clear in the main Hope Street façade of Haworth Tompkins' new building. Here, the movable aluminium shutters which shade the theatre from the sun feature representations of more than 100 Liverpudlians, created from photographs by the artist Dan Kenyon. Whereas the massed statuary on the west front of a medieval cathedral might include saints and biblical figures, normal people are the stars at the Everyman.

The success of the design – which won the prestigious Stirling Prize in 2014 – reflects the strength of the original project 'vision', the clarity with which the Everyman's creative team expressed their identity and needs, and the extent to which the vision was sympathetically and collaboratively developed. The old theatre had originally been built as a chapel before being converted in 1964. With a wide thrust stage, it was popular with actors and audiences. The task in replacing it was to create a sustainable new building which would seem familiar whilst at the same time fixing the old theatre's many technical problems.[3] The new theatre reinterprets the form of the Everyman's previous auditorium within a building twice the size of the old theatre which has enhanced front-of-house areas, learning spaces, and technical facilities. The first all-new theatre by Haworth Tompkins, who had hitherto been known for re-working existing buildings such as the Royal

Court and the Young Vic, it is a tactile piece of architecture which avoids the sterile slickness of much contemporary design. Instead, it celebrates the textures and colours of the materials from which it is made. These materials give it a sense of place, history, and, indeed, theatricality. They create a welcoming, informal backdrop for actors and audiences which delights in humane details and human experience rather than grand architectural gestures.

## History and Context

Writing in the early 1980s, the historians George Rowell and Anthony Jackson recognised the significance of the Everyman's work, writing that 'there can be no doubting that Liverpool theatre has in the past fifteen years undergone a sea-change, and for that the Everyman must be held primarily responsible'.[4] The theatre was founded in 1964 by Peter James and Terry Hands, who sought to stage 'serious modern plays which [they] felt were being neglected by the Liverpool Playhouse'.[5] Students from the nearby university became especially keen patrons; by the end of the 1960s, the Everyman was known for its youth and education work. During the 1970s, the theatre came to be regarded as a major 'alternative rep', avoiding the 'safe' quality which sometimes characterised regional theatre for something more radical: outgoing, bold, and rooted in the community.[6] Poetry by Roger McGough was read in the basement bar, the first plays by Alan Bleasdale and Willy Russell were staged in the auditorium, and actors including Julie Walters, Pete Postlethwaite, Bill Nighy, and Jonathan Pryce came to prominence there.[7] Conditions in the former chapel, however, were poor for both audiences and actors,[8] although some improvements were made in 1977 when the theatre gained a new street-facing block.[9]

The theatre struggled in the 1990s after losing its subsidy.[10] In 1999, Liverpool Merseyside Theatre Trust was formed to manage both the Everyman and the Playhouse, a late nineteenth-century proscenium-arch theatre which had been boldly extended in the late 1960s.[11] The financial difficulties which had been faced by

C1.2   The 'old' Everyman in 2014, shortly before it was demolished. The building to the right was also demolished and its site incorporated into the rebuilt theatre

both theatres meant that neither was in a position to bid for Arts Council England (ACE) Lottery funding during the capital projects boom of the mid-1990s.[12] In 1999, ACE recognised that Liverpool had missed out and earmarked some £6 million for the two theatres.[13] Essential health and safety work was done to the Playhouse in order to secure its theatre licence, but it was clear that much more was needed. Both theatres were by now in poor condition, had failing technical systems, lacked space on site where work could be created, and offered limited opportunities to generate income beyond ticket sales.[14] During 2002–03, various options were considered, including the construction of a new building elsewhere in the city as a replacement for both the Everyman and Playhouse.[15] However, these options were expensive, coming in at some £60–80 million (at 2003 prices). They were also dependent on the progress of other redevelopment schemes, without which the new theatres might have become marooned in partly rebuilt areas of the city.[16]

In summer 2003, Liverpool Merseyside Theatre Trust appointed new joint chief executives, namely Deborah Aydon (executive director) and Gemma Bodinetz (artistic director). Aydon later recalled that their work initially fell into three distinct areas.[17] The first concerned the artistic and organisational development of the Trust. The second related to planning for European Capital of Culture 2008, which was awarded to Liverpool in 2003. The third area was the potential capital project, although this work was initially put on the back burner to allow a focus on the other two areas, and for market research and audience development work to be carried out.[18] However, the physical condition of the two theatres increasingly demanded attention. A project steering group was set up, including board members, the executive team, and external representatives. Aydon acted as Project Champion and Client Representative, while Bodinetz was Design Champion and had to sign off all design decisions.[19] The process was supported by Building Development Director, Robert Longthorne. Steve Tompkins was asked to join the steering group, but instead offered a day's work *pro bono*.[20] In 2005, Haworth Tompkins was appointed to produce a feasibility study. Subsequently, the practice was selected by means of a competitive *Official Journal of the European Union* (*OJEU*) interview to develop detailed proposals for the two theatres.[21]

An initial development plan for the Everyman in 2006 was followed by a more detailed study at the start of 2008. RIBA Stage C (concept design) was reached early in 2010 and Stage D (developed design) that summer, when planning consent was secured. During the period in which the design was being developed, funding applications were also made; the funding package took three years to assemble.[22] Having earmarked £6 million in 1999, ACE increased its offer to £8 million in recognition of the theatres' renewed success under Aydon and Bodinetz, and to encourage other stakeholders.[23] This funding supported all early project development, including land assembly. In July 2009 ACE increased its allocation again, awarding the Trust £12,876,104 in addition to funding drawn down to date. The North West Development Agency awarded £206,625 in 2007 as a 50 per cent contribution towards the final Feasibility Study, and contributed £1.7m to the purchase of the Everyman building in 2008. £6 million came from the European Regional Development Fund in spring 2011, allowing work to begin on site.[24] Support was also received from

private individuals, and trusts and foundations, while Liverpool City Council remained an important strategic partner throughout.

## The 'Vision'

The underlying premise was that the retention of both theatres on their existing sites would be more effective and efficient than a single new building elsewhere, with the Everyman being completely reconstructed and the Playhouse being restored and altered.[25] Of the two projects, it was decided that the Everyman should come first, not least because it was in worse condition than the Playhouse. There were also new opportunities to expand its footprint by acquiring adjacent properties.[26] (In this respect, the site acquisition process also included the purchase of the theatre's freehold, with the sale completing in nail-biting fashion, just twenty minutes before the deadline which had been imposed by the funders.[27]) In developing the final strategy, various options were tested, some involving a larger site than was eventually settled upon. It was decided to buy fewer properties and to use the resulting savings to develop the theatre site more densely.[28] In parallel, the possibility of retaining the existing auditorium was studied ('both as a sustainable re-cycling option and to preserve the original patina of the space') before it was concluded that 'structural, economic, logistical and technical criteria will almost certainly require a rebuild of the theatre in its entirety'.[29]

The 'vision' was summarised at RIBA Stage C as 'the creation of an informal, intense and welcoming performance space and a convivial foyer/bistro, along with much improved, accessible back-of-house facilities, rehearsal space and new Theatre and Community spaces'.[30] There would be a new auditorium, albeit one which evoked its predecessor:

> The advantages and disadvantages of the existing auditorium have been examined in the Development Plan: the thrust stage, three-sided seating block, relatively low ceiling and unpretentious décor are all regarded by the [trust] as germane to the Everyman's identity

69

and have served the theatre well throughout its recent history, whilst the lack of servicing capability, technical obsolescence and difficulty in adapting the staging configurations when required (especially for incoming touring productions) are equally embedded issues that cannot be solved satisfactorily without major change, most significantly the re-siting of the stage at ground or tailgate level.[31]

The new auditorium would retain the wide thrust stage of its predecessor, but would be easier to use and would enjoy significantly better technical facilities and equipment. For audiences, the space would be recognisable, but would be more comfortable. There would also be more seats, and in this respect, financial sustainability was emphasised:

> The new building is intended to strengthen the Trust's financial base by providing increased revenue. Increased attendances will bring increased box office revenue. A new catering operation – whether in-house or contracted-

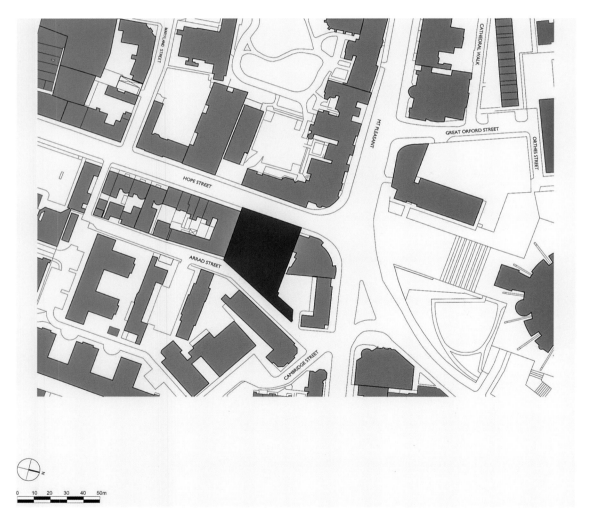

C1.3    Everyman Theatre, site plan showing the footprint of the expanded theatre

out – will provide a new income stream. The new building needs to support sponsorship income by providing space(s) conducive to corporate hospitality. It should allow for income generation from hires, whether on a larger scale from occasional conferences or on a smaller scale from hiring out individual spaces. It is essential that the cost of operating the new building does not reduce the project's positive impact on the business model. At every stage of decision-making, cost-in-use must be considered alongside capital costs, including the lifespan of equipment and materials; maintenance and cleaning of the building and equipment, and operational staffing requirements.[32]

With there being cuts in Liverpool City Council's culture budget after 2010, the need to generate income in as many ways as possible became increasingly significant.

The potential for a low-energy building was also stressed from an early stage, partly as a way to minimise running costs but also as an aim desirable in itself. Reference was made in the 2008 feasibility study to an 'exemplar sustainable theatre building that uses energy efficiently and consequently reduces running costs'.[33] Accordingly, the design team tender instructions required sustainable construction, low carbon design and consideration of sustainability in use, and a BREEAM (Building Research Establishment Environmental Assessment Method) rating of 'Excellent'. Tompkins and the design team embraced the idea, using the project to explore their interest in the design of major naturally ventilated public buildings.[34] Accessibility, too, emerged as a key consideration, being understood as something more than meeting legislative requirements.[35]

In addition to its practical elements, the 'vision' also had a more intangible side. Gemma Bodinetz set out the organisation's ambitions in an appealingly poetic fashion:

> The Everyman auditorium is waiting to be recontextualised within a thriving theatrical engine. Discovering it behind the dreary and poor back and front of house facilities is akin to

a surgeon finding that miraculously his elderly, emaciated, unloved patient has the heart of an Olympic athlete. It's a heartbeat worth transplanting.[36]

The need for the building to maintain the atmosphere of its predecessor was repeatedly emphasised:

> Any new theatre must remain as unpretentious, friendly and welcoming as the current building, whilst resolving the many practical problems that have made the continued running of the theatre less and less efficient and cost effective.[37]

Such ambitions would have implications for the theatre's architecture:

> Too grand and reverential and it will lose the right to put on daring young work by unknown writers. What is more it will fail to encourage the diverse and youthful audience that is critical to its survival. On the other hand if the design seems too inconsequential, too everyday, it will let down not only its neighbourhood and its city but will take the very magic away from one of the most glittering art forms there is.[38]

It was hoped that the result would be 'a technically advanced and highly adaptable new theatre that would retain the friendly, democratic accessibility of the old building, promote the organisation's values of cultural inclusion, community engagement and local creativity, and encapsulate the collective identity of the people of Liverpool'.[39] The challenge for Haworth Tompkins and their team – including theatre consultants Charcoalblue and engineers Alan Baxter and Associates – was to find an architecture which would express these ideas.[40] How did they respond?

## The Design

Haworth Tompkins was founded by Graham Haworth and Steve Tompkins in 1991. In 1997, they were commissioned to redesign the Royal Court in London. A steady stream of theatre work followed, which continues more than twenty years later.[41] During the late 1990s and early 2000s, these projects comprised either restorations with some new construction (the Royal Court, the Young Vic), or temporary 'pop-up' theatres in 'found' spaces (two temporary venues for the Almeida Theatre), rather than completely new buildings. Such projects encouraged the architects' interest in texture and materials, and their view that theatre architecture should engage with time and place.[42] Haworth Tompkins' theatre work has often explored the idea that these buildings are 'layered' structures, to which each generation of users (and designers) adds something. The building thus serves as a kind of 'tape recorder' of its history,[43] with Tompkins suggesting that the task of the design and client team when faced with an existing building is to consider 'how to intervene in a building's history, and add to it with a story of your own'.[44] Furthermore, the architects have also long had an interest in reforming the design process. In 2007, Tompkins co-wrote an article with Andrew Todd which called for the process to become 'more engaged', with all parties

being 'more experimental, more informed, more responsive, more communicative, and more aware of the real lives of our completed buildings'.[45] As they put it, 'the need to be vulnerable, to trust peripheral vision, to change our minds, to explore obscure diversions and repeatedly to test our progress against an informing idea, is common to both fields, but too rarely do we share our creative processes with sufficient candour'.[46]

Haworth Tompkins' remodelling of the Young Vic between 2005 and 2007 demonstrates these ideas well. This theatre had been created in 1970 on a wartime bombsite, when what was intended as a temporary auditorium was designed for the director Frank Dunlop by Bill Howell of Howell Killick Partridge and Amis (HKPA).[47] The auditorium, built from concrete blocks and exposed steelwork, was attached to the only surviving building on the site, a house and butcher's shop which was repurposed as the theatre foyer. Haworth Tompkins extended the building to create new foyers and turned the old foyer into the box office (retaining its worn butcher's tiles as a memory of its original

C1.4   Young Vic, London, as reconstructed by Haworth Tompkins, 2005–07

function). The auditorium was extended upwards to add seating and improve its technical capabilities; extra space was also wrapped around the auditorium, meaning that what were previously its exterior walls are now inside.[48] In other words, the building preserves memories of its history, both before and after it became the Young Vic, with both this history and the architecture itself being seen as essential parts of the theatre's identity. Similarly, as was discussed in Chapter 3, Haworth Tompkins' work at Battersea Arts Centre over the course of more than a decade saw a series of interventions being made on an incremental basis.[49] Rather than begin the capital project with a clearly defined outcome (as others had proposed), a more flexible, collaborative approach was taken, in which some changes were made to accommodate particular productions while other alterations were tested and prototyped before being fully implemented.

According to Tompkins and his colleague Roger Watts, the Young Vic project can be understood as one in which a new building was 'grown' from the 'seeds' of the auditorium and the butcher's shop.[50] The Everyman, too, required a similar approach. Now, however, the 'seed' was less tangible, comprising not a surviving building but rather the history and atmosphere of the old theatre. A further challenge, as Tompkins and Watts saw it, was to avoid perfection.[51] Any existing theatre – indeed, any existing building – inevitably imposes constraints on its users. A new building, by contrast, offers the chance to avoid such constraints. Yet theatre-makers often enjoy problems, reacting against their buildings in ways which turn out to be productive and creative. Tompkins and Watts thus sought in the Everyman to 'build in complexity, build in some recalcitrance', as well as 'memory and texture'.[52] They later recalled that they valued having had time to develop their response:

We had an unusually long time to develop the original concept with the Everyman team through extended feasibility and research work. The ideas of thrust stage auditorium, legible public façade, brick skin and expressed ventilation funnels remained constants from the early sketches and models but detailed

fabric design and space planning went through several, closely related incarnations in response to the developing brief, to funding targets and to detailed land negotiations.[53]

These ideas were discussed with 'everybody – from artistic director to stage door keeper'.[54] External consultation was also a keynote of the project, as the design and client team sought to build understanding among external funders, stakeholders, contractors, and the public.

The Everyman's location on Hope Street places it on a significant axis in central Liverpool, a historic street which links Giles Gilbert Scott's Anglican Cathedral of 1904–78 with the Metropolitan Cathedral, designed by Frederick Gibberd in 1962 and completed in 1967. At its north end, around the Everyman, it comprises a mixture of three-storey, red-brick eighteenth-century terraced houses and stone and brick commercial buildings whose scale and presence reflects Liverpool's nineteenth-century prosperity. Also prominent is the Philharmonic Hall of 1939, a brick building designed by Herbert J. Rowse which is evocative of contemporary Dutch and Scandinavian modernism. Within this environment, the Everyman needed to hold its own whilst retaining a degree of 'edginess', as has already been noted:

The position of the Everyman on the ceremonial route between the two cathedrals is another significant aspect of the project and an important factor in the evolution of the elevation and massing of the new building. Our instinct is that there is no place here for a purely frivolous or insubstantial architecture, but rather the theatre should take its place as another permanent site for public celebration and congregation in the city.[55]

The theatre's Hope Street frontage forms part of a continuous terrace of buildings on the east side of the street. Haworth Tompkins' elevation is around twice as long as that of its predecessor, as a result of the rebuilt theatre's expanded footprint. It is in two parts. To the right, a small, brick-clad volume connects the main part of the theatre to the adjacent 'Annexe' building. Its materials reflect

C1.5   The Everyman in its Hope Street context, with the Liverpool Medical Institution to the left

the red-brick architecture of its surroundings; its subordinate relationship with the main part of the theatre echoes the way in which the stone-clad, colonnaded Liverpool Medical Institution on the other side of the Everyman similarly has two parts, one much grander than the other.

The main part of the theatre has an elevation with essentially three parts. At pavement level, full-height glazing steps back to make room for café chairs and tables. Above, a projecting balcony allows patrons in the first-floor foyer to catch a breath of fresh air or to watch the world

go by. The Everyman's previous neon signage has been reinterpreted on the balcony front by the artist and graphic designer Jake Tilson, using LED lighting. The upper part of the building is screened by Dan Kenyon's movable panels with their etched depictions of ordinary Liverpudlians. Above the top of the screen, but only really visible in oblique and distant views, are the brick-clad stacks which form part of the ventilation system. Meanwhile the rear of the building is somewhat quieter, and certainly less formal. Here, red brick dominates, picking up on the surrounding buildings.

(*right*) C1.6   The rear elevation of the Everyman, the brick architecture of which echoes its historic neighbours

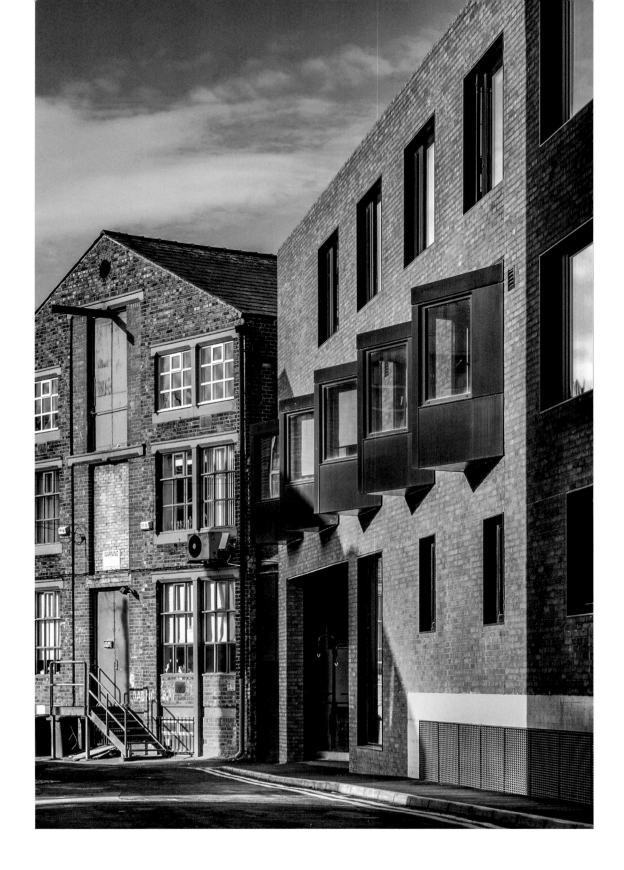

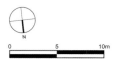

C1.7    Everyman Theatre, plan at level G+0.
This is the main public entrance level, with
the café running along the street front

Key:
  3    Store
  5    WC
  12   Youth and community changing
  13   Stage Door
  14   Actors' quiet room
  15   Stage management
  16   Dressing room
  17   Stage kitchen
  18   Workshop
  19   Auditorium (stage level)
  20   Youth and community studio
  21   Café
  22   Office
  23   Box office
  24   Get-around corridor

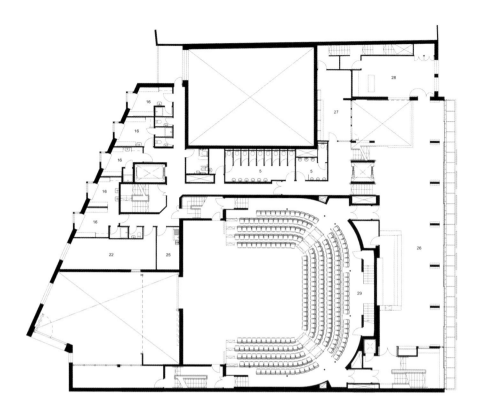

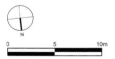

C1.8   Everyman Theatre, plan at level G+1.
This level is that of the main part of the auditorium
and the main foyer

Key:
 5   WC
16   Dressing room
22   Office
25   Laundry
26   Foyer bar
27   Writers' hub
28   Function room
29   Auditorium stalls

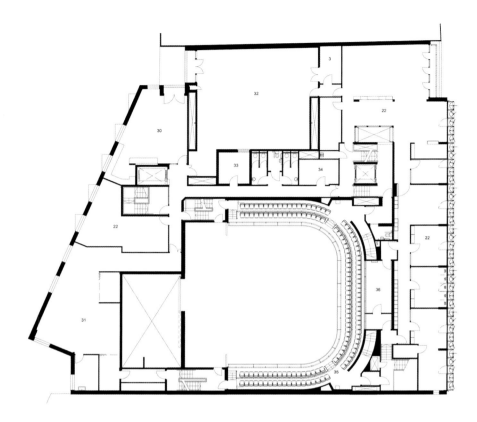

C1.9    Everyman Theatre, plan at level G+2, with the
auditorium gallery, offices, and the rehearsal room

Key:
  3    Store
 22    Office
 30    Green room
 31    Wardrobe
 32    Rehearsal room
 33    Sound recording room
 34    Server room
 35    Auditorium circle
 36    Control room

Tompkins has described the design as a 'palazzo',[56] something which 'has got to be part of an urban wall, it has got to do its duty as a piece of urbanism' but should also 'defer to the cathedrals'.[57] The Hope Street front certainly evokes the scale, presence, and symmetries of Palladio's urban *palazzi*, although those symmetries are disrupted by Kenyon's screens, each of which can be individually angled. The result is a potentially ever-changing ripple of panels on the elevation. In addition, the split between the glazed lower sections of the building and the screens above evokes the bipartite nature of the Everyman's 1977 façade, which comprised a rendered, blank wall above a recessed brick 'colonnade'. The new elevation is, however, much more transparent. Not only can the screens move, but the individuals' portraits are cut through them. As a result, the elevation is more permeable than the previous blank wall; it gives glimpses into the building beyond. The theatre is also more physically accessible. The lower foyer and café are no longer reached via steps but are now at pavement level.

In Tompkins' view, theatre foyers have a significant role to play:

Theatre architecture is not just about performance. It's about how you frame civil society. Where are the spaces in which strangers can meet at peace in a city? That for us is the underpinning idea. If you look at the support space of the theatre as a commercial space like a shopping mall or a branded coffee bar something has gone terribly wrong. You predispose the audience to being in a mood of consumerism rather than human transaction.[58]

The Everyman's foyers have moments of formality, such as the double-height entrance foyer or the processional main stair. There are also more informal touches, however, with Tompkins emphasising the need for 'corners to perch in, places for conspiracy'.[59] In order to make the most of its site and to achieve an efficient arrangement of space (in the interests of economy and environmental sustainability), the theatre is arranged as a series of half-levels, rising up from the entrance. Adjacent to the street is a relatively low-ceilinged café, with exposed board-marked concrete beams and walls of brick, concrete, and timber. Below this café is the reconstituted

C1.10   First-floor foyer, a long space successfully broken up by deep concrete beams and columns

C1.11   Auditorium, showing the mixture of reclaimed brick and board-marked concrete, the perimeter stairs, the wide thrust stage, and the 'lid' of the technical level

basement bistro: dark, cosy, and warm. Above the café, the first-floor foyer is more generously proportioned, evoking the formal *piano nobile* of classical townhouses as well as the way in which the nearby Philharmonic Hall couples a low-ceilinged entrance with more spacious foyers above.[60] The café and foyer run almost the full length of the main part of the elevation, but their length is broken down by a regular rhythm of board-marked concrete posts and beams. The beams at first-floor level, in particular, are deliberately deep in order to articulate a series of smaller areas within the length of the foyer.[61] The upper foyer gives access to an adjacent multi-purpose space divided by means of a sliding shutter from the foyer, for which it can act as an extension. A window, meanwhile, offers views into the theatre's Writers' Hub, allowing glimpses of creativity at work.

The interiors have a consistent, rich palette of materials: board-marked concrete, recycled brick, timber, leather, copper, and cork. White-painted plasterboard and MDF were rejected in favour of materials which might appeal to the senses and which would age well. In this respect, Tompkins and Watts have suggested that they

obsess about sensory experience. What does it smell like? What does it feel like? Will it become tawdry as it ages, or more beautiful?[62]

Furthermore, Tompkins had strong views on lighting:

Lighting is crucial. I'm phobic about lighting that is too bald. A lot of foyers are overlit. The Royal Court has very low levels of light. If you go to the Theatre Upstairs you might easily turn back on the way: you think, I must have gone wrong, this can't be in the public territory. That was what we wanted: the idea of leaving the party and venturing up the dark staircase to the attic.[63]

These themes are also evident in the Everyman's auditorium. It is lined with 25,000 bricks recycled from the old building, which give a warmth and depth to the space, further accentuated by the brown-gold colour of the seating.

The design of the auditorium was carefully developed and tested using card models and a 1:1 scale mock-up of part of the structure. Its position in the building makes it something of an anchor for everything else, as the stage floor is located at a height which facilitates the easy unloading of delivery lorries. As in the old theatre, the stage thrusts forward and is impressive in its width. It is surrounded on three sides by seating. Capacity is up slightly on the old theatre, at 405, and whereas the old auditorium had only a single tier, its replacement has a shallow gallery as well as the stalls. The addition of the gallery has allowed a reduction in the number of rows of stalls seating from twelve to six. Audiences enter the space as a single group from the foyer and then move up to the balcony using stairs located within the auditorium volume itself.

The auditorium has a definite 'lid' in the form of the technical level, which covers the whole space and creates an apparently solid ceiling. Its solidity is, however, something of an illusion. All of the grating which makes up its floor is in fact removable to allow props to be flown or lighting to be installed. Scaffolding poles define areas but allow for easy changes to be made. Much of the technical equipment can be readily unbolted, and there has been an effort to standardise equipment across the Everyman and Playhouse in order to allow staff to work at both sites. Notably, this level is accessible to people using wheelchairs.[64]

Backstage, the attention to detail and experience which characterises the front-of-house spaces continues. Deborah Aydon later noted her dislike of theatres where the backstage areas are poorly laid out or redolent of economy; staff, she argued, deserve as good a deal as customers.[65] Good use is made of daylight, for example in the rehearsal room, and materials have been chosen for their tactile qualities and robustness. Space has been provided for youth and community work, located conveniently next to the stage door. Dressing rooms have projecting bay windows, while there is an airy green room. During 'value engineering', some of the intended basement storage space was lost. However, with the tender process taking place in a falling market, the contract price came in under budget.[66] As a result, some of what had been lost was added back into the project's scope.

The building's natural ventilation strategy reflected the client's aspiration to achieve a BREEAM 'Excellent' rating as well as a desire to minimise running costs. Natural ventilation is unusual for a contemporary theatre auditorium in Britain. Theatres are intensively occupied during performances, but may be less busy at other times. They also see the use of a lot of equipment, some of which can generate a lot of heat. As a result, mechanical ventilation systems have been the norm since the 1960s.[67] During the 1990s, however, the art and science of designing contemporary, naturally ventilated theatres was explored by the architect Alan Short, not least at the Contact Theatre, Manchester (1993–99), which formed a key reference point for the design team along with Wright and Wright's similarly naturally ventilated Hull Truck Theatre (2009, and discussed in Chapter 3).[68]

In the case of the Everyman, air moves through the building by virtue of the stack effect, and so the theatre is, to some extent, designed around its ventilation system. The aim was, according to Jonathan Purcell, the building services engineer, 'to provide a nice, clean, swept path for the air to enter the space at low level, then meet very little resistance as it is allowed to rise from low level to high level in the auditorium; and, finally, to provide a simple route out through the roof-top chimneys'.[69] Air enters through an inlet louvre at the back of the building. Passing through acoustic attenuators, it enters a concrete-encased plenum,

C1.12 Particular attention was given to the backstage areas, which, like the public parts of the theatre, are comfortable spaces for staff, with tactile materials and ample daylight

which serves to cool the air in summer. It then passes beneath the stage, through secondary attenuators, and into a horseshoe-shaped plenum underneath the seating. Grilles below the seats finally allow the air into the auditorium. The heat given off by the audience (approximately 50 kW) and by lighting (usually c. 65 kW is in use at any one time during a performance) causes the air to rise through the lighting gantries to an acoustically attenuated, 2.5-metre-high exhaust air plenum. From here, a large duct, which doubles back on itself, delivers the air to the four louvred exhaust chimneys – nicknamed John, Paul, George, and Ringo by the design team. Early modelling work was important in showing that a fresh air requirement of $5m^3/s$ would flush the 115 kW heat gains from the auditorium. The sizing of the chimneys was critical to achieve the degree of buoyancy needed to meet this requirement as well as the Building Regulations for auditorium air quality. Other areas within the building are also naturally ventilated. The community/rehearsal room, for example, has a similar strategy though with some limited heating of incoming air owing to the lower level of heat gain which the space offers. In addition, the thermal mass of the building is important, with the heavyweight concrete structure serving to temper the air. A night-time purge rids the plenum structures of accumulated heat.

This sort of approach is not without its challenges. Natural ventilation can prove unpredictable in reality, and a certain amount of 'tuning' can sometimes be required.[70] Air handling units were installed at the Everyman just in case the system proved inadequate, but it apparently works well in practice and the mechanical units have hardly been used.[71] The theatre's BREEAM 'Excellent' rating is unusual for an urban performance building. Its achievement here recognises the nature of the ventilation system as well as other measures, such as the extensive amount of material from the old theatre which was recycled, or the use of ground-granulated blast-furnace slag (GGBS) as a cement replacement. GGBS is a by-product from the iron and steel industry, with lower levels of embodied carbon than cement. In this respect, the desire to evoke the atmosphere of the old building through the

reuse of its bricks was a practical and sustainable strategy as well as something poetically inspired.

## Conclusions: 'A Humane Art Form'

The March 2014 opening of the Everyman was positively received. Ticket sales, for example, were strong. The 2014–15 Annual Report (covering the Everyman and Playhouse) reported that the average ticket yield had increased compared with the previous year, and that there was a significant number of new bookers.[72] It concluded that the theatres' value to the Merseyside economy was £15,630,328, a 26 per cent increase on 2013/14.[73] Further increases were reported in 2015–16,[74] when a 'permanent' company was introduced to perform throughout the season in a revival of the classic repertory model.[75]

Architecturally, the building has been acclaimed. Among a field of thirty-three strong contenders, it was one of six projects selected as a RIBA North-West Regional Award winner in 2014. This and other prizes were, however, but a prelude to the theatre's success in the 2014 Stirling Prize. Its victory there – against strong competition including the Shard in London and the London School of Economics' Student Centre – recognised it as Britain's best major building that year. Its success can be explained by several factors. Among these is the extent to which the design is well detailed and fully resolved, as well as the efficiency with which the building meets its functional brief. But also significant is what the Everyman suggests about contemporary theatre – something which can be open and welcoming, formal and informal – as well as contemporary public architecture. It is an important example of sustainable architecture, sustainability here being understood both in terms of the design and material strategy, and the extent to which the building allows efficiencies in use. One of the Stirling Prize judges, Meredith Bowles, concluded that the Everyman is a fundamentally 'radical' proposition.[76]

The Everyman demonstrates what is possible when a passionate, well-informed client organisation with a clear view of its identity and requirements works with a committed, inventive design team. The project offers many learnings, among them the possibilities of environmental sustainability, the value of consultation and collaboration, and the importance of making humane, welcoming architecture. In this last respect, Gemma Bodinetz concluded:

> The choice of Haworth Tompkins was because [they] understood theatre. I remember just before we opened I was sitting in the auditorium getting very overwhelmed by how beautiful the auditorium had turned out, and Steve [Tompkins] made me go outside into the front of house area and said, "I want you to imagine you are a member of the audience coming into that environment, into the auditorium, and feel it." He wasn't talking to me about the soundproofing or soffit. He understood it was a humane art form. That is a very rare thing.[77]

It is nonetheless a highly specific building. Graham Haworth commented after the theatre's Stirling Prize victory that 'the worst thing would be if [people rang up] and said "I want an Everyman"'.[78] In this respect, perhaps the project's ultimate message is the bespoke nature of the best theatre architecture.

# Cast, Doncaster

Architect: RHWL Arts Team

Client: MUSE Waterdale/Doncaster MBC

Structural engineer: Arup

M&E: Arup

Lighting consultant: Arup

Landscape architect: Grontmij

Acoustic engineer: Arup

Theatre consultant: Charcoalblue

Access consultant: Arcadis Vectra

Quantity surveyor: Gardiner and Theobald

Opened in September 2013, Cast – a £22 million building in central Doncaster – is conceived in thoroughly contemporary terms. Its one-word name sets it among a crop of early twenty-first century venues which have sought to avoid the traditional and perhaps off-putting connotations that might come with being called a 'theatre' or 'arts centre', let alone a 'civic theatre'. Instead, we have something less specific, potentially more welcoming, and certainly more easily developed into a snappy brand, among them Home (Manchester, 2015), Storyhouse (Chester, 2017), and Curve (Leicester, 2008). Cast's name at once evokes the idea of a cast of actors as well as Doncaster's history of cast-iron railway engineering.[1] 'Cast' is, of course, also the middle part of the word 'Doncaster'. Cast, which was conceived by the local authority, forms part of Doncaster's emerging 'civic and cultural quarter' (CCQ). It reflects the contemporary interest in using the arts to catalyse urban regeneration as well as a trend to position the arts within 'place-making' narratives. At the same time, it was hoped that Cast would be more than a landmark building. Cast was intended to encourage greater local interest in the arts, and also to transform perceptions of the town. An Arts Council England (ACE) report in 2010 suggested that people in Doncaster had low levels of engagement with the arts.[2] Although the town had a small, active Civic Theatre which was appreciated by amateur groups, residents had to travel to Sheffield, Nottingham, Leeds or York for major professional productions. Doncaster was also the subject of several negative news stories, including much-reported failings in the council's children's services department.[3]

And yet, for all that its name and aspirations seem to be entirely of the moment, Cast does not completely reject the well-established idea that an arts building can be a substantial presence in the townscape. The CCQ is located on the southern edge of Doncaster's town centre. Here, on what was previously an open-air car park to the south of Waterdale, Cast occupies one side of a new public square. To its left is a substantial building accommodating the town council; to the right, an empty site awaits redevelopment. Opposite Cast is the Central Library, built in the 1960s and currently scheduled to move, along with the town's museum, into a new building next to the civic offices. When viewed from the square itself, Cast has real presence. It can be understood as a fairly traditional piece of public architecture, connoting the munificence of the local authority (which provided the majority of the funding)[4] and acting as a significant, symbolic urban landmark. That a theatre could be conceived in these terms was decisively established in Britain by the new subsidised theatres of the post-war decades such as Coventry's Belgrade Theatre (1958), and was continued by some of the major Lottery-funded venues of the 1990s and early 2000s. Indeed, a 'New Performance Venue' (NPV) in Doncaster was first envisaged in the late 1990s. Cast thus reveals the persistence and development of these ideas, as well as the extent to which the arts are now understood to contribute to urban regeneration and the creation of 'place'. At the same time, it demonstrates some of the challenges which arise when a venue is conceived by a local authority rather than the arts organisation which will make the building work in practice. Who is 'the client' in such projects? As we shall see, Doncaster's vision for Cast was informed by specialist knowledge, but the artistic team which inherited the building was critical of some of the financial and architectural assumptions which had been made.

## History and 'Vision'

Doncaster's civic quarter has its origins in the post-war redevelopment of the town centre. During the 1960s, the land south of Waterdale – then dominated by the open paddocks used by a bloodstock auctioneer – was built up, with new roads being cut through; nearby substandard housing was also cleared. Plans for a 'civic centre' in this area had been drawn up by the architect Frederick Gibberd in the mid-1950s.[5] These proposals reflected a trend which had its roots in the 1920s, in which a diverse range of local government facilities were centralised in a single complex for both practical and symbolic reasons.[6] Gibberd was then also busy planning Harlow New Town and was a noted advocate of a 'picturesque' approach to the urban landscape.[7] In Doncaster, he proposed a typically loose, asymmetric arrangement of buildings, including

offices for the town council, a technical college, and a new theatre, all connected by a sequence of pedestrianised public spaces. A revised proposal in the late 1960s included Gibberd's designs for a new town hall, courts, and police station, sandwiched between offices for the National Coal Board and the technical college.[8] Some of what was planned was built, but the site intended for the town hall remained a car park. Meanwhile no progress was made as far as the theatre was concerned. A cinema – originally built as a sports hall in 1921 – had been acquired by the council in the 1940s and was pressed into service as an arts centre; it became the Civic Theatre in the 1970s.[9] With a single rake of forward-facing seats and a proscenium-arch stage below a barrel-vaulted roof, it was much-used by amateur and local groups, and also received small touring productions. However, in the late 1990s it was described by The Theatres Trust as being near the end of its life.[10]

The drive to replace the Civic Theatre came from the body which owned and operated it, namely Doncaster Council. It functioned as a 'receiving' venue run by the council rather than the home of a resident arts organisation, which might otherwise have led the capital project. As a project led by the local authority, Cast (as it became) followed a well-trodden course. As was discussed in Chapter 1, civic theatres first appeared in Britain in the late 1940s. Doncaster's civic arts centre was typical of the early examples, which were often housed in existing buildings taken over by the local authority. From the end of the 1950s, however, newly built civic theatres started to appear across Britain. Some of these venues were well-conceived and carefully designed, but in some cases the 'artistic' side of the vision was less well-developed than the theatre's intended contribution to more abstract narratives of civic pride or urban reconstruction,[11] with the result that technical and backstage facilities could sometimes be inadequate.[12] In Doncaster, as we will see, the project's local-authority origins did not preclude artistic input. However, they had important implications for the terms in which Cast was planned and the facilities which were provided, some of which the eventual artistic leadership questioned.

Proposals for a new theatre were developed within the context of a series of plans for the redevelopment of central Doncaster. Designs by Glenn Howells Architects for an NPV were unveiled in early 2001, featuring 'a lively elevation with lots of projections and activities'.[13] The broader urban context was subsequently elaborated in a masterplan for central Doncaster, which argued for the redevelopment of the civic area and the introduction of cultural uses into it.[14] To lead the implementation of the masterplan, Doncaster Council looked to appoint a private-sector development partner. This kind of public-private partnership became commonplace for major infrastructure projects during the 1990s. The private-sector partner brings specialist experience and finance, potentially reducing local-authority reliance on central government funding whilst also accelerating progress. However, the delivery of an arts building in this fashion was then novel. MUSE, the urban development and regeneration arm of the construction firm Morgan Sindall, was appointed in 2007.[15] The agreement gave MUSE the option to develop various sites in the town centre.

As a whole, the Waterdale project – including new homes, shops and cafés as well as the NPV and civic offices – was intended to be a £300 million investment in the town, delivering 1300 permanent and 265 temporary jobs and adding £40 million gross value to the local economy.[16] Within this context, the NPV was to be 'a very different offering to that of a traditional theatre or the Civic [Theatre]'.[17] The project brief was overseen by two council officers with arts expertise, Huw Champion and Jan Sissons.[18] The concept which had emerged by 2010 was of a 'toolbox for the arts'.[19] A strong emphasis was placed on participation, with Huw Champion recording that 'it is based on excellent cross-community access, and will deliver extensive workshop, participatory and outreach and community programmes, be a vibrant centre for schools and work with young people, and act as a teaching, project and performance resource for Doncaster College, providing professional-level experience in a cutting-edge high street venue'.[20] In this respect, it would also offer a new model for local-government architecture, offering 'exemplar twenty-first century civic facilities'.[21] The NPV was to contain a 600-seat proscenium-arch theatre with flytower, a smaller flexible auditorium, dance and drama studios, education rooms, and associated

backstage and front-of-house spaces, the latter including a café/bar.[22] The building would be a presence within the urban landscape: reference was made to a 'relevant, clear and powerful architectural design that enhances the [civic and cultural quarter] and Doncaster'.[23] It would also be sustainable. The aim was a BREEAM (Building Research Establishment Environmental Assessment Method) rating of 'Excellent' or 'Very Good'.[24]

## Design Development

The masterplan for the Waterdale site was drawn up by the architectural firm Cartwright Pickard, working with AECOM, and included as its centrepiece a new public space – Sir Nigel Gresley Square – on the site of the former public car park. The civic offices are located at the north-east end of this square, replacing buildings previously occupied by Doncaster College. Cartwright Pickard designed the offices, completed in 2012 at a cost of £25 million. Cast, meanwhile, was designed by RHWL Arts Team (now Aedas Arts Team), appointed in 2008. This architectural practice had long experience of arts buildings, beginning with the Crucible Theatre, Sheffield (1971); it had also previously worked with MUSE. The design reached RIBA Stage B in early 2009, when the estimated cost was £18 million. Stage C followed in July 2009, Stage D during 2010, and planning permission was secured the same year. By then, Doncaster residents had elected a new mayor, Peter Davies, whose manifesto promised significant cuts in public expenditure. Davies, a member of the English Democrats, had suggested that 'idiotic schemes like the Civic and Cultural Quarter will be abandoned', but on taking office had little option but to continue, as abandoning the already-signed contracts would have incurred significant penalties.[25] By 2012, Davies' view seemed more positive,[26] but his successor after 2013, Ros Jones (from the Labour Party) was wholly supportive of Cast.[27]

By RIBA Stage B, the fundamentals of the plan and the basic massing of the various elements had been fixed. It had initially been planned that construction would be phased, meaning that some spaces were located in early designs in less than

C2.1    Cast, Doncaster, with the new council offices alongside

optimal locations simply to meet the demands of phasing.[28] At Stage B, however, it was decided to construct the NPV in a single phase, allowing a freer approach and meaning that the education spaces and studios could become the focal point of the main elevation – something which accorded with Doncaster council's emphasis on accessibility and community participation.[29] The larger auditoria were located on either side of these spaces, effectively in the locations they occupy in the executed design. At Stage C, the design was developed in greater detail; some spaces shifted around the building.[30] By this stage, the final cost (excluding fees) was projected to be £17.89 million.[31]

Cast's design, as we have noted, balances participatory intentions with municipal ambition. Sir Nigel Gresley Square has a decidedly 'civic' atmosphere. The elevations of the council headquarters feature, for the most part, a regular grid of large windows, but the location of the council chamber itself above the main entrance is denoted by the use of thin terracotta tiles in shades

of blue, purple, and cream, and by large civic crests. Cast is similarly 'civic' in scale and register. The elevation facing Sir Nigel Gresley Square has full-height glazing, some three storeys tall. The glazing is pushed back; it sits inside a deep 'frame'. The architects emphasised the importance of views of the foyers:

> The glass sizes have been maximized, and designed with vertical proportions to contrast with the horizontality of the portal. Mullions to the curtain walling have been carefully engineered to be as small as possible to reduce visual interruption. Transoms have been designed out entirely to reinforce the vertical rhythm. The glass is low 'e', low reflectance specification to maximize transparency.[32]

The regularity of the elevation is nonetheless interrupted by a solid volume containing the education spaces, and the drama and dance studios. Floating above the main entrance doors, this volume thrusts forwards and upwards, breaking through the glazing and rising above the roofline. Its highly visible location at the heart of the building was intended as a definite statement of the importance of these spaces within the Cast concept, and formed a key feature of the design from Stage B onwards:

> The creative education spaces have been located over the main entrance and act as a canopy. The central location, form and materiality of these spaces express their cultural importance in developing young artists, craftspeople and audiences within Doncaster.[33]

The use of solid cladding to wrap these spaces distinguishes them from the transparency of the rest of the main elevation (although large windows punched through the cladding do allow views of the interior). In early designs, this cladding was, in fact, intended not to be copper. A 'red carpet' was to begin with the paving in the square before entering the foyer and then turning through ninety degrees to rise up as a metal wrapping for the education and drama spaces. As the design developed, copper cladding was substituted for the red panels, but the idea of a wrapping which would grow out of the square remained:

> A "carpet" of hand-crafted copper cladding wraps around the studios, and flows from outside to inside the building over the entrance, leading to the box office inside. Changing

material at ground floor to a coppery stone flag, the "carpet" continues back out through the entrance into the Square, reaching out to visitors welcoming them in.[34]

As one approaches the building, the foyer is clearly on view, running the full width of the main front. Behind it (and again clearly visible) are the solid 'exteriors' of the two larger auditoria, one either side of the entrance. Like the block containing the studios, they are treated as self-contained volumes sitting within the overall envelope of the building.

In the way that glazing is used to reveal the foyers, and in setting up a contrast between a 'transparent' elevation and 'solid' auditorium volumes, Cast follows examples including the Royal Festival Hall, London (1951). In part, this approach can be related to a modernist interest in revealing a building's functional parts, but in the case of theatres it was by the 1960s often also linked with the idea that views into the building, especially at night, would seem 'theatrical'. Furthermore, with policymakers, funders, and theatre-makers alike increasingly keen in the post-war decades to appeal to new audiences, views into a theatre might also serve to demystify it and to tempt potential patrons. As Barry Pritchard of Arts Team suggested of Cast:

> The glazed exterior creates a link between the town's public space and its new cultural heart. From the square visitors can see people moving around in the foyers, café spaces and education suite throughout the day and well into the evening. These spaces form 50 per cent of the building and have not only become a social hub but also a way of introducing a performing arts environment to a new audience.[35]

Doncaster Council, too, wanted an 'active' elevation.[36] In effect, Cast represents the kind of 'modern monumentality' proposed by theorists such as Sigfried Giedion in the late 1940s. As a riposte to conventional ideas of monumentality, which depended on historicist styles, Giedion and others proposed a 'modern monumentality' in which the users of a building would not be dominated by overblown architectural forms.[37] Users' presence, indeed, was essential: they would humanise and complete the architecture.

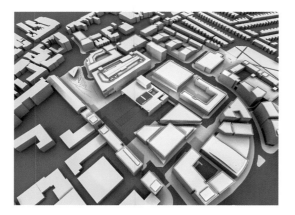

C2.2   Cast within the context of the Civic and Cultural Quarter masterplan, showing the idea of the 'red carpet' extending from Waterdale, across Sir Nigel Gresley Square, and wrapping around the education spaces in Cast

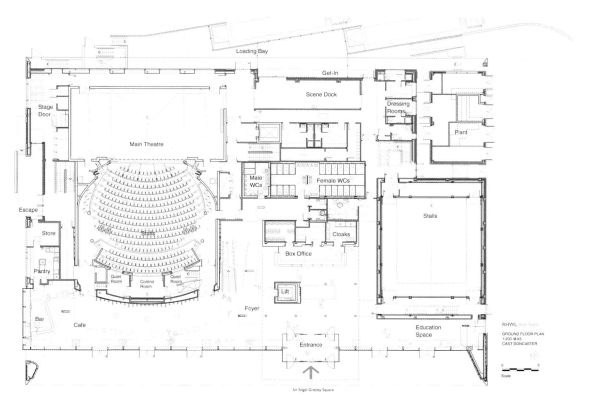

C2.3   Ground floor plan

In accordance with Pritchard's emphasis on the desirability of a 'link' between the town and its 'cultural heart', the foyers are presented as a kind of intermediate zone between Sir Nigel Gresley Square and the auditoria, with some of the materials used outside – including copper cladding and stone paving – continuing internally. Entering below the copper-clad 'box' containing the studios, there is a sense of warm intimacy, created in part by the low, copper-faced ceiling. Oddly, the lift partly blocks the view of the box office and reception counters, but in so doing it adds to the sense of spatial compression whilst usefully being on clear view. To either side, the foyer rises through the full height of the building, creating a sense of spatial release that contrasts with the low ceiling of the entrance, while pale finishes and abundant daylight counter the autumnal tones of the copper. Within

this space, the wall of the larger auditorium, to the left of the entrance, is especially dramatic as it billows, sail-like, into the foyer. Vertical ribs cling to its sinuous form and are strongly illuminated at night. Below it, is tucked the café seating, with oversized standard lamps.

Cast has three main performance spaces, each with its own character. The 'Main Space' (dubbed 'Space 2' during the design process) is a traditional horseshoe-shaped lyric theatre auditorium with 620 seats on two levels and a proscenium-arch stage. The gallery connects to narrow side slips which step down towards the stage opening, animating the side walls. The intention was a contemporary reinterpretation of traditional theatrical luxury and formality. Julian Middleton of Arts Team suggested that the space was planned to be exuberant: the aim was a 'sense

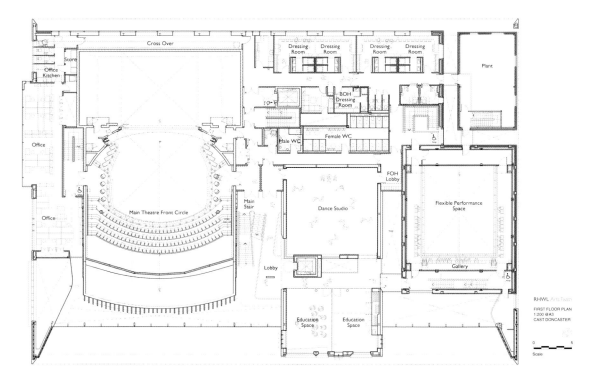

C2.4 First floor plan

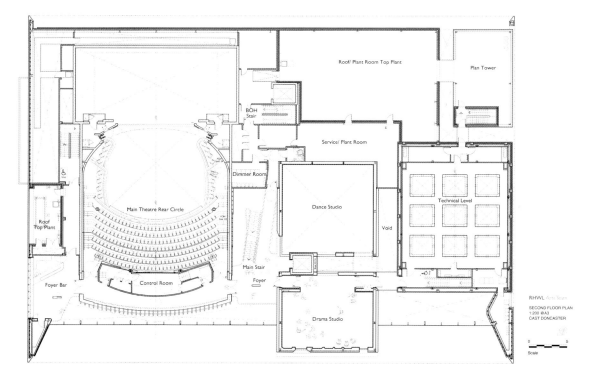

C2.5 Second floor plan

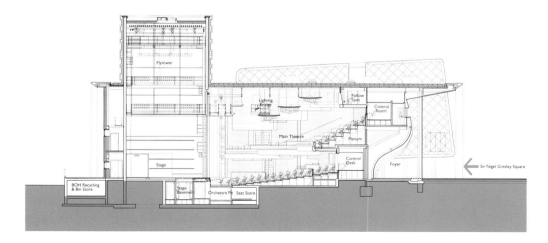

**C2.6    Section through the largest auditorium**

RHWL Arts Team
Main Theatre Section
1:200 @A3
CAST DONCASTER

0                    5
Scale

of joy' which would put audiences 'in the right mood' for productions,[38] which might include classic and new drama, musicals, comedy, dance, and small-scale opera. The colour red dominates, complemented by warm earth tones on the curved balcony fronts. Five 'chandeliers' hang from the ceiling, their form inspired by the cross-section of Doncaster-produced steel rope.[39] The side walls are clad in red-painted timber strips, the stepping in and out of which catches the light in a pleasing way whilst also having an acoustic role.

The so-called 'Second Space' (originally 'Space 1') is a 615m$^2$ flexible space located to the right of the main entrance. It is intended for drama, dance, and music. Described as the 'engine room' of the building during the design process, it can accommodate around 200 seated or 300 standing, and has a decidedly industrial feel which suits its flexibility. Its courtyard layout is fairly typical for flexible auditoria of this size. A narrow gallery runs around three sides of the space, providing a strip of seating. The main level below is flexible, and can be built up with tiered seating and staging in various configurations. Above, an 'egg crate' lighting grid allows for particular flexibility and innovation. Similarly flexible are the

dance and drama studios and education spaces. The dance studio is especially generous, a well-lit, double-height space, while the education spaces are planned in such a way that they can easily be hired out for meetings.

Just as the foyers run across the full width of the building, so too are the backstage facilities organised in a linear strip at the rear of the building. Inevitably more utilitarian, these areas seem reasonably well-planned, though the actors' green room is a small, windowless room. It was a late change to the design: in early drawings the room is dedicated to information technology. Clare Clarkson, Cast's Deputy Director, has suggested that it was initially assumed that Cast would largely be a receiving house, with little need for production facilities or space for actors to spend long periods in the building during rehearsals, but in the event, Cast has created a larger proportion of its own work than was originally anticipated.[40] Given the landlocked site, expansion to accommodate changing needs would not be straightforward.

There were a number of delays to the completion of the venue,[41] and some late changes to the scope of works. Notably, some features which had been omitted to save money, such as an

C2.7 The foyer at Cast, conceived as an extension of the city square beyond, with hard paving materials

C2.8 Cast's box office, tucked below the copper-clad education space and floored with red paving as an extension of the 'red carpet' leading to the street

C2.9   The main auditorium

orchestra pit lift in the Main Space, were reinstated when additional capital funding was secured, with ACE funding being matched by the local authority, MUSE, and New Stages.

## Cast in Use

Cast is owned by Doncaster Metropolitan Borough Council and operated by Doncaster Performance Venue, a registered charity and wholly owned subsidiary of Doncaster Culture and Leisure Trust (DCLT). This body operates a range of facilities across Doncaster at 'arm's length' from the local council. That Cast would be managed in this way was first proposed in 2008, when it was noted that an outsourced arrangement was then not unusual in sports and leisure provision, but was less commonly found where culture and the arts were concerned.[42] Since then, this approach has become increasingly adopted, not only in the arts but also for the provision of library, archive, and museum facilities. Cast is, however, not presented formally to the public as part of DCLT. In fact, shared ticket/box office arrangements were abandoned in 2014–15, despite the higher costs of a stand-alone arrangement, after the shared approach was thought to confuse some audience members.[43]

The Civic Theatre presented a mix of amateur productions and small-scale touring shows. Its operation was thus very different from that planned for Cast, a much bigger building with several auditoria and much greater professional use.[44] There was little audience data available,[45] and it seemed to some that Cast's business plan had been put together partly speculatively.[46] Some of the assumptions which had been used in planning the theatre also seemed to be rather ambitious.[47] It was, for example, assumed that some ticket prices could be significantly more than was charged in the old Civic Theatre.[48] Furthermore, although there had been good artistic input into the briefing process within Doncaster Council, it was not necessarily clear when the building was designed who would eventually run Cast. Kully Thiarai was appointed in May 2012 to be Cast's first director; she joined the organisation full time that autumn.[49] A director with a national reputation, Thiarai had previous experience of capital projects including Curve, Leicester. She quickly became a visible and well-recognised figurehead for the new venue,[50] remaining in post until 2016, when she became the director of the National Theatre of Wales.

Interviewed in 2018, Thiarai was critical of some of the assumptions which had shaped the design of Cast. An apparent lack of professional end-user input during the briefing and design stages meant not only that the business case was problematic, in her view, but also that mistakes had been made during 'value engineering': 'no-one had a strong handle on what was being handed over', she later recalled.[51] Little work also seemed to have been done in programming a theatre which at this stage was due to open in May 2013. Thiarai and her senior colleagues thus had to manage the final stages of the construction project whilst also building up Cast as an organisation and developing the artistic programming. Thiarai also sought to develop a robust senior management structure. She hired a mixture of freelance specialists and experienced permanent staff to work on the business case and organisational structure, and to help with the final stages of the capital project. This expertise would prove essential in navigating the project to successful completion and beyond.

There were two particular challenges. The first concerned the extent to which the planning and specification of the building were adequate for the scale of operation which would be needed to sustain it, and in particular the extent to which technical equipment had been 'value engineered' out of the project to save money but with potentially serious long-term consequences. For example, the automated orchestra pit lift in the largest auditorium had been omitted in favour of a cheaper manual lift, but Thiarai argued that a manual lift was a false economy, as much greater labour costs would be incurred in using it.[52] The cost was, in effect, being transferred from capital to revenue. As a result, she felt it would rarely if ever be used, and she argued for extra funding to allow the inclusion of the lift and other essential technical equipment. At the same time, Thiarai was concerned that the optimistic nature of the business case might mean that there would not be the money to run the building. She 'called in all the favours' she was owed in putting together the programme, but nonetheless had to have numerous 'difficult conversations' with Arts Council England and the local authority.[53] Neither she nor Clare Clarkson, then the Business Development Manager, felt that the building or the organisation was ready, and so the decision was made to delay the opening of Cast until September 2013.[54] In any case, autumn is traditionally a stronger time for theatre than summer.

The management team also had to develop an identity for Cast, and to cultivate a sense of ownership among staff and local people. For Thiarai, this identity revolved around the idea of a cultural 'living room' for the town: a place in which people would feel comfortable.[55] Staff were encouraged to welcome visitors as they would someone coming to their home. The opening weekend was ambitiously programmed. The opening production – *The Glee Club*, a play about 1960s Doncaster miners – was preceded by a free outdoor event. After a wet day, the rain lifted and several thousand people turned up.[56] An open weekend followed, intended to encourage people to come in, experience the building, take part in workshops, and to meet staff.

Although initial sales were strong, it became necessary during 2013–14 to apply for ACE

Intervention Funding (a scheme for organisations supported by ACE as part of its National Portfolio which may be facing acute financial difficulties).[57] As had been feared, footfall projections proved to be a little optimistic, hoped-for additional partner funding was not forthcoming, and the running costs of the building in use turned out to be higher than had been planned.[58] The senior management team had to work hard to make the case for additional funding: it was critical that Cast did not fail as soon as it opened.[59] Doncaster Council and ACE together contributed an additional £310,000 for the years 2013–14 and 2014–15. In March 2014, ACE also confirmed that Cast would remain a National Portfolio Organisation, with an increased grant of £960,000 over the three years from April 2015.[60] Over the course of the following year, 2014–15, 82,152 tickets were sold for 544 performances (over 162 events), generating £947,772.[61] Average attendance levels rose slightly during the year, to 59 per cent. By 2017, the theatre was delivering a surplus and had more 'unique booking households' than comparable venues in Huddersfield or Scarborough.[62] Performances, many of which involved local groups in a 'Home Grown' strand of work, were by now fully complemented with a rich variety of additional activities, including artistic residencies and work with young people.

## Conclusions

In some ways, an obvious precursor to Cast is Salford's The Lowry, a project where the construction of a major building for the arts was initiated by a local authority as the catalyst for the wider regeneration of a vast tract of redundant dockland. Cast is not on the same scale as The Lowry, and Doncaster's CCQ is not Salford Quays, but Cast, like The Lowry, reveals the extent to which the arts have, since the late 1990s, become integral in narratives of place-making and regeneration. A landmark building supplies a civic focus and is intended to act as a source of civic identity; it forms part of a bigger regeneration project bringing together the public and private sectors. In Doncaster, the realisation of the project in spite of the challenges of economic austerity and restricted local-authority budgets is especially significant, and demonstrates the persistence of a belief in municipal patronage. The story is nonetheless a salutary one. Thiarai is clear that the project could have been stronger had the final end-user been involved earlier in the briefing and design process.[63] Certainly the process of opening and developing the building was onerous, and there are useful lessons which might be learned.

To focus on the building alone, though, is at the same time not the whole story. Cast was intended to attract new audiences in an area where engagement with the arts was low. In so doing, the ambition was not so much cultural 'education' as empowerment: to expand horizons, develop community and social relations, and to foster new skills. As Thiarai put it, the local lack of engagement with the arts stemmed not from 'a lack of aspiration, it's just a lack of experience'.[64] Doncaster's willingness to invest at a time of economic austerity is noteworthy, as *The Guardian* pointed out in an extremely positive account of progress early in 2014, a welcome 'good news' story for Doncaster after previous accounts of failures.[65] In 2013, Bob Johnson, the council cabinet member for regeneration, leisure and culture, reflected on the long journey:

> Like all these long term projects, when we set out on it the world was a different place. But it was a commitment [...] we thought it was important to continue.[66]

Thiarai echoed his views, concluding that

> It's really important that people feel there's a cultural life in a place, however hard life is. The arts can't change the world in terms of fixing the lack of jobs or the economic woes of the country, but [they] can give people hope and opportunity and entertainment and a space to think about other ideas than just the daily grind.[67]

C3.1  Storyhouse in the early morning sun

# Storyhouse, Chester

Architect (lead): Bennetts Associates

Architect (delivery): Ellis Williams Architects

Client: Cheshire West and Chester Council

Project director: Graham Lister

Contractor: Kier Construction (Northern)

Structural engineer: WSP

M&E: Foreman Roberts

Strategic project manager: Buro Four

Acoustics: Sandy Brown Associates

Access consultant: David Bonnett Associates/CW&C Access Team

Furnishings & fit out consultant: Demco Interiors

In the heart of Chester city centre is a former Odeon cinema. Designed in the office of the architect Harry Weedon and opened in 1936, the building's pared-back geometric forms, sheer brick surfaces, and prominent tower make it a typical example of the Odeon style of the 1930s, a style inspired by such modern architects as Hans Poelzig, Erich Mendelsohn, and Willem Dudok. The Odeon finally closed its doors in 2007. Ten years later, the building reopened, having been reworked, extended, and renamed 'Storyhouse'. This £37 million project, an innovative and well-received fusion of theatre, cinema, and library, was generously funded by the local authority, Cheshire West and Chester Council to the tune of £32.5 million,[1] with additional support from Arts Council England, MBNA Bank, and trusts and charities. The main theatre auditorium can be arranged in a 500-seat thrust format for in-house productions or as an 800-seat proscenium-arch theatre for medium-scale touring shows.

Storyhouse's value as a case study is several-fold. It contains an imaginative mix of different functions. It was realised collaboratively, with strong and clear leadership, and was delivered on budget and very nearly on time. It demonstrates extraordinary commitment by the local authority to a cultural project, in spite of a change in political leadership. It also shows how a significant piece of architectural heritage, Grade II listed, can be successfully reimagined.

## Context and Chronology

Storyhouse partly replaces the Gateway Theatre, a 500-seat theatre which opened in 1968 as part of the Forum shopping centre.[2] This location on the one hand embedded the Gateway in the commercial heart of Chester, but also limited its possible expansion and made it vulnerable when proposals were tabled for the redevelopment of the shopping centre early in the twenty-first century. After the Gateway closed in 2007, those proposals stalled, leaving Chester without a professional theatre.[3] The gap was filled by Chester Performs, a group which began staging plays in Grosvenor Park in 2010 using a temporary structure. Audience numbers grew rapidly, as did the organisation's

C3.2    Chester Odeon in 1937

ambitions, and it was soon producing festival events.[4] Popular as its shows were, however, was there a more permanent solution? An opportunity presented itself with the reorganisation of local government in Cheshire. In April 2009, two-tier local government in the county came to an end. A new unitary authority, Cheshire West and Chester Council (CW&C), was brought into being, replacing the previous county council and three district councils. The resulting financial savings created something of a windfall, and some, such as Councillor Stuart Parker, CW&C's executive member for culture, leisure, and regeneration, realised that some of the money could be productively spent on a new arts centre.

Several locations were considered and a certain amount of feasibility work was done before

the Odeon building won out.[5] Compared with alternative sites on the edge of the city centre, its location at the junction of Hunter Street and Northgate Street in the civic core was a significant advantage. As it stood, the building was too small to accommodate everything required, but it was proposed that the adjacent eight-storey office block (Commerce House) be demolished, creating ample space for expansion.[6] The height of Commerce House set a useful precedent for a new theatre flytower, while its basement could be repurposed, potentially minimising the impact of construction on Chester's rich Roman and medieval archaeological heritage.[7] The area to the north of the Odeon also offered space for a second, smaller extension. Meanwhile, the bus station on the other side of Hunter Street was scheduled for redevelopment. There was, therefore, the potential for the revamped Odeon to contribute to – and benefit from – the transformation of this wider area. Accordingly, the Odeon was acquired by CW&C, while Chester Performs was identified as a possible user of the new arts centre.

The design team was appointed in June 2012, led by the architects Bennetts Associates and including the theatre consultants Charcoalblue.[8] Following a ten-week study, assisted by the arts business planner Bonnar Keenlyside, RIBA Stage B (design brief) was reached in September and an application for capital project funding was submitted to Arts Council England (ACE), based on a £43 million scheme. In early 2013, however, ACE rejected the project team's application.[9] The news was disappointing, but encouraging feedback was provided.

Shortly before this news was received, the team had been joined by a specialist project manager, Graham Lister, who had considerable experience of major theatre-building projects. In the wake of ACE's decision, Lister took the opportunity to re-focus and strengthen the 'vision'. A specially convened Partnership Board was set up. This board was intended to build cross-party, cross-function consensus, and to ensure that everyone involved felt that they had a stake in the project.[10] Under an independent and experienced chair, the arts specialist Grahame Morris (who had worked with a similar group at Curve in Leicester),[11] it included councillors from the ruling Conservative and opposition Labour groups, as well as key CW&C officers, representatives of Chester Performs and the library service, and a delegate from Arts Council England. Later, the group was joined by representatives of the project's major funders as well as members of the design and construction teams. The board had no executive function (it was not the client) but was intended to promote collegiality and a shared understanding of the project. Its initial tasks included the development of the design brief; business planning was a key focus later on. Meetings were held approximately every six weeks, with members of the group receiving a 'user friendly high level dashboard report' which summarised key information including successes, issues, progress, risks, business planning updates, and stakeholder communications.[12] Morris later recalled the real value of having politicians on the board, despite initial misgivings: they were able to 'proselytise'

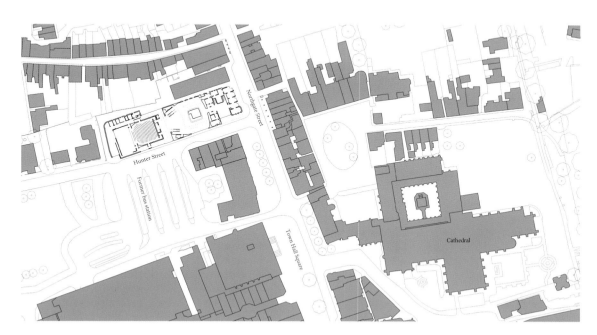

C3.3   Storyhouse, site plan with ground-floor layout as built

about the project among their colleagues.[13] Lister also noted the fundamental contribution to the project generally of Charlie Seward, CW&C's Deputy Chief Executive, who advocated for the project at a high level.[14]

Few if any significant areas of dispute were noted at board meetings.[15] In this respect, Morris' independence and experience meant he was seen as an 'honest broker' while the inclusion of Conservative and Labour politicians meant that the group was productively seen as being above and beyond immediate party-political concerns.[16] Its ability to generate consensus became especially critical when the political leadership of CW&C changed. Storyhouse had been conceived during a period in which CW&C had been Conservative-led, but Labour won the May 2016 local elections. Responsibility for culture and leisure thus passed from Storyhouse's long-time champion, Councillor Stuart Parker, to Councillor Louise Gittins. Gittins later recalled how the Labour group had previously treated the plans for a new cultural centre with some scepticism.[17] However, Labour's view had changed, not least as the centre's likely benefits for Chester became clear.[18] The Partnership Board smoothed the way, ensuring 'buy-in' from both political parties.

During 2013, much work was done to ensure that the business case and operational model were convincing. A revenue budget was agreed with CW&C, allowing various workstreams to be pursued. These streams included stakeholder management, audience development, business planning, fundraising, board development, branding, library integration, communications, and legal/governance structures.[19] The resulting business plan sought to ensure that the running costs of the building would be covered entirely by non-ticketed income.[20] Development money also allowed Chester Performs to scale up its operation. The group was now not only the nominated lessee of the theatre, but would oversee and manage the whole building on completion. The library would be their sub-tenant, paying an annual charge.[21]

A revised brief capturing these ideas was produced in autumn 2013.[22] Local authority cabinet approval was subsequently secured for a £37 million building while a fresh application to ACE for Stage 1 funding also proved successful, with

the project receiving exceptionally high scores and an enthusiastic response.[23] Lister later noted that although ACE's contribution formed a limited percentage of the overall budget, it was crucially important as a statement of confidence in the project, encouraging not only the local authority but also trusts, foundations, and commercial sponsors.[24] RIBA Stage C (concept design) was reached in early 2014, planning consent was secured in autumn that year, with construction work proper beginning the following spring. Alex Clifton, artistic director at Grosvenor Park since 2010, formally became the centre's artistic director in May 2015.[25]

As building work progressed, a new departmental structure was established and new staff were recruited in view of Chester Performs' significantly expanded scale of operations.[26] 'Storyhouse' was announced in 2016 as the new name of both the organisation and the building. Devised by branding consultants, it avoids the connotations of 'cultural centre' or even 'theatre' and reflects the centrality of 'stories' to the books, films, and performances that together are found at Storyhouse.

## The 'Vision'

The ideas which collectively formed the 'vision' for what became Storyhouse represented the ambitions of several groups. Chester Performs, first of all, was keen to re-establish a permanent professional theatre in the city. The group played an integral role in the theatre briefing and design process from the outset as a 'user' client group, drawing where necessary on specialist external expertise, including a 'client theatre adviser', Simon Mills. For Cheshire West and Chester Council, meanwhile, the project was bound up with the revitalisation of the city centre. The 'One City Plan' set out ambitions for the period 2012–27, calling for 'the city to "live" rather than simply exist, to be of the highest quality, repositioned as a contemporary city that lives up to its residents and visitors expectations'.[27] The lack of a 'significant performing arts venue' was explicitly cited in the plan, which called on the council to 'enhance the contemporary cultural and civic offer'. An early design report took up the idea:

Chester Theatre has aspirations to be a producing theatre of major significance, with a reputation extending beyond the north-west of England and ideally overseas. The offering within the theatre will be of significant artistic value. As a direct result the theatre will act as a regeneration catalyst for Chester, attracting visitors and making Chester a more attractive place to live, which in turn will encourage business to re-locate to the area.[28]

Finally, campaigners in Chester and beyond were keen to see the Odeon building revived and restored in a manner befitting its Grade II listing. A Heritage Statement was prepared by a specialist consultant, Purcell, which assessed the significance of the building. Although its exterior was reasonably intact, the auditorium had been compromised:

The original interior of the cinema auditorium was the visual highlight of the 1936 building. The interior plasterwork and ceiling are formed into a series of streamlined motifs which were illuminated with concealed lighting and focused the eye on the main cinema screen at the west end of the room. Photographs taken in 1936 highlight both the drama of this effect and the scale of the main space. Secondary features such as banded veneered panelling encircle the space at dado level and form the front of the orchestra pit. The banded veneer panelling is also carried over existing doors at stage left and right which give access to the WCs and backstage areas. In the current building the overall effect of these features has been considerably reduced by the introduction of multiplexing in the 1970s and 1990s which crudely divided the space into three, then five smaller screens.[29]

The need to respect the historically significant parts of the Odeon whilst potentially radically reworking less significant areas in part explains why Bennetts Associates and Charcoalblue were appointed. They had recently completed the well-received refurbishment of the Royal Shakespeare Theatre (RST), Stratford-upon-Avon, a building similar in age and style to the Chester Odeon and a project which similarly combined sympathetic restoration and radical intervention. Simon Erridge, who had

led the Bennetts team working on the RST, would also be project architect in Chester. Potentially, given that the Odeon was listed at a lower grade than the RST, there was scope for even bolder thinking.[30]

At the start of the project in 2012, it had been decided that the arts centre would also include a replacement for Chester's 1980s central library:

Integrated with the development, the existing City library will relocate to the building, enhancing both the offering the theatre provides, as well as widening the range of literature, literacy and learning activities the library can deliver. This joined up approach will make this unique development more effective and sustainable providing greater benefits to the community.[31]

Although at this early stage it was suggested that the library service would occupy a discrete part of the building, it was nonetheless stated that 'the library must "bleed" into the foyer and become an integral part of the building blending with the theatre'.[32] (This form of words anticipates the extent to which, in the realised building, library books are found throughout the foyers and café.) The foyers, meanwhile, would 'focus on engaging the theatre with the town, not providing an insular environment with fine dining'.[33] Multiple entrances would promote this sense of engagement; it was suggested that the foyer could be conceived as a kind of 'street'.

A 200-seat studio theatre was included in the 2012 brief, along with a two-screen cinema. As far as the main theatre auditorium was concerned, it was established that it should be able to accommodate the in-house productions of Chester Performs as well as touring shows. Chester Performs favoured a projecting thrust stage, with the audience sitting around three sides of the performance area. It believed that this kind of actor/audience relationship was central to its identity as an organisation and as a producing theatre group.[34] Around 550 seats was felt to be right, artistically and economically, as popular shows can be spread over several nights or weeks. Touring shows, however, are different in two ways. Artistically, they typically require an end-stage or proscenium-arch layout. As far as the auditorium economics are concerned, meanwhile, these shows often play for fewer nights in a venue, and so a larger capacity is needed than is usually the case in 'producing' theatres in order to maximise revenue. For many years, major touring shows favoured venues seating 1200 or more. There seems to have been little appetite for such a large theatre in Chester, however, not least because venues of this size are close at hand in Liverpool, Salford, and Manchester. Furthermore, as Gary Young of Charcoalblue pointed out, not only is there now a much larger 'medium-scale' touring circuit, playing in theatres of c. 800–900 seats, but even major shows are now often being staged in more economical ways than hitherto.[35] They can be installed and demounted in a matter of days rather than weeks, and can fit into smaller venues.

Three initial design options were tested at RIBA Stage B.[36] All three presumed the demolition of Commerce House to the west plus a second extension to the north. In Option A, the former cinema auditorium was reworked as a theatre, with its shallow-raked gallery being removed and a shorter, steeper, gallery being inserted to create good views of the stage as well as a sense of compression and community. The library was positioned along Northgate Street. This option was rejected, however, because the position of the auditorium, stage, and backstage areas blocked easy access to the western extension; there would be no continuous foyer through the building. Option B turned the main theatre auditorium through ninety degrees and created a long foyer parallel with Hunter Street, linking the original 1936 entrance with the cinemas and studio theatre in the western extension. This option was set aside because it was felt that the main theatre auditorium still formed a significant blockage in the middle of the building. There were also concerns about the extent to which the flytower might overshadow adjacent properties, while the necessary excavation to create a new stage basement would conflict with known archaeological remains. In Option C, therefore, the main theatre auditorium and associated spaces were moved entirely to the western extension. The studio theatre was located in the centre of the building, the library remained on the Northgate Street front, and the cinema

auditoria were placed in the projected northern extension. This option was felt to have many advantages: functions and activity were well spread through the building, animating it all day; it created a continuous foyer which could potentially open onto Hunter Street; the flytower occupied the least sensitive position; and the stage basement re-used the existing Commerce House basement. Option C was duly selected and a round of consultation took place with the local authority's planning department and English Heritage.

Following the production of the revised brief in autumn 2013, the target cost was cut from £43 million to £37 million.[37] The cinema was reduced to a single screen while the site area shrank. The proposed northern extension was abandoned; the only extension would be on the site of Commerce House, and would accommodate the theatre auditorium and studio. Significantly, the revised brief promoted a more integrated approach to the planning of the building:

> Stage C commenced with a client review workshop […]. The key comments arising from that workshop concerned the potential to provide greater integration between the uses in the building, with more physical and spatial links between the Library, Cinema and Theatre. Strategies for the staffing and management of the building had also progressed since Stage B and this introduced the potential to share staff and staff spaces, and to avoid the need for separate centralised theatre box-office and library reception desks.[38]

Or, as Lister, who encouraged this development, put it in 2017:

> The building would be run by an Arts Council funded organisation, working alongside the city library service. To customers there should be no visible divide between functions, whether they were borrowing a book, seeing a show or visiting the cinema.[39]

What emerged now was much more compact, made better use of the original building, and was judged operationally superior to the earlier scheme.[40]

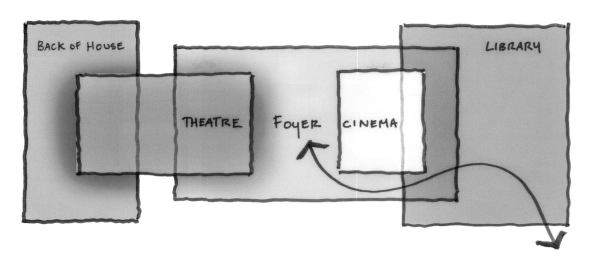

C3.4   Early concept diagram

C3.5   Section as built. The original cinema auditorium houses the new cinema box, with the foyer and library wrapping around it and continuing into the rest of the 1936 building (to the right). To the left are the newly built theatre auditorium, studio, and backstage areas

## Storyhouse as Built

The view of Storyhouse from Town Hall Square is dominated by the tower at the corner of the building. Three narrow bands of windows slice vertically through its brown-brick elevation and are accentuated at night by lighting. Just below the roofline, large illuminated letters spell out 'STORYHOUSE'. The original 1936 design depends for much of its effect on the playing-off of vertical and horizontal elements. The tower thus contrasts with the sheer cliff of brickwork which makes up the long Hunter Street elevation, the horizontality of which is emphasised by the presence of continuous bands cut into its lower part; the upper part features a regular rhythm of projecting courses of bricks. A second, smaller tower interrupts this frontage and supplies a second vertical emphasis. Towards Northgate Street, meanwhile, large windows give views into

the former shops and offices that now house part of the library. This elevation ends with a gently rounded corner.

The elevations of the new western extension play with the forms and materials of the earlier cinema. The two parts of the building are clearly related. The roofline of the 1936 structure continues into the extension, for example, while the new flytower's brown textured brick surface recalls the earlier structure. At the same time, there is a clear difference between old and new. For example, much of the extension is faced in panels of opaque cast glass, arranged in broad horizontal bands. At the junction between old and new is an entrance into the foyer, aligned with an as-yet unbuilt street which will approach from the south. Above this entrance, a full-height window of clear glass has narrow fins which pick up the vertical rhythms of the original corner tower. At roof level, meanwhile, a copper-clad box housing

C3.6   The newly built part of Storyhouse, which contains the theatre auditorium, studio, and back-of-house areas. Its forms and materials draw upon those of the original Odeon

C3.7   Foyer, looking towards the theatre auditorium. The translucent cladding of the cinema 'box' can be seen upper left

the studio theatre projects forward in deliberately sculptural fashion.[41]

If one enters through the 1936 entrance, there is no reception desk nor any other obvious sign of security or authority. To the right is the children's library. Ahead, the Odeon's twin stairs survive, with walls faced in bands of dark and light timber which curve invitingly around the corners. To the left of the entrance, meanwhile, is the former cinema auditorium. At the centre of what were the stalls are the kitchen and bar, while the walls are lined with library books. There are lots of sofas and easy chairs of decidedly domestic style, rather than the kind of corporate 'contract' furniture one might expect. Along the Hunter Street side of the building, the café's long tables enjoy views of the street through a large window inserted into the previously blind elevation. The upper part of the former cinema auditorium, meanwhile, is largely given over to the 'box' which contains the new cinema. Finished in translucent, back-lit cladding, this 'box' is encircled by the library galleries, which are pulled back from the cinema volume in order to create views through the building. From these galleries there is also access to what was originally the Odeon's upper foyer, and to a more conventional quiet reading room.

Having passed through the café or around the cinema 'box', the visitor arrives at what was originally the front of the 1936 auditorium. This area survives largely intact, its soaring height contrasting with the more intimate spaces elsewhere in the building. Intended to accommodate pre-theatre and interval gatherings, it can also be used for informal performances. The swooping proscenium arch remains. A series of superimposed galleries cuts across behind it, combining a steel structure with bright red and black panels. Accessed by a broad stair that rises through the proscenium arch itself, the galleries lead to the various levels of the theatre. The framed view of these galleries and the stair through the proscenium arch invites a reading of the space as a kind of minimalist, geometric stage set, in which audience members become players. It brings to mind the way in which the architect of the National Theatre in London, Denys Lasdun, argued in the 1970s that the National's foyers were as much a performance space as its auditoria, albeit one inhabited by the public rather than professional actors.[42]

The steel and painted plywood used in the new part of the foyer are also found in the main theatre auditorium. In proscenium-arch format,

C3.8  Foyer bar/restaurant

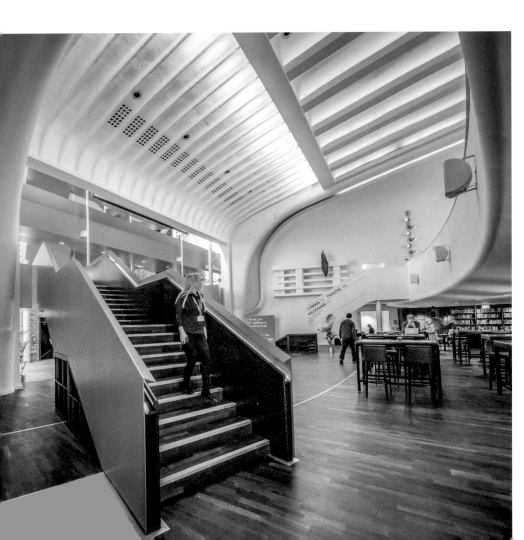

C3.9  Looking towards the 'proscenium arch' which once housed the cinema screen, and which now opens through to the newly built theatre and studio

the audience occupies three levels, that is, stalls and two galleries. The proscenium opening is 10 metres wide and 8 metres high. It can be reduced to 8 metres by 6 metres to offer full-height flying over the stage area, which has a total width of 20.3 metres and a depth of 11 metres. To convert the space to thrust-stage format, the stalls are adjusted using modular rostra to create a consistent level. On top of this level the thrust stage (7 metres by 6 metres) and adjacent seating are then built, connecting with the lower gallery. To the rear of the thrust stage is an opening, 5 metres high and 10 metres wide, which can accommodate an extension to the thrust stage inside the flytower and which offers the opportunity to use the flying system to provide a backdrop for the thrust stage. The means of transformation is deliberately low-tech: there are

no complex mechanics or systems to go wrong. Such an approach is made possible by the relative infrequency with which the auditorium will be reconfigured, essentially four times a year.

In many ways, the auditorium recalls Bennetts' and Charcoalblue's RST. Like Storyhouse, the RST has a tightly packed, characterful auditorium with a 'technical' aesthetic, and Storyhouse evidently benefits from the extensive thinking which went into the RST. Storyhouse also sits within a longer line of 'courtyard' theatres. As was discussed in Chapter 1, this form, which has its roots in galleried Elizabethan inn-yards and closely packed eighteenth-century theatres, was rediscovered in the 1970s, with the theatre consultant Iain Mackintosh and others presenting it as an antidote to what they saw as the bland perfection of forward-facing modernist auditoria.[43]

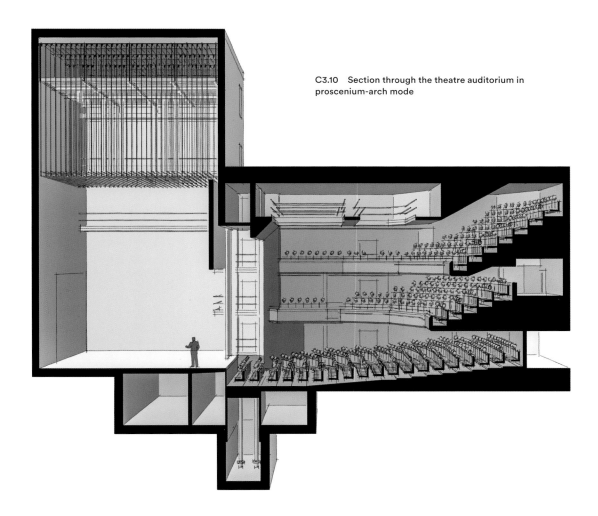

C3.10   Section through the theatre auditorium in proscenium-arch mode

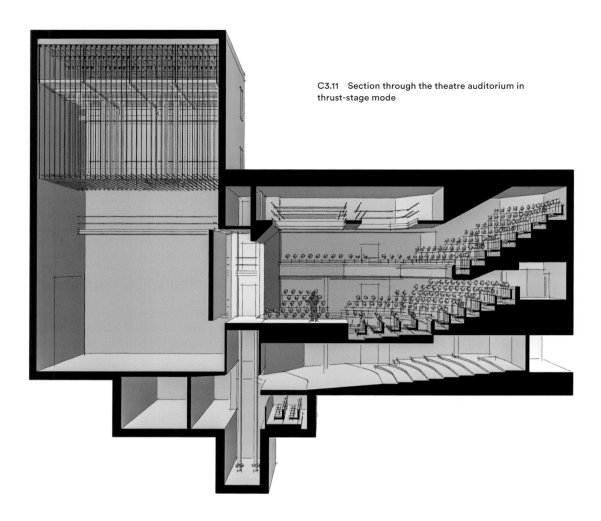

C3.11  Section through the theatre auditorium in thrust-stage mode

## Building Storyhouse

As originally conceived, Storyhouse was to be procured traditionally, not least in the interests of maintaining design quality.[44] However, CW&C's Project Delivery Manager, Jane Hetherington, was keen to consider alternatives.[45] Hetherington pushed for the use of a contractor-led team selected from the 'North-West Construction Hub' framework. The Hub, established in 2009 in order to deliver public building projects, comprises a range of contractors who have 'pre-qualified'. In effect, selecting a contractor from the Hub makes the appointment process less onerous for a client organisation. A 'mini-competition' is held with the Hub's pre-qualified contractors, with it being possible to make an appointment within six weeks

of an initial approach. At Storyhouse, potential contractors were assessed against two measures. The first, design quality, was weighted at 70 per cent, while price was weighted at 30 per cent. (The Hub involves pre-set rates to some extent, meaning that price variation was, in fact, limited.) A 'two-stage' appointment was made. The first stage allows a contractor to become involved in the design process, potentially shaping it in useful ways, while the second stage comprises the actual contract to build the building. The winning contractor was Kier, with Bennetts Associates and Charcoalblue continuing on the project; it was the first time that Charcoalblue had experienced a 'Design and Build' contract.[46]

Kier's appointment took place at RIBA Stage C, partly because it was believed that early contractor involvement would improve Kier's understanding of the design and the need for quality, and partly because it was hoped that Kier's involvement would lead to less 'value engineering' later on.[47] The aim was that Kier's views on buildability and cost would shape the design while their input would serve to de-risk the project as much as possible. In this respect, any project involving an existing building involves risks. For example, services and structure may not be adequately documented and so require assumptions to be made; there may also be such hazards as asbestos. Chester's archaeological heritage posed a further challenge. Typically such risks would be priced into the contract, and, if they turned out to be real, could delay completion. In Chester, Kier's early appointment made it possible to carry out tranches of demolition and site investigation work prior to the second-stage contract being signed. As a result, it was hoped

that there would be fewer nasty surprises once the builders were fully on site.[48]

It was initially planned to use an NEC 'option C' contract. This is a 'target cost contract', where the out-turn financial risks are shared in an agreed proportion between the client and the contractor. However, an NEC 'option A' contract was ultimately used. It comprises a priced contract where the risk of carrying out the work at the agreed prices is principally carried by the contractor. Hetherington later suggested that the 'onerous project management' needed by option C prompted this change.[49]

Construction proceeded relatively smoothly. Value engineering was reported to be limited, largely affecting the specification of technical equipment; the auditoria and stage were protected as much as possible, with cuts being made in other parts of the building.[50] Lister had always argued that Bennetts Architects should lead the design until RIBA Stage E, later than is often the case in

C3.12    The auditorium in proscenium-arch mode

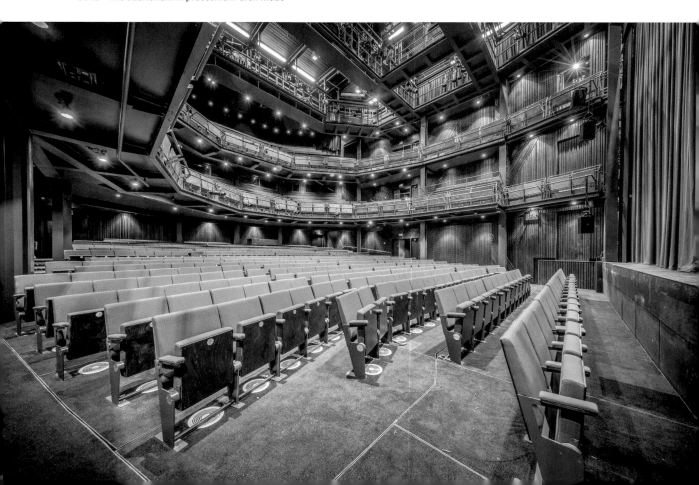

'Design and Build' projects, in order to maintain the integrity of the design.[51] In the event, although Ellis Williams Architects took over the delivery of the building at this point, Bennetts was retained in a kind of monitoring role by the client organisation on account of the complexity of the scheme.[52] Young later felt that it would have been more cost-effective for the architects and theatre consultants to have remained novated to the contractor (as is more usual in a 'Design and Build' contract) rather than the client.[53]

Some changes were made to the design during construction. For example, the children's collections were relocated to the part of the library housed in the former shops on Northgate Street, while there were also changes to the kitchen arrangements serving the café. Poor weather and the discovery (despite the earlier site investigations) of unforeseen asbestos then delayed the programme. It had been planned to open Storyhouse in autumn 2016, a target which Kier had always felt was likely to prove challenging.[54] The eventual opening came in May 2017, time also having been allowed for technical systems to be commissioned and for staff to get used to the new building. Yet, although the opening was thus delayed, the building was delivered on budget for £37 million, a significant achievement.[55]

## Storyhouse in Use

Storyhouse was borne initially of the need for a new arts centre, but the vision grew and soon also included a library. What could have been solely a pragmatic move – rehousing the library service in an efficient way at a time of financial austerity – in fact served as the catalyst for a novel type of building. Other library/theatre combinations have maintained some degree of spatial and organisational separation between the two functions, as one finds in Birmingham (where the theatre dates from 1971 and the library was built in 2012), or Corby (2010). However, in Chester, library books are found through the building and so the library is in effect open whenever the building is open. It would be nearly impossible to close it whilst leaving the café, theatre, or

cinema in use. Perhaps inevitably, this blurring of typological boundaries has not proved universally popular. Some readers apparently long for a more traditional, quiet study environment.[56] Indeed, Rob Wilson in the *Architects' Journal* felt that library users had got 'the raw end of the deal', commenting that

> despite a couple of nooks, it represents poor provision for those library-goers who might just want to sit down to concentrated study or to read, in what remain primarily distracting, busy circulation spaces. At worst, the books can appear like "storytelling" shop-dressing.[57]

At the same time, there have been many new visitors, with over 1000 new readers' tickets being issued within the first month of opening.[58] Evidently the new approach does suit many. The balance is a tricky one; reader expectations clearly have to be carefully managed. However, at a time of nationwide cuts to library opening times and library provision more generally, the fact that Chester not only has a new library but also one which enjoys long opening hours is surely an achievement.

Storyhouse benefitted from strong leadership, effective project management, and a clear 'vision'. A collaborative approach to briefing, design, and construction brought together a range of professionals whose enthusiasm for Storyhouse as a building and set of ideals drove things forward. Chester Performs was passionate in its commitment to the city and determined to secure a replacement for the Gateway Theatre. Conservative and Labour members as well as the officers of Cheshire West and Chester Council shared the view that a new arts and cultural centre would animate the city centre whilst also developing the local economy and offering new opportunities to local people. The capital project benefitted from experienced leadership, with Graham Lister's knowledge helping a client body which had not previously attempted a project on this scale. Grahame Morris praised Lister's contribution: 'a bloody good project director' who 'led from the front'.[59] CW&C's post-completion review of the project also emphasised the importance of Lister's work in facilitating the emergence of a shared 'vision' by means of the Partnership Board, and keeping the project on track.[60]

Storyhouse feels like a real success. 500,000 visitors were expected in the first year of opening; more than one million in fact passed through its doors. In late 2017, Alex Clifton reported that 48 per cent of visitors come to spend time in the building, whether meeting friends, having lunch, or just passing the time, while 150 groups meet at Storyhouse.[61] The result, he concluded, is a 'community living room'. While some of the design team perhaps inevitably felt that the design and build approach led to compromises in design quality,[62] the building has won several awards, and has been celebrated for its creative approach. It is surely a model for a new kind of inclusive, welcoming, accessible public architecture.

C4.1    Tara Theatre, Earlsfield, with the 'banyan tree' spreading across the walls of the building

# Tara Theatre, London

Architect: Aedas Arts Team

Client: Tara Arts

Main contractor, QS, and CDM co-ordinator: HA Marks Ltd

Structural engineer: engineersHRW, incorporating Jane Wernick Associates

M&E: Atelier Ten (to RIBA Stage D); Clear Springs (from RIBA Stage E)

Project manager: Cragg Management Services

Acoustic consultant: Arup

Theatre equipment consultant: Theatreplan

BREEAM consultant: Sol Environmental

Sustainability consultant: Sam Hunt

Building control: Butler and Young

Fire consultant: Trenton Fire

The train from London Waterloo to Earlsfield takes around twenty minutes, passing through Battersea before reaching busy Clapham Junction. Earlsfield Station is one stop further south. The station sits high on an embankment. From the platforms, the view is one of roof tiles, chimneypots, and treetops. Almost hidden at first glance, a building clad in golden render peeps through the trees at the southern end of the London-bound platform. If one descends to the station entrance at street level and passes under the railway lines, this building reveals more of itself. A golden box seems to have crashed through the slate roof and the corner of a Victorian end-terrace shop. Its rendered surface and large areas of glass contrast with the yellow London stock bricks and the sash windows of its older neighbours. Running across the render and the glass is an abstract representation of a tree. One might perhaps assume that its presence is inspired by the vegetation on the adjacent embankment, but it is, in fact, a reference to the banyan, India's national tree, and to the idea that people might gather below a tree to watch a performance. It marks out this building as the home of Tara Theatre, created in the late 1970s as Britain's first Asian-led theatre company.

Tara was co-founded by Jatinder Verma in 1977 and came to occupy 356 Garrett Lane, Earlsfield, in 1983. Here, a former mission hall became a 50-seat auditorium. The company's work attracted increasing attention and critical acclaim, with Verma, still leading the company more than forty years later, being awarded an MBE in 2017 for services to diversity in the arts. Supported by Arts Council England (ACE) revenue funding, Tara has become a leader in UK Asian theatre. Much of its audience comes from the local area – some 49 per cent in 2013 – but it also enjoys a wider London catchment.[1] Between 2014 and 2016, its building was reconstructed to designs by Aedas Arts Team in a £2.7 million project, funded by ACE (70 per cent) as well as individuals, trusts, and foundations, including Equity Charitable Trust and Equity's local branch. Although the theatre was able to acquire a sliver of land from Network Rail, the footprint of the old building largely had to be maintained. The challenge was thus to add a significant amount of extra support space (including a new rehearsal room, larger offices, and improved backstage facilities) and to increase the auditorium capacity on a highly restricted site. Arts Team's response was creative, playful, and collaborative. For a modest sum, Tara's building has been transformed, giving the theatre a new image whilst opening up new artistic possibilities. One hundred and twenty-five square metres of additional floorspace has been squeezed onto the site, an increase of almost 50 per cent. And yet, the spirit of the past has very deliberately not been lost. Julian Middleton of Aedas Arts Team concluded of the work that 'while this is a complete rebuild, the old Tara building is still present'.[2]

## The 'Vision'

356 Garrett Lane, Earlsfield, is an end-of-terrace former residence and shop with a single-storey extension to the rear, originally a mission hall. Tara acquired the property in 1983, initially as a rehearsal and development space for what was then largely a touring operation.[3] Over the course of the next thirty years, the building also became a formalised performance venue, with the hall serving as a 50-seat auditorium. Although piecemeal alterations were made, there was no comprehensive re-visiting of what the building provided. By 2011, the theatre was in poor condition. It was noted that the demands of artists and audiences had increased, but that conditions in the building were limiting what could be done.[4] The roof had not been repaired since the 1980s and was leaking. The building was energy-inefficient, and was inaccessible beyond the ground floor to anyone with restricted mobility, while its technical infrastructure was failing.[5] The basement had low headroom and could only be used for storage.

Verma later noted that the organisation briefly considered moving elsewhere and starting again before concluding that the Earlsfield building was their home.[6] Verma and the team, including the resident designer, Claudia Mayer, therefore developed a brief for its transformation. Central to this 'vision' was the idea of a dialogue across cultures, places, and time: something which could embody the idea of an Asian-led theatre company presenting a programme of work from around the

globe in London, occupying a Victorian building in the twenty-first century.[7] Verma also noted the significance of the project as Britain's first complete capital development for an Asian arts group.[8]

At RIBA Stage C – concept design – the 'vision' was summarised as follows:

> The vision at the heart of Tara Arts' proposed renovation is to create an imaginative fusion of the global and the local in its building in south-west London. The global and the local expressed both as arts practice and as sources of inspiration for the components in the fabric of the building. This vision, while remaining true to Tara's history of making art from the dialogue between East and West, looks to the future by establishing the conditions for the sustained development of cross-cultural arts practice. Central to these conditions is the creation of an exceptional, numinous performance space with an earthen floor which gives tangible expression to the Asian in south London and a separate rehearsal space that allows for the development of new and experimental work.[9]

The building would make a clear statement of its environmental sustainability. Along with low-energy technologies, recycled materials would figure prominently including timber, reclaimed bricks, and earth. The company asked that the auditorium capacity be doubled to 100, with better acoustics, ventilation, and technical infrastructure. There would also be specific space for rehearsals, more room for administration and backstage functions, and improved technical equipment. Finally, the whole building was to be made accessible, with the old, domestically scaled stair being replaced and lift access being introduced.

## Design History

In 2011, the possibility that Tara might acquire the strip of land between their building and the railway embankment led to a feasibility study by Haworth Tompkins.[10] This report proposed an extension on the railway land, containing circulation; the rest of the building would be freed up for performance and administration.[11] However, in the first of what Verma

C4.2 Tara Theatre: architects' working concept model. The building has been expanded upwards, but its footprint remains largely unchanged

later called the project's 'sticky moments', Network Rail turned out only to be willing to surrender the land if it could maintain a right of access for maintenance, meaning that very little could be built on it.[12]

RHWL Arts Team (now Aedas Arts Team) was appointed in 2012 following a selection process organised by Nick Cragg of Cragg Management Services. Arts Team's subsequent RIBA Stage C report contained the fundamentals of the executed scheme, and came with a price of c. £2 million.[13] The document outlined the possible reconstruction of the auditorium in order to increase capacity and improve its facilities. Above the foyer – the former shop at street level – it proposed a rehearsal room, with two floors of offices above that. The uppermost of these two floors would be an addition to the building, intended to compensate for the inability to build on the former Network Rail land. A new stair core was squeezed into the corner of the building, adjacent to the street and the railway land, which was conceived as an open-air extension to the foyer. Two options for the extension of the basement were outlined in the report, one involving a greater degree of excavation than the other. At RIBA Stage D, the design was refined, partly for affordability, but the basic content of the scheme and the relationships between its spaces were not fundamentally altered. The planning application was made in August 2012.

**C4.3** Section through Tara Theatre. The foyer is adjacent to the street and leads to the auditorium in the former mission hall at the rear, the roof of which has been raised. Above the foyer is the rehearsal room. The previous attic has been replaced by two floors of offices

## The Design

The design revolves around the idea of a group gathered on the ground below a banyan tree in order to watch a performance. The banyan is found in many Indian villages, but the idea that performance might be shaded and framed by a 'tree of life' or 'tree of knowledge' was felt to resonate in many cultures.[14] It prompted the architects to think about the use of natural materials – mud, earth, lime render – and the role of craftspeople in using these materials to produce art and architecture.[15] As noted above, an abstracted representation of the banyan tree cuts across the surfaces of the new part of the building, at the corner of the original terrace. The tree stands proud of the extension's solid, gold-rendered surfaces (in what the architects likened to the traditional craft of pargeting); the 'branches' of the tree are also applied to its glazing. The extension is thus intended as 'a distinctly Asian inspired object' which 'sets up a contrast in materiality and detail with the original terrace'.[16] The idea was that 'the building literally becomes

an interplay between East and West, old and new, theatricality and urban context',[17] in order to connote Tara's cross-cultural agenda. The original frontage, meanwhile, has been completely rebuilt in facsimile. Previously hidden behind a layer of white paint, its yellow brickwork now glows. The original pediment above the entrance has been recreated: just as before, it collides with the first-floor window.

The entrance leads straight into a cosy foyer, with a few chairs and tables plus a counter at the rear which serves as a bar, café, and box office in one. On busy evenings, the new outdoor terrace offers extra space. There are stairs and a lift down to the basement, the public part of which houses the toilets. The basement also accommodates a communal dressing room, an actors' toilet and shower, and small wardrobe area. Back in the foyer, doors opposite the street entrance lead into the auditorium. Similar in scale to the Donmar Warehouse and the Winterflood Theatre at City of London School (both of which were key references for the designers), this space is asymmetrical, compact in plan yet generous in its 6 metres height. Compared with the previous configuration of the auditorium, the floor area has been increased by annexing the adjacent space formerly occupied by toilets and the control room; the roof has also been raised.

The auditorium has 98 seats, recycled from the temporary Courtyard Theatre at Stratford-upon-Avon. Several seating arrangements are possible, including thrust staging, in-the-round staging, or cabaret. In all these formats, the main part of the audience sits in tiers to the right of the entrance, with the remaining audience members being seated alongside or around the stage. The front row comprises continuous benches, suggesting informality and evoking the concentrated 'groundlings' of the Elizabethan theatre. Stairs lead down to the actors' basement area; they can be covered over if not required. Entrances otherwise are made through the same door as is used by

audiences. The acoustic is good, with the adjacent railway line being virtually inaudible.

Natural materials give character and warmth. Verma was keen to break away from the 'black box' aesthetic of the old theatre in favour of something more distinctive and memorable.[18] The walls are thus made of sand-blasted brick in shades of brown and yellow, and of timber. Lighting brings out the colour and texture of the materials. It was originally planned that the seat coverings would come in a range of colours. In the event, they are all red, but the colour sits well alongside the brick and timber. Daylight streams in through a high-level window on the left-hand wall, which can be easily closed off using a screen salvaged from India. The playing area itself, approximately 5 metres by 6 metres, has a surface made of (visible) straw and red clay from the Jurassic coast. An earth floor was central to Tara's 'vision'. It continues the metaphor of a performance below the banyan tree, and has

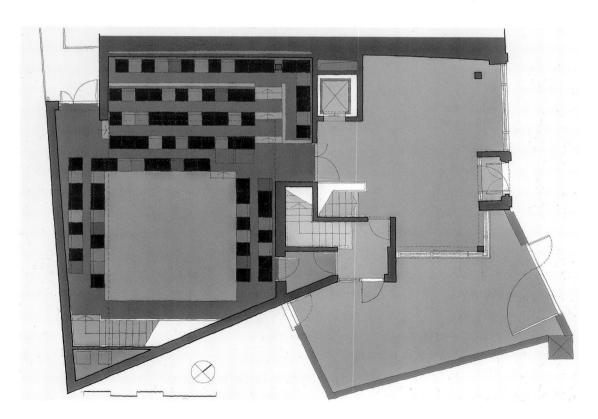

C4.4    Ground floor plan, showing the auditorium in a 'thrust' stage layout

C4.5   The auditorium: an atmospheric space in which texture is important. The door is one of several items of Indian architectural salvage. Above, a window gives views into the space from the main staircase. The control room is above left

a warm, organic appearance. Although it looks as if earth has simply been compacted in the middle of the floor, the surface has in fact been sealed with linseed oil and so can easily be swept or vacuumed. The theatre's technical manager, Tom Kingdon, has pointed to the compromises inherent in the form and materials of the auditorium: its asymmetry, the lack of dedicated actors' entrances, and the inability to cut into the floor.[19] In his view, however, any theatre space has built-in compromises. A detailed specification has been produced for visiting companies so that they know what to expect.

The technical infrastructure was devised by the theatre consultant, Theatreplan, following wide consultation with Tara and the building's users.[20] The brief was to future-proof the system and to build in spare technical capacity for equipment which might be installed later.[21] A fixed technical grid is placed approximately 5.4 metres above the floor level. There are four internally wired bars in one direction and four plain rigging bars in the other. It has a deliberately 'lived-in' appearance whilst also being up-to-date. A 'rusty' look was chosen for lighting bars and socket boxes in order to 'blend in seamlessly'.[22] At first-floor level, a large window gives views into the auditorium from the control room, which has its own en-suite toilet – a move which *The Stage* suggested makes Tara the envy of many London theatres.[23] Tie-lines from the control room to the performance space and throughout the building include lines for audio, video, ethernet, communications systems, cue lights and loudspeakers.[24]

Back in the front part of the building, a stair leads up from the foyer to the rehearsal room and company offices. On the first floor, the rehearsal room spans the width of the building and is approximately the same size as the playing area. It enjoys ample daylight from the building's original sash windows as well as the expansive glazing on the corner of the theatre extension. From Verma's perspective, large windows were essential to make the room pleasant to use. They also celebrate the theatre's urban location by allowing views out whilst offering passers-by glimpses of creativity in progress.[25] In addition to its use for rehearsals, the room can accommodate small performances and meetings. One floor further up, the former attic has been removed. A full new floor level houses the main administrative office, from which a spiral stair leads to the

top floor, where Verma and Mayer work. This penthouse office, cosily lined with books and almost domestic in feel, has views across the Earlsfield roofscape from its large windows. As one ascends through the building, the inter-relationship of the theatre's administrative and creative areas is clear. Many theatres segregate offices from technical areas, but at Tara to reach the offices it is necessary to go past the rehearsal room, opposite which is a window into the auditorium. Verma and Mayer have suggested that this inter-relationship keeps the staff in touch with each other and with what is going on.[26]

Two further themes run through the building. The first is the way in which spaces 'double up'. The use of the rehearsal room for performances and meetings has been mentioned, but also notable is the way in which the foyer counter is a box office, café, and bar in one, and the extent to which storage is cleverly integrated (and made a feature) throughout the building. Every last inch of the building works hard, in often creative ways. The second theme is the use throughout of pieces of Indian architectural salvage. Some – including many of the doors – are integrated into the building; others are more obviously 'applied' decoration, but

C4.6   Tara's new rehearsal room is light and airy. Space is at a premium, and so the room also doubles as storage. As elsewhere in the building, the doors have been salvaged

are none the worse for it. They are set off by bright colours on the walls and in the glazing. For Verma, the inclusion of the salvaged objects, purchased by Mayer and Julian Middleton on a special trip to India, formed a demonstrable statement of Tara's heritage as well as its wish to create a dialogue between east and west, old and new.

## Process

Tara's final cost – £2.6 million – represents a 25 per cent increase on the original budget, the over-run being largely attributable to unforeseen costs associated with Network Rail's approvals process.[27] Securing funding was not straightforward, with Verma noting that a low 8 per cent success rate in funding applications might be the product of 'the scale, location, and perhaps "ethnic" flavour of the project'.[28] The building was procured as a Design and Build project, with the architects being novated to the contractor at RIBA Stage E in the interests of cost certainty and deliverability.[29] Julian Middleton later reflected that the project was perhaps not a typical Design and Build job, but that this approach took away many of the cost risks that would otherwise have been present.[30] He spoke positively of the contractor, HA Marks, chosen following a selection process held in the theatre itself. The firm not only had experience of working next to a live railway but was also a family-run business; it therefore gelled with Tara's family-like ethos. The contractors had to contend with the constrained site. The adjacent road and railway severely limited what could be kept on site and the number of people who could work there.

The theatre was formally opened by the Mayor of London, Sadiq Khan, in September 2016. During the next six months, it hosted 141 performances, featuring 360 Black and Minority Ethnic performers and playing to around 7,000 people.[31] There was considerable demand to hire the auditorium even before marketing material had been prepared.[32] The completed building was reviewed by Robert Bevan in the *Architects' Journal*, who worried that the Indian architectural salvage had overtones of colonial 'plunder' which, he argued, its use in an 'Asian cultural building'

did not quite overcome. He also suggested that some of the architectural detailing had been compromised in the transition to Design and Build.[33] Nonetheless, Bevan noted the popularity of the building, praised its witty moments and strong character, and concluded that it was 'endearingly dotty' in its synthesis of forms and inspirations. He pointed out that Tara fitted well with a tradition of creative small London theatres such as the Tricycle/Kiln in Kilburn. It has won several prizes. Its emphasis on low-energy technologies – including solar panels and a pair of 'green' roofs – won it *The Stage*'s 2017 Award for Sustainability. Other accolades include Best Project Design – London Construction Award 2016, and a Culture and Community Award from the New London Architecture Awards 2017.

Reflecting on their capital project, both Verma and Mayer emphasised the extent to which it was 'artist-led', conceived by and for the group who were going to use the building.[34] Verma pointed out that there is always a 'client' in building projects, but that this figure can sometimes be elusive. At Tara, however, the client was very much present: it was possible to put a face to the name, with Verma aiming to be on site every day during construction.[35] Verma and Mayer also valued the expertise of their architects, with whom they enjoyed a good relationship. Arts Team's experience of theatre design meant that they 'knew what they were doing' and that it was possible to have an informed 'real conversation' about what might work.[36] Mayer likened the process to that of putting on a production: 'it's how we do shows', she later reflected.[37] Nonetheless, in Verma's view, there is an 'element of luck' in choosing a design and construction team, just as there is with casting for the stage.[38] Someone who is promising on paper and auditions well may not live up to their promise. Fortunately, Verma and Mayer felt that the selection process had turned out well at Tara; we have also noted Middleton's positive view of the contractor's involvement. Verma further noted the steep learning curve that came with being a client, commenting that 'there is a different language' and noting that the design team and project manager had both played critical roles in inducting him into the terminology of RIBA workstages and procurement routes.[39] Many might resist this language, he suggested, but he felt that as a client it was critical to learn the jargon in order to be able to make informed decisions. He emphasised his day-to-day involvement: 'building a theatre needs its creative head to get down and dirty'.[40]

The creative team is pleased with the finished building. Without compromising the essence of the organisation or the place, Verma concluded, the project has been productively transformative.[41] Previously, the theatre was utilitarian, but now it positively attracts performers, performing groups, and audiences. Not only that, Verma mused, but it has also allowed him to say, proudly, 'I run a theatre.'[42]

C5.1 National Theatre, London, in 1976: Denys Lasdun's 'townscape sculpture' in which people supplied 'movable ornament'

# National Theatre, London: NT Future

Architect: Haworth Tompkins

Client: National Theatre

Main contractor: Lend Lease and Rise Contracts

Structural engineer: Flint and Neill

Services engineer: Atelier Ten

Project manager: Buro Four

Quantity surveyor: Aecom and Bristow Johnson

Acoustic engineer: Arup

Theatre consultant: Charcoalblue

Signage consultant: Jake Tilson

Mid-morning, and the ground-floor foyers of the National Theatre (NT) in London are already busy. People make their way to the café, where staff are meeting at small tables while others tap away at laptops. On the long benches outside the Lyttelton Theatre auditorium, students are working, some alone, others in small groups with friends. Some visitors make a beeline for the bookshop, where they can browse publications about theatre, literature, and theatre architecture. The upper parts of the foyer are perhaps a little quieter, but even here, people are working, chatting, and enjoying the ambience. As the day goes on, the buzz steadily increases. Later, theatre patrons start arriving for the evening's performances. Theatre-goers mingle with those who have popped in for a drink or meal, like the couple that Rufus Norris, the National's director since 2014, met on the terrace one night, who had stopped for a drink without realising that they were at a theatre.[1]

One suspects that Denys Lasdun, who designed the NT, would have approved. For Lasdun, the foyers were a fundamentally public place, to be used and enjoyed.[2] Accordingly, he provided spaces of varying scale and character. The foyers serving the National's largest auditorium, the Olivier Theatre, have a definite formality in their paired, symmetrical stairs, while the foyers by the proscenium-arch Lyttelton Theatre are more informal and asymmetric, with galleries providing ample opportunity for people-watching. So do the theatre's external terraces ('strata', as Lasdun called them), whose regular horizontal rhythm breaks up the NT's river-facing elevations. In 1976, when the theatre opened, J.M. Richards, then the editor of the *Architectural Review*, concluded of the building that 'it's been deliberately made incomplete without people'.[3] Lasdun, for his part, referred to a 'townscape sculpture' whose visitors were 'movable ornament'.[4]

Between 2008 and 2015, the restoration and improvement of the National's foyers formed part of the 'NT Future' project, an £80 million scheme designed by Haworth Tompkins which also tackled the theatre's setting, its backstage and education areas, and its smallest auditorium, the flexible Cottesloe Theatre.[5] Whereas previous proposals for change at the National had sometimes been guided by a sense that the building was a problem which needed to be solved, NT Future was founded on a positive view of Lasdun's architecture. The project was guided by a strong artistic, administrative and architectural 'vision', and benefitted from a well-developed understanding of the building's significance. This understanding was built up collaboratively, and was captured before design work began in a Conservation Management Plan. As a whole, therefore, NT Future demonstrates how a major work of twentieth-century modernism – listed at Grade II* – can be sympathetically reworked to meet twenty-first century needs.

## Background and 'Vision'

The idea of a British 'National Theatre' can be traced back to the nineteenth century, although it was not until 1938 that a foundation stone was laid on a site in South Kensington.[6] Work was suspended during the Second World War, during which time the theatre's location was moved to the South Bank of the Thames, then a run-down industrial area.[7] An Act of Parliament was passed in 1949 authorising construction and committing £1 million to the project,[8] but little progress was made until the early 1960s, when the London County Council made a substantial offer of further funding.[9] A National Theatre Company was created under Laurence Olivier, and was initially based at the Old Vic. Who would design its permanent home? The architect Brian O'Rorke had prepared several proposals during the 1950s, but O'Rorke's work seemed increasingly old-fashioned in the face of a rising generation of younger, more deliberately avant-garde designers,[10] and so interviews were held to find a replacement.[11] The winner was Denys Lasdun, who secured the job after a modest performance in which he promised to engage collaboratively with what turned out to be an often fractious and divided client body.[12] Lasdun (and his talented team) initially worked on proposals for a combined National Theatre and Opera House, to be built on a site between County Hall and the Hungerford Bridge, but the Opera House was soon scrapped and the theatre site moved (once more) to the east of Waterloo Bridge.

Lasdun's self-proclaimed 'townscape sculpture' was built between 1969 and 1976. A veritable

theatre factory, housing three auditoria and a host of associated public and backstage areas, the building is characterised by its controlled geometries, its external strata, its boldly massed skyline, and by the use – internally as well as externally – of precisely finished, board-marked concrete. The National Theatre was one of the last great projects of the post-war Welfare State consensus, representing the optimistic faith placed in architectural modernism and the public sector during the 1960s. In the more architecturally cautious and politically turbulent 1970s, some welcomed the design, but others were unsure. The director Michael Elliott wondered whether building for 'posterity' in materials which might require a 'bomb to move them' was right for theatre,[13] while for those committed to the emergent 'High Tech' architecture the NT seemed like a relic of a previous age.[14] Worse was to come: by the end of the 1980s, with the reception of modern architecture having sunk to its lowest ebb, the building was frequently a target for open criticism.[15] The director Richard Eyre wondered in 1988 how it could be 'turn[ed] into a theatre'.[16] Several changes were made in 1997 by Stanton Williams Architects, including the expansion of the Lyttelton foyer, alterations to the Cottesloe foyer, and the glazing-in of the porte-cochère to accommodate a new bookshop. Lasdun himself was publicly unhappy with the results.[17] The extent to which the bookshop obscured the original entrance sequence was a particularly sore point. Originally, the main entrance was on a diagonal axis aligned with the Olivier Theatre's stage, with patrons entering the building on the diagonal and then ascending via a pair of staircases to the Olivier auditorium level.[18] Nonetheless, by this date the theatre had been listed at Grade II*. The NT was among the first post-war buildings to be listed, and its high grade – II* rather than the more usual II – attests to its architectural quality and international significance.

In 2003, the NT welcomed new leaders. Nicholas Hytner became Artistic Director, and Nick Starr Executive Director. Both had previous experience of the National, and so were aware of the building's strengths and weaknesses. Significantly, both were enthusiastic about it.[19] Starr, for example, had grown up in south-east London, and remembered the theatre being built. For him, it represented a 'vision

C5.2    The riverside front of the National Theatre in 2017, with the pedestrianised square created in the 1990s and, below Jake Tilson's sign, the revised entrance to the building on the critical diagonal axis

of the future' and stood as a symbol of the 'white heat' optimism of the 1960s; he was 'impatient' with those who had 'arguments with the building'.[20] Rather than treat the building as a 'found space' or something to fight against, the team concluded that Lasdun had 'got it right' on the whole.[21] The challenge was to enhance Lasdun's vision, to make it work where necessary, and to update the building whilst respecting what was there.

A strategic review of the NT's operations was launched.[22] One strand took in the building. Several issues were emerging. The first was simply a matter of age. Much of the original 1970s technology remained, and replacements had

sometimes been tackled in an ad hoc manner.[23] The 2013–14 Annual Report would conclude that some of the theatre's technical equipment was 'close to breakdown'.[24] There were particular questions concerning the Cottesloe Theatre: could it be updated to work more efficiently? A second objective related to the improvement of the theatre's setting. Although the alterations of 1997 had not been universally welcomed, the closure of the road which originally ran around the theatre had been positively received. Removing the road had allowed the creation of a pedestrianised 'Theatre Square' between the NT and Waterloo Bridge.[25] This space recognised – and contributed to – broader changes on the South Bank. When the National opened, there was no riverside walk to the east. Most visitors in 1976 arrived either by car (being dropped off below the porte cochère) or on foot from the west. Lasdun's location of the service entrance and the bins at the theatre's north-eastern corner was thus a logical move. However, with the subsequent creation of an extended riverside walk and the opening of new attractions such as Tate Modern in 2000, more and more visitors arrived from the east, having to pass the bins as they did so. The potential for change was made clear early in the twenty-first century when well-received alterations were made to the nearby Royal Festival Hall and Queen Elizabeth Hall. Service roads were removed, the 1960s system of elevated pedestrian walkways and decks was simplified, and the insertion of new restaurants and shops into the complex not only created connections between the Festival Hall and the riverside but also further animated this area. In Starr's view, these changes – and the sympathetic £111 million refurbishment of the Festival Hall in 2005–07 more generally – were a 'game changer' for the National.[26] They suggested the possibility to make more of the theatre's riverside location.

A further issue concerned the south side of the theatre. Lasdun had treated this area as the back of the building. Many of the technical departments were housed here, in a block whose elevations lacked the strata of the other sides, being instead faced in grey brick. The fortress-like appearance of this side of the theatre and the presence of coach parking both suggested that the National had turned its back on the residential neighbourhood to the south, something excusable, perhaps, in the 1960s when much of this area was derelict, but which was problematic fifty years later.

A third ambition related to the NT's provision for educational activities. Hytner wrote in the theatre's 2006–07 Annual Review that 'it is increasingly becoming our responsibility in the theatre to look beyond the work we do on our stages, and to offer, besides the performance of the great drama of the past, everything an audience might want to fully appreciate it'.[27] The National's education department had come into being in the 1980s, but was located off-site. By 2007, however, it was noted that there was

growing public interest more generally in the process of 'making theatre', with some 20,000 people a year taking part in backstage tours:[28]

> The current commercial and critical success of the theatre has led to new and increasingly diverse audiences coming to the building with a variety of expectations about what the National might offer as a cultural experience. The National can no longer rely upon the majority of its audience to possess a working knowledge of the canon (classical, or theatrical), but there is also recognition of a growing and more sophisticated interest in theatrical process amongst audiences. Increasing enthusiasm towards Platforms, backstage tours and online resources demonstrates that while audiences may have more limited "inherent" knowledge, they also have a greater appetite for the broad educational role of a National Theatre.[29]

Although the ideals which had inspired Lasdun's design had been fundamentally democratic, there was (as one would expect of a theatre designed in the 1960s) greater separation between the 'public' face of the theatre and its backstage workings than was implied by this new focus.

Finally, the National's management was contending with a changing financial context. The NT had been conceived at a time of generous public subsidy for the arts, but as levels of subsidy began to fall in real terms during the 1980s, greater emphasis was placed not only on box-office income but also other sources of revenue, including catering.[30] The trend was amplified following the 2008 economic crash and the 2010 election of the Conservative/Liberal Democrat coalition government. Between 2010 and 2017, the National's Arts Council England grant decreased in real terms by 24 per cent.[31] The direction of travel was highlighted in 2007:

> The National has in the past maintained a healthy balance between ticket sales, public funding and trading activities. Historically, the revenue generated by trading operations has been strongly associated with audience numbers, but there has been a recent growth in catering profit following renovation of facilities

that has exceeded increased performance attendance. This has highlighted the opportunity for commercial activities to deliver a more sustainable source of income that could support the growing amplifying activities, ensure maintenance of the building, and sustain affordable ticket prices.[32]

Significantly, it was felt that these 'commercial activities' should be managed in-house rather than being contracted out (as was the case for the Festival Hall's new riverside units), in order to 'build and sustain the NT brand' and secure 'a balance between profit-making and promotion of the theatre'.[33]

The project which developed from these aspirations was named 'NT Future'. It was steered internally by a small team, the members of which changed over time but eventually included Lisa Burger, Paul Jozefowski, Anna Anderson, and John Langley, alongside Hytner and Starr. The aims were sympathetically to improve the National Theatre building (especially the foyers), to enhance provision for education, to create better connections between the theatre and its setting, and to create larger workshops. In this last respect, the existing workshops were increasingly unable to keep up with the expanded scope of the National's shows, as well as its growing programme of touring.[34] It was decided early on that the workshops should remain on site, rather than being moved out of London, in order to maintain the National's 'company' ethos.

## The National Theatre Conservation Management Plan, 2007–08

Although Lasdun himself was no longer alive to keep a watchful eye on the building, the team was mindful of the mixed reception given to earlier changes as well as the growing extent to which twentieth-century modern architecture now interested heritage groups. In order to build consensus about the significance of the building, Haworth Tompkins was commissioned in 2007 to produce a Conservation Management Plan for the NT. Nick Starr was familiar with their work from his time at the Almeida Theatre in the late 1990s,

when the firm had designed a temporary home for the Almeida at Gainsborough Studios.[35] In preparing the plan for the National, the architects collaborated with the historian Barnabas Calder (who had recently completed his PhD thesis on the design of the building) and the architect William Fawcett of Cambridge Architectural Research, who had produced a similar plan for a contemporaneous Lasdun building, the University of East Anglia.

The 'Conservation Plan' was developed in Australia in the early 1980s as a way to elucidate the underlying 'significances' of a building or place.[36] In the mid-1990s, the idea was formally brought to the United Kingdom under the aegis of the Heritage Lottery Fund (HLF), which required major applications for funding to be supported by a conservation plan – or 'Conservation Management Plan', to use the HLF's term.[37] Such plans usually begin with a discussion of the history of the building or site. They then consider its overall importance as well as the relative value of its constituent spaces or parts. This value may not simply be a matter of design quality or its place in architectural history, but may be related to events which have happened in the building or the associations which it has for the public. At the end of the document, formal policies set out a strategy to maintain and enhance the building's significance. By identifying exactly what about a building is important, or which parts of it really matter and why, the plan should make it possible to make informed arguments for change, not least when making an application for Listed Building Consent, as the plan offers a more refined analysis of its subject building than is often the case for the actual list entry. Crucially, the process of researching and writing a plan is as significant as the final document, offering the opportunity to build understanding.

Completed in late 2008 and weighing in at nearly 300 pages, the 'Conservation Plan for the National Theatre' was intended as a 'reference guide to the qualities of the NT's architecture, underwritten by both the theatre and by statutory conservation bodies' as well as 'a framework within which any future changes or repairs to the building should be developed'.[38] It begins by narrating the history of the site, including the development of Lasdun's design and subsequent changes to the building. It then provides a succinct description of the overall significance of the theatre, with a paragraph on each of five sub-categories: 'architectural significance', 'urban significance', 'cultural significance', 'theatres significance', and 'back of house/production significance'. A detailed analysis of issues and opportunities follows, covering factors including the theatre's changing physical context, new ideas of what theatre should be, and the National's developing operational requirements. Next come the policies, which aim to protect the overall significances of the building. They are followed by a more detailed discussion of the spaces around and within the building. Each is given an overall grade indicative of its significance. In addition to each space (or type of space), other features were also considered, including, for example, the signage in the front-of-house areas.

Perhaps unsurprisingly, the plan affords greatest significance to the theatre's north, east, and west elevations, that is, those with strata, as well as the main public spaces inside the building. The analysis is impressively fine-grained. Thus, for example, the north-east corner of the building, graded 'B' overall, is broken down as follows:

Raking buttresses and elevated strata: A
Olivier Theatre double escape stairs: C
Brickwork infill under elevated strata: C
Goods-in and Waste-out: D
1997 Alterations: E
Blue/Green room terrace: C[39]

Subsequently, this grading would be used to support the removal of the goods-in and waste-out bays and the creation here of the theatre's new café.

The HLF's own documentation notes that a Conservation Management Plan can easily become a kind of reactive box-ticking exercise, undertaken by those seeking money simply to satisfy HLF requirements.[40] Although the National certainly intended to approach the HLF (from which it later secured £2.5 million), its plan was a thorough exercise, carried out well in advance of proposals being developed. In this respect it represented the HLF's 'ideal', in which this sort of document forms a routine part of the management of major historic buildings. At the National, the process of producing the plan allowed a shared understanding of the

building to be developed.[41] It gave the National's staff community much-needed 'thinking space', while Haworth Tompkins benefitted when they subsequently came to prepare detailed design proposals because they had already had the opportunity to get to know the building and the organisation. Furthermore, early dialogue with external organisations was constructive.[42] These groups included the Twentieth Century Society (the amenity society concerned with post-1914 architecture), English Heritage, representatives of the local authority and the South Bank Centre, and the so-called 'Lasdun Group', made up of ex-employees of Lasdun's practice. Having been consulted during the preparation of the plan, these bodies essentially signed up to the completed document, potentially easing the course of future applications for planning permission and Listed Building Consent.

## NT Future, 2008–15

In December 2008, competitive interviews were held in order to appoint a design team to produce a masterplan for the National Theatre.[43] From a list including Allies and Morrison, David Chipperfield Architects, Dixon Jones, and Levitt Bernstein, Haworth Tompkins was selected – an appointment which recognised the knowledge they had gained by producing the Conservation Management Plan, as well as their reputation as theatre specialists.[44] The project architect was Paddy Dillon, who was also working on the restoration and extension of the concert hall at Snape Maltings. During the next eighteen months, the theatre's wish-list was boiled down into a series of options, which were tested and costed.[45] Haworth Tompkins' response featured four key moves: the creation of new workshops to the south; the reconfiguration of the north-east corner of the building; the restoration of the main foyers; and the reconstruction of the Cottesloe Theatre and its foyer.

An extension was always earmarked for the south side of the NT. Consideration was given to using this new building for the learning studio and education, but to do so would not have optimised inter-departmental relationships in the rest of the theatre. Instead, the extension, named the Max

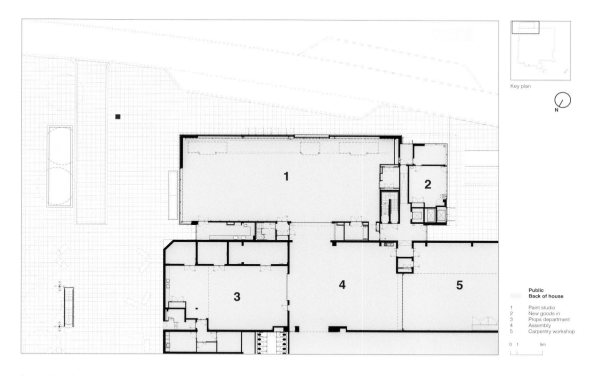

Key plan

N

Public
Back of house

1    Paint studio
2    New goods in
3    Props department
4    Assembly
5    Carpentry workshop

0  1                    5m

C5.3   Max Rayne Centre: ground floor plan. The building contains the new paint studio (1) and goods in (2) at this level, and connects into the 1976 backstage building

Rayne Centre after Lord Rayne, chairman of the NT board between 1971 and 1988, houses improved facilities for some of the National's technical departments. The retention and expansion of the technical facilities on-site underlined the NT's commitment to the production side of theatre and, as we have noted already, its 'company' ethos. The opportunity was taken to reveal something of the theatre-making process to the public, with, for example, a new high-level walkway offering views of the scene-painting studio as well as the Props and Scenic Construction workshops.

Describing the Max Rayne Centre, the architect Steve Tompkins has referred to 'a lightweight vessel moored alongside the mothership'.[46] It sits in front of the eastern half of the NT's south elevation, with the connection between old and new being recessed so that the new building appears to be a discrete object. In this respect, there are parallels with the way in which the original workshop block

– brick-clad, and cubic in form – similarly reads as something separate from the 'public' parts of the theatre to the north, with their concrete surfaces, their strata, and their more complex forms. The Max Rayne Centre has a recessed, dark-clad base, similar in height to the concrete plinth of the 1976 building alongside it. On top of this base sits a substantial block which projects forward over the pavement. Its elevations are defined by regularly spaced, narrow aluminium fins, creating a vertical rhythm which counters the NT's prevailing horizontality whilst nonetheless echoing the spacing and material of Lasdun's windows. Between the fins are set-back panels of mesh and glass. They bring a sense of depth to the elevation, like the strata on the north front, and as a result contrast with the monolithic brick surface of the original south elevation.

The second key move took place at the north-east corner of the building, where Lasdun's service

C5.4   Max Rayne Centre, seen from the east in 2018. The building forms a discrete volume 'moored' alongside the 1976 south elevation

yard was located below giant raking struts. In view of the way in which the riverside walk had developed since 1976, as discussed already, the decision was taken to move the service yard and to put this area to 'public' uses. Rather than try to design an extension or an isolated pavilion for a café, the architects opted not to compete with Lasdun's architecture, which already had significant public presence.[47] Instead, the space behind the struts was cleared in order to make space for the new café ('Kitchen') and bar ('Understudy'). The industrial aesthetic of these areas hints at their history as 'back-of-house' space. They have a less formal quality than the theatre's foyers, partly as a

result of their low ceilings and simple finishes: their concrete, for example, is plain, rather than richly board-marked. Externally, the space alongside the café and bar has been re-landscaped, and a large seating area has been created adjacent to the riverside walk.

Within the foyers, meanwhile, much of the architects' work was to strip away later accretions and to enhance Lasdun's architecture. The most significant change is at the main entrance. The controversial alterations made in the 1990s – that is, the glazing-in of the porte cochère – were largely reversed. The doors have been relocated to a point between their 1976 and 1997 locations.

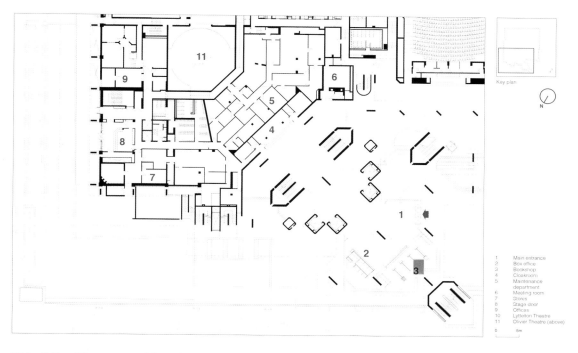

C5.5   National Theatre, ground-floor plan at the north-east corner before NT Future. The 1976 porte-cochère is shown as enclosed in the 1990s, with the off-axis entrance (1), box office (2), and bookshop (3)

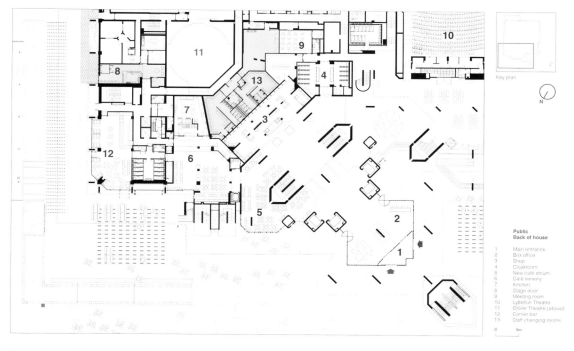

C5.6   National Theatre, ground-floor plan at the north-east corner as of 2018, following NT Future. The entrance has been restored to the significant diagonal axis (1), with a new box office to one side (2). The bookshop has moved (3), while (6) is the new café and (12) the new bar. (5) is the Pigott Atrium

131

More importantly, the axial sequence has been restored. Visitors once more enter the building between Lasdun's paired staircases. Having arrived in the foyer, the new bookshop is straight ahead, in what was previously a cloakroom. To the left, the architects took advantage of the depth of the exterior strata to expand the foyer. A new glazed wall has been set closer to the river than Lasdun's original. Its glazing features a mixture of large and small panes. Specifically, it reprises the form of one of the screen walls on the other side of the main entrance, in the Lyttelton foyer, which had previously been extended in a similar way. That wall was essentially mirrored by Haworth Tompkins, creating a symmetry about the porte-cochère which strengthens the axiality of the design. Practically speaking, this move has created the Pigott Atrium, a soaring space which rises through the building and enjoys brilliant views across the Thames to Somerset House. It connects to the new 'Kitchen' café.

Throughout the foyers, three priorities have been juggled: the reinstatement of features which had been lost; a desire to celebrate the original architecture; and the freedom to intervene in ways that are decidedly contemporary. The balance of these priorities at any one moment was informed by the assessments of the Conservation Management Plan. Within the bookshop and café, for example, Haworth Tompkins had particular latitude, because these areas are new creations within spaces originally deemed to be of secondary value. Elsewhere in the foyers, new furniture is balanced by the restoration and celebration of the tactile and spatial qualities of the original architecture. New lighting brings out the rich texture of the board-marked concrete, while signage by Jake Tilson reinstates the Serifa typeface originally used in 1976. Concerns about legibility and a desire to update the theatre's image meant that much of the original signage had been removed in the 1990s, but, having researched the original design intent, Tilson produced an improved version, with the colour of the lettering and the way that the signs are illuminated being carefully tested to ensure readability.

The final strand of NT Future comprised upgrades to the Cottesloe Theatre, renamed the Dorfman Theatre in recognition of a £10 million donation by the entrepreneur and philanthropist Lloyd Dorfman. The circumstances of the Cottesloe Theatre's conception meant that its foyer had never worked brilliantly well. Although a studio auditorium was part of Lasdun's brief, the need to save money meant that its completion was deferred in 1968.[48] The space itself nonetheless survived, because Lasdun had cunningly arranged it in such a way that it formed part of the main building structure. When in 1974 the money was found to fit out the auditorium, the job was handed to Iain Mackintosh of Theatre Projects Consultants. The 'courtyard' which Mackintosh designed had

C5.7    The new Pigott Atrium, viewed from the riverside walk. The glazed screen was added to enclose what was previously outside space, below the projecting strata

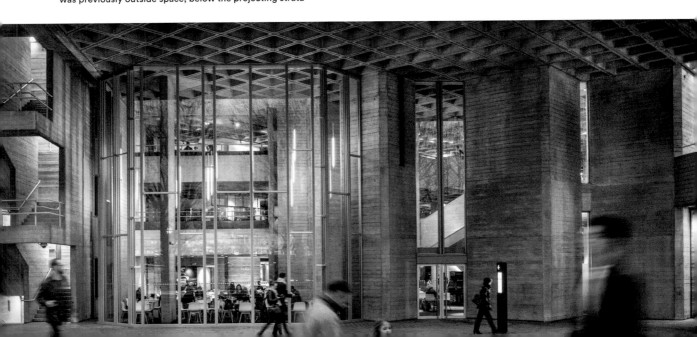

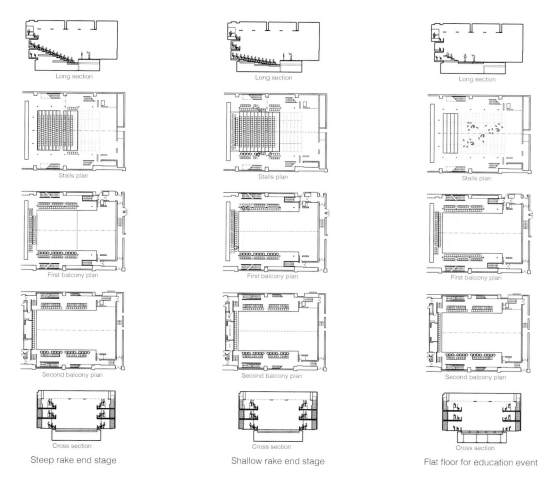

C5.8 Some of the possible arrangements of the Dorfman Theatre auditorium

a significantly greater capacity than Lasdun had intended, and so its foyer – accessed separately from the rest of the building – was always too small. Although the stairs were reconfigured in the 1990s, this change seemed not to have helped.[49] The task, therefore, was to re-organise the foyer to create more space. It now gives access not only to the auditorium but also to the adjacent Clore Learning Centre, created within the space liberated by the move of the workshops into the Max Rayne Centre. This facility comprises a room for talks, workshops, and screenings on the ground floor (the Cottesloe Room). Above, the Duffield Studio is a large

workshop area, designed to introduce participants to the technical side of theatre production.

The Dorfman auditorium itself is now closely associated with the NT's education department whilst also continuing to serve as a much-loved venue for performances. To enhance its flexibility, it has been reworked and updated in collaboration with theatre consultants Charcoalblue.[50] The result was judged by Mhora Samuel, then director of The Theatres Trust, to be 'distinctly different' in its sense of spaciousness, its colours and its textures, whilst respecting the Cottesloe's 'original intent'.[51] There are about 150 more seats than previously.

C5.9   Dorfman Theatre, viewed from the stage. This space, previously the Cottesloe Theatre, was a pioneer 'courtyard' auditorium

The previous retractable steep rake of seating has been replaced by new, folding seats. Motorised elevators allow a variety of configurations to be created more quickly and efficiently than before, something which is essential if the auditorium is to be used for education activities during the day and performances at night. A shallow-rake format is possible for the first time since the 1980s, while it is possible to create a flat floor by folding the seats and setting the elevators at stage level.[52] All of the balcony seating can be individually moved, while seats are now wider than before and have more legroom; much effort was expended by Charcoalblue in design development and prototyping. From a production perspective, two of the overhead bridges have been extended, while ladders have been replaced with stairs, resulting in

a time saving of 20–30 per cent during fit-ups. A new LED lighting system allows lighting states to be preset for different users, allowing education group leaders to come into the auditorium and select their preferred lighting state without the need for a theatre technician.

## Process and Fundraising

Planning consent was secured in 2010, with construction beginning the following year. The southern extension and learning studio were completed in 2014, as was the Dorfman auditorium. Work on the foyers continued into 2015. There were some delays, caused in part by the usual difficulties of working with an existing building, the complexity of integrating old and new mechanical and electrical services, and the discovery of large quantities of asbestos.[53] The National Theatre's Anna Anderson and Paul Jozefowski later recalled that it had been necessary to take a flexible approach to the management of the project. For example, the initial plan to keep all staff in the building while construction was in progress, involving a series of Tetris-like moves, was abandoned in favour of the logistically easier solution of temporarily hiring space elsewhere.[54] This move turned out well. It broke down barriers between departments and created connections which persisted after the return to the South Bank.[55] In this respect, it is important to note the extent to which capital projects can contribute to institutional change.

For performers and the public, the theatre remained open throughout. Temporary signage and staff were deployed to help visitors. Attention was paid to the likely effects of noise on rehearsals and performances, not least as the vibrations caused by construction work can travel through concrete buildings in unexpected ways. A 'noise hotline' was set up.[56] Members of the National team recalled the value of regular meetings with the construction

team which allowed the contractors to learn how theatre worked, with Anderson and Jozefowski also emphasising the importance of treating the contractors well.[57] They suggested that the way in which theatre-making is a practical team endeavour shaped their attitude.

In 2013, with the Cottesloe Theatre out of action, a temporary theatre was built on the riverfront. Its name for the first year of its existence, The Shed, reflected its bright red timber walls. The timber, in turn, evoked the moulds in which Lasdun's shuttered concrete had been formed; indeed, it could be read as the inverse of Lasdun's building. A monolithic object, it was distinguished by the tall 'chimneys' at each of its corners, which formed part of a stack-effect natural ventilation system for the 200-seat auditorium, which was designed by Haworth Tompkins and Charcoalblue. Plugged into the Lyttelton foyers in a deliberately makeshift way, The Shed stood as an antidote to the apparent permanency of Lasdun's concrete and reflected Steve Tompkins' enthusiasm for a more provisional approach to theatre design along the lines advocated by Michael Elliott in 1973.[58] In this spirit, the architects conceived the Shed as an 'R&D project' which offered 'potential to

C5.10    The Shed, the temporary theatre at the National used between 2012 and 2017

experiment, without agonising about how it will weather and what future generations will think'; 'it's not something you'd want to keep', Tompkins concluded.[59] It proved a popular space and survived until 2017, being renamed the 'Temporary Theatre' after the National's one-year licence to use the name 'The Shed' had expired.[60] Lessons from its design were applied in the reworking of the Cottesloe/Dorfman auditorium.

Fundraising continued into the construction period, with the initial £70 million target being raised to £80 million, in part due to the theatre's success in raising money but also in recognition of some of the challenges of the building project – the aforementioned asbestos, for example – as well as increased construction costs. Dorfman's £10 million donation was a landmark moment in the fundraising campaign. Other significant sums were raised from Arts Council England (£17.5 million), the HLF (£2.5 million), the Clore Duffield Foundation (for the learning centre), while a contribution of £7.5 million came from the profits of the National's hugely successful production of *War Horse*, which had transferred into the West End and then had gone on an international tour. Overall, 140,000 donations were received, testament to the significant place that the theatre – and its building – have in the country's cultural landscape.[61]

## Conclusions: The New National Theatre is Yours

Like much of the practice's work, Haworth Tompkins' approach to the National Theatre can be understood in terms of layers. Lasdun's concrete is conceived as a permanent base onto which other, perhaps more transient layers can be added, including brick, timber, and people.[62] Lasdun himself had suggested such an approach, telling Richard Eyre in the 1980s that he welcomed changes to 'the "fittings" but not the "room"',[63] and producing his own proposals in 1989 for the addition of lightweight awnings and tented

structures to the strata.[64] Whereas in the 1990s Stanton Williams largely sought to contrast their additions with Lasdun's architecture, Haworth Tompkins' changes drew on the forms, rhythms, and ideas which had inspired Lasdun (and which had been documented in the Conservation Management Plan). Particular attention was given to the restoration of the concrete where necessary, drawing on new research in order to try to make the repairs as imperceptible as possible.[65] On the south side of the building there is greater contrast between old and new, but even there, as we have seen, the Max Rayne Centre relates in its forms and materials to the rest of the building.

Looking back, Steve Tompkins reflected that every theatre job is a bespoke commission, but that the National required a particularly careful approach owing to the nature and strength of Lasdun's architecture.[66] He contrasted it with the practice's contemporaneous work at Battersea Arts Centre, which is also listed at Grade II*. Whereas Battersea could take a playful, sometimes provisional and often creative approach (not least following the fire of 2015), much of the National had a certain 'purity' and 'austerity'.[67] Even if Haworth Tompkins' work in both cases could be understood as the addition of new layers to a historical framework, Lasdun's architecture demanded careful handling. The long period of learning about the building and planning for its future at the start of the capital project was thus valuable. For Paddy Dillon, meanwhile, the project also offered a valuable opportunity to reflect on the nature of theatre organisations as clients. He has suggested that they have much in common with people commissioning extensions to their own homes: they are the end user for what will be built, and they are passionate about their project.[68] He also felt that they have much in common with architects, being creative and used to risk, change, and dialogue. Certainly at the NT, the results have been worth the long wait. 'The new National Theatre is Yours', declared posters in 1976. NT Future has restated that ideal for the twenty-first century.

# Theatre Royal, Glasgow

Architect: Page\Park

Client: Scottish Opera

Main contractor: Sir Robert McAlpine

Structural engineer: Arup Scotland

M&E consultant (including lighting design): Max Fordham

Quantity surveyor: Capita

Project manager: TX2

CDM co-ordinator: CDM Scotland

Acoustic consultant: Sandy Brown Acoustics

Theatre consultant: Charcoalblue

Fire engineer: Atelier 10

Graphics: Studio Arc

'A special building' was what the General Manager of Scottish Opera, Alex Reedijk, wanted from the transformation of the company's Glasgow base, the Theatre Royal.[1] This £13 million project was completed in late 2014. It involved the demolition of some of the historic theatre's foyers and the construction of larger front-of-house areas in a building which gives the theatre a significantly greater presence in the Glaswegian streetscape. As the architects, Page\Park, put it:

> Attending the Theatre Royal will be a special experience. One of the challenges for the design team has been to make a special and memorable corner at the junction of Hope Street and Cowcaddens Road. You won't miss it! It will be as if a little bit of the splendid interior has escaped and flourished on the street edge, the auditorium and the lantern crowning of the busy junction, working together to celebrate performance in the city. It will be a fun building to visit; to climb through the levels will be exhilarating, guiding the visitor to the entrance to the auditorium but framing at the same time the city around. Each level will be a surprise from the open feel at the ground level, the theatricality of the dress and upper circles and the panoramic views of the balcony terrace.[2]

The result is a tower of 'gilded' metal fins and glass panels. Inside, it contains dramatic curved stairs that seem to float through a stacked series of sumptuous new foyers in a highly successful example of contemporary theatricality.

## History and 'Vision'

Glasgow Theatre Royal is managed by Ambassador Theatre Group (ATG), which leases the theatre from its owner, Scottish Opera. Fifteen weeks of opera are programmed each year, with the rest of the schedule being filled by touring shows. The theatre was originally constructed in 1867 and then reconstructed following fire damage to the designs of the prolific theatre specialist C.J. Phipps in 1879 and 1895.[3] It was the birthplace – and then one of the flagships – of the Howard and Wyndham touring circuit during the first half of the twentieth

C6.1   Theatre Royal, Glasgow, after the completion of the new foyers. The exuberant form of the theatre extension celebrates a major corner in the Glasgow street grid by suggesting the 'theatricality' of theatre

century. In the mid-1950s, however, it met the same fate as many other large Victorian theatres. With the post-war subsidy regime favouring repertory theatres with resident companies rather than the previously dominant touring circuits, and with theatre facing growing competition from television, the Theatre Royal closed. For nearly twenty years it housed studios for Scottish Television (STV). In 1974, with STV having constructed new buildings on the adjacent site, the theatre was offered to Scottish Opera, which had been founded by the conductor Alexander Gibson in 1962. It reopened in autumn 1975 with c. 1500 seats.

Scottish Opera's acquisition of the building was a sensible move. Plans to build a major theatre suitable for opera in Edinburgh were collapsing as a result of rapidly increasing costs, while Glasgow's projected cultural centre – intended to include a new concert hall, the Citizens Theatre, and the Royal Scottish Academy of Music and Drama – had also stalled amid financial difficulties.[4] The conversion of the Theatre Royal from television

studio to theatre was overseen by Arup Associates (fresh from working on Snape Maltings) and the theatre consultant John Wyckham.[5] Achieved in less than a year for £2 million (one-tenth of the cost of the long-mooted Edinburgh project), it involved a degree of historical 'reconstruction', especially in the case of the foyers,[6] something which was to prove important when Scottish Opera began to consider further improvements in the twenty-first century. Meanwhile the auditorium was significantly upgraded in the late 1990s. Despite having been built for drama rather than opera, it functions very satisfactorily. The Theatres Trust has commented that 'the Theatre Royal feels like a miniature version of grand European opera houses and has fulfilled its role very well'.[7]

The Theatre Royal's commercial origins meant that its street presence was relatively muted until its recent transformation. Like many Victorian theatres, it was originally screened by shops, which were cleared away early in the twentieth century. From the 1930s onwards, the theatre presented a long, fairly plain façade towards Hope Street with only a minor flourish at the entrance, which was capped by a tower and dome (later demolished).[8] In addition, like many of its contemporaries, the theatre had separate entrances for each part of the auditorium (that is, for each price of seat). Plans to combine the foyers in the 1975 reconstruction were only partly carried out.[9]

In 2008, Scottish Opera was able to buy an adjacent 'gap' site, and began thinking about how the Theatre Royal's public face could be improved.[10] Scottish Opera's plans were further catalysed by the announcement in late 2007 that Glasgow was to host the 2014 Commonwealth Games, something which brought the possibility of funding for associated cultural projects. The architectural practice Page\Park was appointed. A local firm with significant expertise in public architecture, relevant arts experience included the refurbishment and extension of Eden Court, Inverness.

Page\Park's initial task was to produce a Conservation Statement. This document – shorter than a full Conservation Management Plan – outlined the history of the theatre and the significance of each of its constituent spaces.[11] It was produced in consultation with Historic Scotland and Glasgow City Council, essentially securing the authorities' 'buy-in' for the assessments which were made. Page\Park was then re-appointed through an *OJEU* process to develop outline design proposals to RIBA Stage B, and subsequently to take the project to completion. Their team included Arup Scotland (structural engineering), Max Fordham (mechanical and electrical engineering), Sandy Brown Acoustics, and the theatre consultant Charcoalblue. Initially conceived as an £8 million project,[12] the final cost in 2014 was £13 million.[13]

The aim was to transform how the Theatre Royal was seen and experienced by the public,[14] in

C6.2   Theatre Royal, Glasgow, before the construction of the new foyer

terms of the journey 'from street to seat'.[15] It was noted that the theatre did not compare well with refurbished venues in Aberdeen, Edinburgh, and Inverness, despite Glasgow being Scottish Opera's national base: 'in Glasgow there is no major theatre with contemporary public foyers and facilities to match other major Scottish cultural centres.'[16] It was feared that the increasingly 'inadequate' building was 'not of a standard to meet raised public expectations nor with the capability to grow future audiences'.[17] Areas of concern included the theatre's 'undemocratic' separate foyers, which were cramped and congested at performance times.[18] In addition, the building was confusing to navigate while its upper levels were inaccessible for anyone unable to climb stairs. Furthermore, many seats in the auditorium had poor views of the stage, and there were problems with the ventilation system.[19] It was feared that revenue was being lost as patrons turned away.[20]

The core goals of the capital project were the improvement of the auditorium and the extension of the foyers, which would be reconfigured as a space in which to welcome visitors all day with good coffee, comfortable seating, and wi-fi.[21] The building was to be 'special', connoting the essence of theatre and fitting in to a longer tradition of generous public architecture. This 'vision' was elaborated into eleven objectives:

1. to provide direct and clear wayfinding for the public on axis with the rear of the auditorium at each of the key levels of the theatre, the stalls, the dress circle, the upper circle and the balcony;

2. to relocate the bar provision currently at the rear of the auditorium into new foyers at each key level to the north of the building;

3. to introduce a new stair access to this foyer so that there is a clear vertical visible route connecting all the key levels;

4. likewise to connect all the critical levels by lift provision both for the public and service accesses;

5. to provide at each level significant cloaks and toilet facilities in a visible location and in numbers sufficient to support a comfortable visit;

6. to relocate and re-provide the service provision to the building as a whole;

7. to upgrade and extend the office and hosting accommodation currently within the northern Hope Street wing;

8. to provide an improved entrance foyer with associated welcoming café bar, box office and shop;

9. to provide meeting and education facilities;

10. to improve the environment of the main auditorium;

11. to improve the seating layout to improve sight lines to the stage.[22]

It was noted that these improvements would benefit not only Scottish Opera but also the other companies playing at the theatre during the rest of the year.[23]

## The Design

Rather than confine themselves to the theatre's newly bought gap site, Page\Park proposed the demolition of part of the existing building, containing the café and offices, in order to create a 450m$^2$ site to the north of the auditorium.[24] In doing so, they were guided by the assessments of significance contained in the earlier Conservation Statement, which had identified these areas (fitted out in 1975) as being of little value. Page\Park's proposals were developed in discussion with representatives from various departments of Glasgow City Council, Historic Scotland, and The Theatres Trust, as well as Scottish Opera and ATG staff.[25] Public consultation events were arranged with residential and commercial neighbours, and with major commercial and arts-related neighbours. Scottish Opera staff toured venues in Britain and beyond for inspiration.

Most of the principles of the final scheme are evident in Page\Park's initial design proposals. From the outset, the project included the creation of a landmark structure at the Hope Street/ Cowcaddens Road junction. Corner sites were emphasised by Glasgow's nineteenth-century architects; in particular, Page\Park sought to respond to the ornate tenement on the opposite side of Hope Street, designed in 1903 by the firm of Honeyman, Keppie and Mackintosh. In describing their concept, Page\Park referred to the way in which many modern theatres feature a glazed elevation which gives direct views of the curved wall of the auditorium beyond.[26] Such an approach was not possible at the Theatre Royal, however, owing to the position of the auditorium on the site, and so a different approach was developed:

> The beauty of the internal curvilinear auditorium form has no expression on the external face of its containing box. The resolution of this conflict [is] the decision to scallop the corner out of the notional urban block within which the enlarged Theatre Royal complex sits, the wings of the scallop reading as extending from the rear of the new auditorium entrance. By this means, the contemporary sense of the foyer wrapping around the auditorium is transformed into the auditorium extending to wrap around the foyer. The eccentric orientation of the main theatre block is resolved by canting the new scalloped foyer to engage with the corner on Hope Street and Cowcaddens Road.[27]

In plan, the Theatre Royal extension comprises an oval volume containing the foyers and stairs, set at 45 degrees to the auditorium. This geometry means that the narrow end of the oval fits snugly into the Hope Street/Cowcaddens Road corner. Its curved form also recalls that of the horseshoe-shaped auditorium. It reads as, if not a mirror image of the auditorium, then at least a closely related sibling, something which is also true of its appearance, as we shall see shortly.

The architects argued that there were historically two main approaches to façade design within Glasgow city centre.[28] One was fairly plain and ordered, and developed on a property-by-property rather than whole-block basis; the other was bolder in scale, and more expressive and exuberant in form, though no less individualistic.[29] Buildings demonstrated the wealth of their owners and served as an opportunity for 'show', with corner sites offering 'a means to enhance individual expression'.[30] The result was a varied streetscape:

> Look along the main streets of the city centre and what stands out is the variegated texture of the receding planes of the façades framing activity between. That texture comprises a number of characteristics, variations in plot width, height and depth of façade.[31]

On the basis of this analysis, they justified their Theatre Royal proposals:

> Fundamentally, the proposal is made up of a corner and two wings embedded into the street architecture of Hope Street and Cowcaddens Road.
>
> - the central corner composition reflects the exuberant Glasgow tendency
> - the wing to Hope Street in line with the more restrained aspect of the Theatre Royal adopts the severe modest position
> - the wing to Cowcaddens Road likewise adopts the severe persona, but canted to meet the neighbouring setting.
>
> This attempt to reconcile the exuberant and severe is facilitated by the creation of visual gaps between the corner and its two wings.[32]

The curved street elevation of the oval 'drum' which contains the foyers has alternating vertical bands of gold-coloured steel cladding (evocative of the auditorium's gilded surfaces) and wide panes of glazing. The need to accommodate the ductwork for the foyers' natural ventilation system as well as the location here of deep structural columns gives the elevation a visible depth and solidity often missing from contemporary architecture, allowing it to serve as an effective 'anchor' for the theatre at this busy junction as well as counterbalancing the weighty stone tenement opposite. At ground level, the elevation steps back, creating a covered area below the main part of the 'drum'; a useful shelter in the often wet west of Scotland climate as well as a welcoming gesture at the entrance. To either side of the 'drum', meanwhile, the 'solid'/'severe' side of Glasgow architecture is given form in polished concrete surfaces which echo the proportions and detailing of the theatre's historic street front.

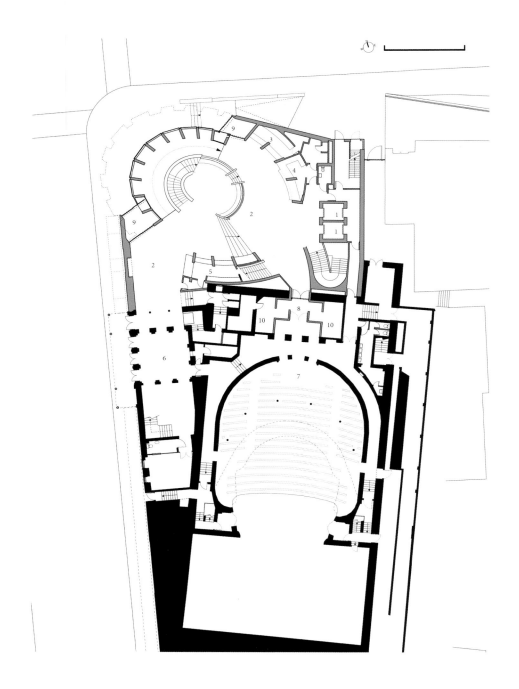

C6.3 Stalls level plan

Key:

1   Lift
2   New foyer space
3   Bar
4   Café
5   Box office
6   Historic foyer/entrance
7   Auditorium
8   Acoustic lobby
9   New entrance
10  Cloakroom

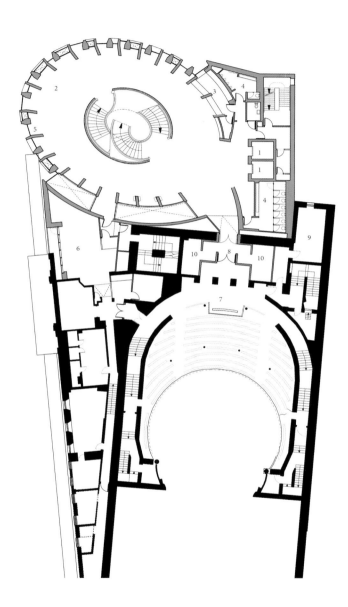

C6.4   Plan at upper circle level

Key:
1   Lift
2   New foyer space
3   Bar
4   Toilets
5   'Niche'
6   Office
7   Auditorium
8   Acoustic lobby
9   Plant
10  Cloakroom

C6.5   Architects' model of the new foyers

As one enters the building, the 'old' entrance foyer is to the right. It has been transformed into a heritage gallery with interactive exhibits about the history of the building. (From here, the previous main stair leads up to what is now a function room.) The box office counter is straight ahead, while around to the left is the coffee bar. The foyer is dominated by the curved stairs in its centre, which are seemingly suspended in the space. If one looks up the stairs from the ground floor, there is a playfully complex clash of geometries and a real celebration of form (and of the engineering that has made these structural gymnastics possible). They lead to the dress circle foyer and then to the upper circle foyer, the latter being a double-height space ideally suited to informal performances, with audiences watching from the stair. From hereon up the stair is tighter and more circular in plan than those below. It

leads to a much-used education suite and to the balcony foyer, where there is a roof terrace.

Each foyer has a similar plan in the interests of navigational ease and simplicity of servicing, with the location of the bars, toilets, and the auditorium entrance being consistent on each level (with the exception of the entrance/stalls foyer, whose toilets are located in the basement). The foyers' structural columns are relegated to the perimeter of the spaces, with the floors being cantilevered in one direction towards the central stairs. The depth of the columns is such that large niches are created around the edge of the foyers. These niches offer places for groups to meet; they have loose seating that can be easily rearranged. Within each is the solid rear side of the ventilation duct, which features numbered shelves onto which interval drinks are delivered. There is also space for the display of material relating to current

C6.6    Stalls level foyer

C6.7    Upper foyer, showing the deep niches created by the structural columns. Each has a numbered shelf to which interval drinks can be delivered, as well as space for posters or archive material

C6.8 Glasgow Theatre Royal, auditorium. One of the goals in the design of the new foyers was to bring the curved forms and rich materials of the auditorium out towards the street

productions or, in another example of the way in which heritage material is effectively displayed throughout the building, Scottish Opera's history, using so-called 'boxes of curiosity'.[33] The different location of the duct in each bay as well as the varied arrangement of shelves, posters, and archive displays makes each of these nooks unique, but at the same time the shared forms and materials (and the attention to detail) result in a strong sense of consistency. The forms were usefully refined through the construction of a full-size mock-up at design stage.[34]

Throughout, there is a certain richness to the finishes as well as a luxurious enjoyment of space, both of which seem entirely appropriate in this kind of building; Page\Park's project architect, Nicola Walls, referred to the glamour of 'a night at the opera'.[35] The stairs evoke the traditional idea of seeing and being seen at the theatre as well as the materials one might expect of this building type. They have a deep red carpet, while the balustrading and handrails are finished in leather,

in a bespoke shade of 'Theatre Royal claret'. The underside of the stair is also red. It stands out in an environment otherwise dominated by the creams and greys of marble, polished concrete, and birch ply, bringing something of the colour and texture of the auditorium out into the foyers. (Incidentally, all of the joinery was made in-house, in Scottish Opera's own workshops.) The colour red also figures prominently in *Butterfly*, a large tapestry by the artist Alison Watt, which serves as a reference to Scottish Opera' origins; its first production under Alexander Gibson was *Madame Butterfly*.

As far as the auditorium itself is concerned, the changes are less obvious but no less significant. Audiences now enter on the central axis, rather than at the sides. Cloakrooms are neatly provided in the acoustic lobbies at each level. Reseating has improved the sightlines, meaning that the number of 'restricted view' tickets has been halved (with a consequential benefit to ticket income, despite a slightly lower capacity), while wheelchair positions are no longer confined to the stalls.

C6.9   Theatre Royal by night. The junction between old and new is carefully detailed, with the lines and proportions of the historic theatre continuing into the new building

The foyers are naturally ventilated. Outdoor air enters ducts located in the depth of the elevation and is heated if necessary, while noise is also attenuated here. The air then passes into the foyers. The stack effect means that it rises through the space before being exhausted at roof level. This natural ventilation strategy represents an environmentally responsible approach, but is also a pragmatic move. The increased amount of plant required to improve conditions in the auditorium meant that, when designing the foyers, it was thought critical not to increase the servicing load any further. The result is a pleasingly integrated approach. All too often, 'sustainability' is applied as a veneer to otherwise business-as-usual architecture. At the Theatre Royal, however, the use of the depth of the elevation as an integral part of the ventilation strategy – and the way in which this depth also serves to some extent as solar shading against the evening sun – is a welcome demonstration of how low-energy considerations, structural design, and the need for a weighty, 'civic' image can be productively brought together.

## Building and Using the Theatre Royal

A two-stage contract was adopted because it was thought desirable that the contractor, Sir Robert McAlpine, should join the team early as a result of the complexity of the new building as well as the need to understand the historic structure. Fundraising continued during the period in which the design was being developed, with substantial sums being received from the Scottish Government (as a result of the Theatre Royal being the Commonwealth Games' flagship cultural project) as well as the Heritage Lottery Fund and private organisations, whose names are commemorated in locations including the foyer 'niches'. The cost of the project increased from £8 million to £13 million as its scope was refined and its complexity was fully detailed. Limited 'value engineering' took place, with the main complete omission being a set of actors' flats which had initially been proposed.[36] Actually doing the work on a restricted city-centre site was challenging. The challenge was compounded by the wish to

keep the theatre open as much as possible. Careful programming was needed.

Ultimately the theatre was only 'dark' for fourteen weeks.[37] However, the construction period was extended from 20 to 26 months, with full re-opening being postponed twice. Reedijk commented on the realities of joining a new building to an old one:

> Any time we looked at that back wall, the north gable, there was another thing we had not expected. It is a 150-year-old wall that's had so many interventions over the years, it's had so many uses, interventions, apertures opened and closed, and particularly where we have been physically joining old and new together we have bumped into so much.[38]

Other unexpected problems included the presence of unknown cabling below the pavement.[39] Temporary bars and toilets were pressed into service,[40] and the eventual completion of the project in December 2014 missed the Commonwealth Games by several months. Relationships seem sometimes to have been strained. While Reedijk praised the design team for their commitment and noted the valuable role played by the project manager, he noted that the sometimes adversarial nature of construction is different from the ethos of theatre: 'we live in a world where the show *must* go on'.[41]

The building has won several awards, including Cultural Building of the Year at the Royal Incorporation of Architects in Scotland (RIAS) Awards 2015, and Best Leisure/Culture Building at the Scottish Design Awards 2015. Reviewing the theatre for the *Architects' Journal*, Rory Olcayto felt Page\Park's work to be entirely appropriate in its setting, invoking the critic Ian Nairn, who in the early 1960s characterised Glasgow's architecture as a 'topographical epic with the buildings as incidents'.[42] And yet, to see Page\Park's work only as an 'incident' perhaps plays down its strengths. The project, like many theatre schemes, was borne of chance: the opportunity to acquire adjacent land, and the chance to secure funding as a result of Glasgow's Commonwealth Games win. Scottish Opera's 'vision' was nonetheless very clearly articulated, and was informed by an understanding of the opportunities presented by the site as well as the extent to which 'architecture' could transform their operations and image. It was developed by a sympathetic design team, aided by a reasonably generous budget.

Ultimately, the new foyers are sophisticated, practical spaces which invite visitors to linger. Externally, the design is rooted in a close reading of its surroundings, whilst also being shaped by its environmental strategy. It makes a bold statement of the Theatre Royal's presence, one which is significantly more inviting than its previous, rather more austere public face. Reedijk contrasted the Theatre Royal's former introversion ('rather like a masonic lodge') with its new-found urban presence. This, he concluded, is entirely appropriate for a building not only conceived in resolutely public terms but which is also full of 'professional show offs'.[43]

# Perth Theatre

Architect: Richard Murphy Architects

Client: Horsecross Arts

Main contractor: Robertson Construction

Structural engineer: Arup

M&E: Buro Happold (design); FES (build)

Quantity surveyor: Red Skye Consulting/Robertson
Construction

Project manager: Robertson Construction

CDM co-ordinator: McLeod and Aitken/Robertson
Construction

Acoustic consultant: Arup

Theatre consultant: Charcoalblue

Conservation: Simpson and Brown

Perth Theatre is a masterclass in space, texture, and the creative juxtaposition of old and new. This historic theatre has been comprehensively transformed: its auditorium has been restored, its backstage areas have been reconfigured, and a new studio auditorium has been built. New areas for community and education work have been created, along with a spacious bar and restaurant. Everything is linked together by a newly built, triple-height foyer. Here, oak, concrete, polished plaster and steel sit alongside the rough bricks of what was once an exterior wall. Areas of bright lighting are juxtaposed with more atmospheric corners. The rich contrasts between materials, the complexity of some of the detailing, and the careful separation of old and new all bring to mind the work of the twentieth-century Italian architect Carlo Scarpa.

Completed in December 2017, the £16.6 million redevelopment of Perth Theatre was, in the words of the project architect, 'a long journey' which took nearly a decade from start to end.[1] During that time, the designers, Richard Murphy Architects, produced and secured planning consent for three complete schemes. While much of the original project 'vision' was preserved, funding challenges meant that some of the facilities which the client, Horsecross Arts, had originally sought were lost. Nonetheless, what could have felt like a compromise has emerged with real character and integrity. It demonstrates the tenacity sometimes needed to succeed in building for the arts.

## History and 'Vision'

Perth Theatre opened in 1900, having been designed by the Dundee architect William Alexander.[2] Its original layout reflects this Scottish city's historic form, in which the principal streets largely run east–west and are linked by 'vennels' (alleyways) and yards. The theatre was built behind a tenement on the north side of the High Street, with just a narrow entrance from the street, between two shops. A corridor steps up through the tenement building into a small foyer with an ornate iron and glass roof, which in turn connects into the auditorium at dress circle (middle gallery) level. Patrons with seats in the cheaper parts of

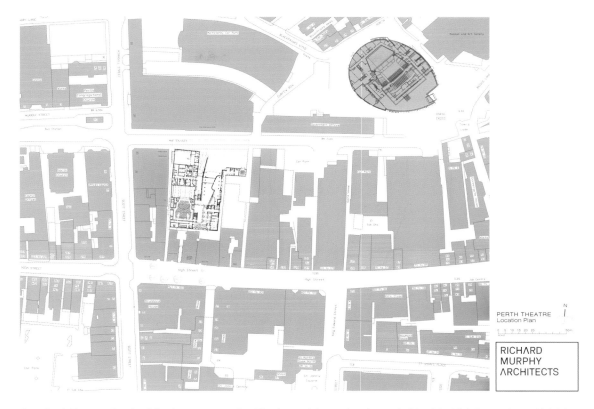

C7.1   Perth Theatre, site plan following reconstruction. The theatre is located on the north side of the High Street, from which it is accessed via a narrow corridor. Further along Mill Street is the ovoid Perth Concert Hall, also run by Horsecross Arts

the theatre originally entered elsewhere, however. The cheapest seats in the pit were accessed from the adjacent Cutlog Vennel, while a third entrance originally led to the 'gods' (the upper gallery).

The auditorium, which originally seated 950, was reconstructed after a fire in 1924. By the mid-1930s it housed a successful repertory company.[3] The theatre building was acquired by the Scottish Arts Council during the 1960s, with ownership subsequently passing to Perth Town Council (now Perth and Kinross Council). The resident repertory company benefitted from the post-war system of subsidy for the arts, and under the direction of Joan Knight between 1968 and 1993 developed a strong reputation.[4] Alterations were made to the building with the support of the Scottish Arts Council in 1967, including the removal of 200 seats

in the 'gods'.[5] Major changes followed in the early 1980s, when the Edinburgh architects Gordon and Dey oversaw the construction of new buildings to the east and north of the auditorium, which had been listed at Category B in 1977.[6] The northern extension accommodated dressing rooms and a studio auditorium, while the eastern block housed offices and a popular restaurant as well as a rehearsal room and workshop. These works, which cost nearly £2 million, came towards the end of the post-war 'Housing the Arts' boom, during which – as was discussed in Chapter 1 – Arts Council money supported the construction or remodelling of major regional theatres around Britain.[7]

By 2007, the building's services were failing.[8] In addition, although attempts had been made to create accessible routes through the theatre, circulation remained complex.[9] The rehearsal room was located far from the dressing rooms, while the studio auditorium was not connected to the foyers. By this time, the theatre was managed by Horsecross Arts, a charity which had been created to run the then-new Perth Concert Hall. Its chief executive, Jane Spiers, had recently overseen the refurbishment of the Tolbooth Arts Centre in Stirling and arrived in Perth keen to tackle the theatre's problems. The local authority was similarly keen to improve the building, with culture and the arts being core strands in its vision for the regeneration of the city.[10] As a result, a design competition took place in 2008, overseen by the Royal Incorporation of Architects in Scotland (RIAS). It was won by Richard Murphy Architects. This award-winning practice had been founded in Edinburgh in 1991. Major arts projects undertaken by the firm include the Fruitmarket Gallery, Edinburgh (1993), Dundee Contemporary Arts (2000), and the Tolbooth, Stirling (2006). The project architect at Perth Theatre was Bill Black.

A 'compact brief' was drawn up.[11] As well as improvements to the auditorium and backstage areas, priorities included the construction of accessible front-of-house facilities with improved catering provision, and the creation of more space for education/community work. A feasibility study indicated that the theatre's aspirations could be achieved for £8 million.[12] However, as we shall see, the theme for much of the next decade was the mis-match between this estimate and the likely cost of the actual design proposals. That the final cost was double the initial estimate is a familiar story in theatre architecture and one we will encounter again later in this book. The reasons can vary, but one issue is the fact that feasibility studies are sometimes undertaken by a different set of consultants from those who carry out the actual project.[13] Although often well-informed, these documents can embody different assumptions from those which shape the final brief (for example, about the extent and nature of new building or refurbishment). In addition, they may be drawn up without the detailed knowledge of an existing building which emerges in subsequent surveys. The creativity of the early design process, too, can sometimes see a brief being developed or changed as initial ideas are tested and new possibilities are considered.

## Design Development and Delivery

During 2009, conservation specialists Simpson and Brown produced a Conservation Plan for the theatre, which narrated its history and identified the parts of the building – principally the auditorium and the conservatory foyer – which were of particular significance.[14] All of the 1980s extensions were deemed to be of 'neutral' significance, paving the way for their removal or remodelling. In the event, Richard Murphy Architects proposed only the demolition of the 1980s restaurant/workshop block to the east of the auditorium. The northern (backstage) extension was to be retained and reconfigured.

Planning consent was secured in 2010. However, the proposals then stalled, not least because of a lack of funding. During 2012, the project's scope was reviewed and the design was revised. A new scheme was submitted for planning approval in 2013, and again was successful. However, it also stalled, once more partly for financial reasons but also because Horsecross Arts went through a period of organisational change.[15] The artistic director, Rachel O'Riordan, moved to Sherman Cymru Theatre in Cardiff. In addition, the chief executive departed, while concerns in late 2013 about the organisation's financial health led to the resignation of some of the members of its board.[16] A new chair was appointed, namely Magnus Linklater, one-time chairman of the Scottish Arts Council, while Gwilym Gibbons became chief executive. Five new directors joined the three city councillors who had remained on the board. In the wake of these changes, a further review of the design was carried out during 2014,[17] with a particular focus on its cost. A fresh planning application was made in summer 2015. In the meantime, the theatre closed pending the start of building work, which took place in 2016–17.

During the evolution of the design, a number of the facilities originally proposed were lost, including a dedicated space for youth theatre and some of the community rooms.[18] However, there are some important constants which connect the proposals. All three schemes are broadly similar in their basic arrangement. Technical/production areas are consolidated into the 1980s northern extension, with the 1980s eastern extension

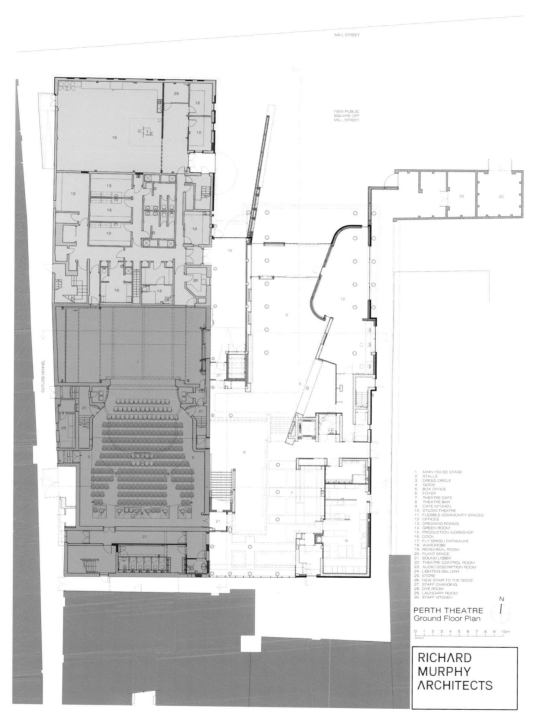

1. MAIN HOUSE STAGE
2. STALLS
3. DRESS CIRCLE
4. 'GODS'
5. BOX OFFICE
6. FOYER
7. THEATRE CAFE
8. THEATRE BAR
9. CAFE KITCHEN
10. STUDIO THEATRE
11. FLEXIBLE COMMUNITY SPACES
12. OFFICES
13. DRESSING ROOMS
14. GREEN ROOM
15. PRODUCTION WORKSHOP
16. DOCK
17. FLY GRIDS / CATWALKS
18. WARDROBE
19. REHEARSAL ROOM
20. PLANT SPACE
21. SOUND LOBBY
22. THEATRE CONTROL ROOM
23. AUDIO DESCRIPTION ROOM
24. LIGHTING GALLERY
25. STORE
26. NEW STAIR TO THE 'GODS'
27. STAFF CHANGING
28. DYE ROOM
29. LAUNDARY ROOM
30. STAFF KITCHEN

**PERTH THEATRE**
Ground Floor Plan

0 1 2 3 4 5 6 7 8 9 10m
SCALE

RICHARD MURPHY ARCHITECTS

C7.2 Perth Theatre, ground floor plan (at Mill Street level) following reconstruction

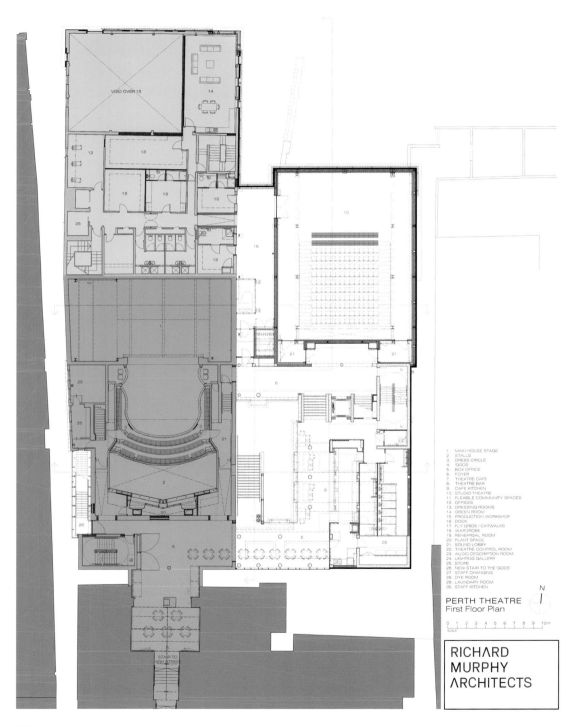

1. MAIN HOUSE STAGE
2. STALLS
3. DRESS CIRCLE
4. 'GODS'
5. BOX OFFICE
6. FOYER
7. THEATRE CAFE
8. THEATRE BAR
9. CAFE KITCHEN
10. STUDIO THEATRE
11. FLEXIBLE COMMUNITY SPACES
12. OFFICES
13. DRESSING ROOMS
14. GREEN ROOM
15. PRODUCTION WORKSHOP
16. DOCK
17. FLY GRIDS / CATWALKS
18. WARDROBE
19. REHEARSAL ROOM
20. PLANT SPACE
21. SOUND LOBBY
22. THEATRE CONTROL ROOM
23. AUDIO DESCRIPTION ROOM
24. LIGHTING GALLERY
25. STORE
26. NEW STAIR TO THE 'GODS'
27. STAFF CHANGING
28. DYE ROOM
29. LAUNDARY ROOM
30. STAFF KITCHEN

PERTH THEATRE
First Floor Plan

0 1 2 3 4 5 6 7 8 9 10m
SCALE

RICHARD
MURPHY
ARCHITECTS

C7.3   Perth Theatre, first floor plan (High Street level) following reconstruction

being replaced by a new structure containing a foyer running north–south alongside the historic auditorium. This new foyer connects the original High Street entrance with a new entrance on Mill Street, which was previously the rear of the theatre. Above this new entrance is the studio auditorium, arranged as a courtyard space with a flexible stalls area and two symmetrical side galleries. The 2010 and 2013 proposals had 232 seats; as built there are around 200. The prominence of the Mill Street entrance itself was partly driven by the impossibility of achieving a level way into the foyers on the High Street side of the building. As we have noted already, the High Street entrance leads into a corridor which steps up into the original foyer at dress circle level. The steps could not be removed without acquiring the basements below, which were not in the theatre's ownership. Efforts to purchase them were unsuccessful.[19] As a result, Mill Street has become the theatre's main public face, with the new principal entrance leading into the stalls-level foyer, from where there is lift access to the rest of the building.

A further constant in all three sets of proposals is the basic arrangement of the foyers, with a restaurant at stalls level and a bar on the level above, although some of the detailing changed from one scheme to the next. The restaurant in the 2010 proposals sits behind a wavy 'crinkle-crankle' screen, for example, which does not figure in the executed design. The size of the foyers also varies, with the 2013 scheme being slightly more spacious than its predecessor. Bill Black recalled that the aim was to 'take out the tightness' in the layout and so approximately 50 square metres was added to each level.[20] Of this move, Richard Murphy commented:

> When a scheme sits around you have second thoughts about it. There has been a slight rearranging and the plans have been made slightly more rational.[21]

In the executed (2015) scheme, the floor area of the new-build part of the theatre was reduced slightly and more of the existing structure was retained or remodelled.[22] For example, earlier proposals to alter the area between the conservatory foyer and the auditorium were abandoned, meaning that an additional accessible entrance from Cutlog Vennel – that is, as close to the High Street as was possible without reconstructing the original way in – was lost.

In the interests of cost certainty and efficient delivery, the building was procured through the Scottish East Central construction hub (formally known as 'hub East Central Scotland').[23] This organisation is a partnership between public- and private-sector organisations which was set up in 2012 to deliver public and community buildings. It is supported by the Scottish Futures Trust, an infrastructure delivery company set up by the Scottish Government as an alternative to the Private Finance Initiative. Black praised the 'creative' on-site team, whilst noting that the procurement method added a degree of distance between the architects and the building users in that the architects' connection was to the 'hubco', which dealt with Perth and Kinross Council, which in turn dealt with Horsecross Arts.[24] As the project neared construction, certain aspects of the 'vision' were the subject of robust debate among the team. To take one area of discussion: was it really worth re-opening the 'gods' to gain just seventy-four seats, when doing so would require the creation of additional public circulation? There was also discussion of some of the design detail: for example, the polished plaster walls which are a significant feature of the foyers were questioned, as were certain other details, such as the architects' wish to integrate lighting into the main foyer stair. The designers and the construction team worked hard to try to preserve the level of resolution and sophistication which the architects believed was a critical part of their concept, whilst achieving an affordable result. Other areas in which savings were made included the furniture and equipment budgets, while changes were made to the specification of the building services: hot water, for example, is heated at 'point of use' in the toilets.[25] In total, these changes are reported to have saved around £5 million.[26]

## Perth Theatre in Use

At night, the Mill Street face of the theatre positively glows. The new entrance is deeply recessed and brightly lit. Above it, the solid wall

C7.4   Mill Street frontage. By night, the translucent rainscreen glows. A wall leads out from the entrance, hiding the loading bay, functioning as a bench, and making space for posters

of the studio auditorium is clad in translucent cast-glass panels and is backlit with LED lighting. A digital screen offers a glimpse of the delights within. The elevation is taller than it needs to be in order to screen rooftop plant and to give the building a strong presence in the streetscape. Glazed panels have also been used to re-clad the retained 1980s wing, giving the whole frontage a consistent appearance. A large window has been cut into its corner, giving views into (and from) the green room. The location of the production workshops and stage means that dock access has had to be maintained on this side of the building, and indeed the service entrance is adjacent to the main public entrance. Space where a 16-metre articulated lorry can unload into the theatre is screened by a low wall, which usefully incorporates a seating plinth and space for posters. This wall has been painted red, bringing a touch of the bright

colours of the interior out into what is, by day, a deliberately monochrome area.

The wall funnels visitors towards the entrance. It continues inside the building, leading patrons past a spacious new box office into the main part of the foyer. This space rises through the full height of the building, and might be interpreted as an indoor version of one of Perth's historic yards. On one side it is overlooked by two steel-fronted galleries; on the other side it is dominated by the rough brickwork of the auditorium's east wall, which was originally outside. Warm in colour and rich in texture, this wall is washed by daylight from a slot-like window at the rear of the foyer as well as a narrow skylight above. The ground floor of the foyer houses the restaurant; one level up is the bar. Seating benches are cut into the gallery balustrade at bar level, which steps in and out as a result. When the benches are occupied and the galleries are busy, the feeling is very much one of peopled space. The bar level also gives access to the studio auditorium, which has been named after Joan Knight. The top-most foyer, finally, leads to the upper part of the studio, the community room, and the 'gods' in the historic auditorium.

The detailing is typical of Richard Murphy Architects. It is sophisticated and well-resolved, and has survived the cost-cutting needed to get the theatre built. One might conclude, perhaps, that it demonstrates that good design need not be expensive. As the *Architects' Journal* put it:

Vertical planes of vivid polished plaster are edged in dark metal trim, balustrades and barriers are articulated in detail, providing various degrees of transparency and places to sit or to stand. Structural concrete is exposed and legible, reinforcing the circulation and clarity of the plan and section. Oak wall and ceiling linings are tactile and give warmth while also modulating the acoustics of the various volumes. Signage, also designed by the practice,

is well incorporated into the finishes and overall design.[27]

Throughout, the colours used on the walls signify the functions of the spaces: orange indicates 'auditorium'; red refers to 'circulation'; the bar is blue. The lighting strategy avoids bland uniformity for dramatic contrasts of light and shade. Particularly effective is the bright illumination of the orange-painted lobbies that lead to the main auditorium, glimpses of which are evident through openings in the brick wall. Elsewhere, lighting washes over board-marked concrete, bringing out its texture. Other areas are more intimate, with darker tones and dimmer lighting. Black notes that the aim was to recreate the cosiness of the old foyers, 'the world hiding away from the weather'.[28] In doing so, low slab-to-slab heights (necessitated by the floor levels in the historic building), colour, lighting, and materials all play their part. The result, like Liverpool's Everyman Theatre, shows how a contemporary sense of theatricality can be achieved.

C7.5    Looking back towards the Mill Street entrance, with the box office on the right. The lighting design avoids uniformity for contrasts of light and shade

C7.6    The main foyer, with the brick wall of the auditorium to the right. The space feels like a covered-in version of one of Perth's historic yards

C7.7    The new Joan Knight Studio, a courtyard auditorium with character

The historic auditorium has been redecorated, the seating has been reconfigured, and the ventilation system has been replaced. Now with c. 500 seats, it is a compact, intimate space. Behind the stage, dressing rooms have been refurbished. The former studio is now a well-located, spacious workshop with immediate access to the dock entrance and stage. Above this area, the former garment store was repurposed as a rehearsal room with potential community use. The new Joan Knight studio, meanwhile, is a space of deliberate character, rather than an anonymous 'black box'. Oak linings and black-painted steel give consistency with the foyers; the oak slats also conceal services and have an acoustic function. The seating is retractable: initial performances made use of a transverse arrangement as well as the more usual end-on configuration.

## Conclusions

The road to the reopening of Perth Theatre was long and sometimes bumpy. Horsecross Arts has seen changes in its personnel and governance; the designers have had to re-visit the scheme several times; fundraising, too, was challenging. Although substantial sums were secured from Creative Scotland, the Heritage Lottery Fund, the local authority, and the Gannochy Trust, among many others, a small shortfall remained when the theatre eventually reopened in December 2017.[29] The challenges faced along the way make the final result all the more creditable. The building has won several awards, and been nominated for more. Now the task for Horsecross Arts is to continue to develop their audience and to build on the opportunities offered by their renewed building.

Bill Black is content with the outcome, feeling that '90 per cent' of the original 'vision' has been achieved, spatially and in terms of architectural detail.[30] For Horsecross Arts' Peter Hood, the extent to which the original brief has been maintained reflects the way in which the organisation started

C7.8   The restored main auditorium

with a clear view of its end goals. Any theatre setting out on a capital project, he suggests, needs to start at the end and work backwards, rather than 'starting at the beginning and wondering where you'll get to'.[31] Black, meanwhile, notes the tenacity required:

Unless you have a benefactor, it's hard work. You need to know what you want to do. A good design team will find a way, however hard it is – though the route is hard.[32]

# Citizens Theatre, Glasgow

Architect: Bennetts Associates

Client: Citizens Theatre

Quantity surveyor: Turner and Townsend

Structural engineer: Struer Consulting Engineers Ltd

Theatre consultant: Theatreplan

Services engineer: Max Fordham

The River Clyde divides Glasgow city centre from the Gorbals, Laurieston, and Hutchesontown districts immediately to the south. Until the 1950s, these areas were characterised by cramped and decaying nineteenth-century tenements, and were regarded by planners and politicians as 'slums'.[1] During the 1950s and 1960s, their Victorian buildings were largely replaced by a mixture of low-rise flats and tower blocks. The contemporary appearance of these buildings distinguished them from what had gone before, as well as from the historic architecture of the city centre, north of the river. Their layout amid grass and car parking rather than the traditional street grid also set them apart. However, many of the 1960s buildings, in turn, became the targets of criticism during the 1980s and 1990s. In addition to growing general unease about some forms of post-war architecture and urban planning, a number of the Gorbals blocks were afflicted by serious construction and maintenance problems.[2] Today, the area is gradually being rebuilt once again. The tower blocks are making way for new buildings, the design of which often nods to historical precedents. Amid the building sites and the fenced-off areas reserved for future development is one of the few survivors of this area's nineteenth-century history, the Citizens Theatre. Previously known as the Royal Princess's Theatre and constructed in 1878, the theatre's well-preserved Victorian auditorium and significant collection of historic stage machinery stand as beacons of continuity in this rapidly changing environment.[3]

In early 2013, Bennetts Associates was appointed to reconstruct the theatre's foyers, studio auditorium,

C8.1   The Citizens Theatre in the 1970s. The historic auditorium is screened by a tenement block; the bus is passing its rather modest entrance. Next door is the Palace Theatre, with its more ornate front

and backstage areas, which had grown up in a slightly ad hoc fashion around the core of the 1878 auditorium. The architects had recently completed the re-working of the Royal Shakespeare Theatre, Stratford-upon-Avon, and were also working in Chester on what would become Storyhouse. The Citizens Theatre's £21.5 million capital project, to be completed in 2020, will improve the auditorium and stage, and will secure the theatre's historic fabric. Previous extensions will be swept away, with new foyers, a new studio theatre, and enhanced technical areas all being wrapped around the auditorium. The theatre will be fully accessible, and will offer a legible, spacious, and welcoming environment for visitors, audiences, and staff. Its ability to earn income from catering, conferences, and external bookings will be increased. Within the context of the Gorbals/Laurieston masterplan, meanwhile, the theatre will not only have a stronger presence within the streetscape but will also, it is hoped, stimulate further developments and a sense of community. In this respect, the Citizens Theatre project – and its funding – reflects a number of agendas, bringing together the theatre's aspirations for a safe, sustainable building with those of its funders relating to such things as inner-city regeneration and architectural conservation.

## 'Vision' and Funding

The Citizens' Theatre Company was founded in Glasgow in 1943 by a group led by the playwright James Bridie and the art curator Tom Honeyman.[4] Intended as a stepping stone towards a fully professional Scottish National Theatre, the group began work at the city's Athenaeum Theatre before moving in 1945 to the Royal Princess's Theatre. When their lease expired ten years later, the building was acquired for the company by Glasgow Corporation. Presenting a mixture of British and European work with new plays by Scottish authors, the Citizens flourished. It was a significant beneficiary of the new system of public subsidy for the performing arts, introduced after the Second World War.[5] The Close Theatre, opened in 1965, was one of the first studio auditoria within a repertory theatre complex in Britain.[6] The theatre came to particular

prominence after 1970 under the well-received co-directorship of Giles Havergal, Philip Prowse, and Robert David McDonald.[7] It not only developed an ambitious and bold approach to production but also sought to appeal to a diverse audience through the sale of cheap tickets. During the 1960s and early 1970s, a replacement theatre was included in plans for a new multi-auditorium cultural centre in the heart of Glasgow city centre; critic John Elsom wrote in 1971 that a new building would give the company the surroundings its work deserved.[8] In the mid-1970s, however, the scheme was judged to be unaffordable and was abandoned, although the Citizens seems never to have been keen to leave the Gorbals anyway.

Until 1977, the auditorium was screened from the street by a four-storey stone tenement. More prominent, in fact, was the adjacent Palace Theatre, which had an elevation with giant Doric columns topped by statues. Entry to the Citizens was through a narrow entrance leading into a courtyard in front of the auditorium's stone wall. The tenement and the Palace Theatre were demolished in 1977. Twelve years later, the Citizens acquired what The Theatres Trust's gazetteer described as an 'undistinguished yellow brick frontage'.[9] At ground level, the only opening was the main entrance; a band of windows above gave restricted views in. The foyer itself was largely top-lit, with a central bar area and several changes of level. The preserved statues from the old Palace Theatre were relocated here. A subsequent extension in the 1990s added further back-of-house facilities.

By 2011, the Citizens was beginning to show its age. A survey revealed that some £3.5 million of remedial work was required.[10] Dominic Hill, recently appointed as the theatre's artistic director, later recalled his first tour of the building, during which the extent to which water was pouring in – not least below the stage – was all too apparent.[11] Furthermore, the ad hoc way in which the building had grown made it difficult to navigate, problematic in its multiple level changes, and perhaps also unwelcoming for visitors sent to a rear door. Hill noted: 'a lot of the work that connects with [the] community, the learning work, at the moment takes place at the end of labyrinthine corridors at the back of the building,

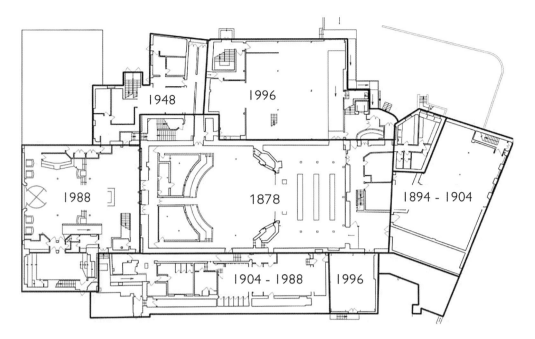

C8.2    The Citizens Theatre, plan prior to reconstruction showing how the building had grown up over time

C8.3    The Citizens Theatre prior to the demolition of the foyer

which are completely inaccessible, freezing cold. Rain pours in.'[12]

The announcement by Creative Scotland of a capital funding round gave impetus to plans for change during 2012–13, not least as it was believed that there might be no further funding rounds for some time thereafter.[13] In addition to necessary repairs and conservation work, other priorities emerged, including a flexible 150-seat studio auditorium, additional space for learning and outreach activities, improved rehearsal and administration spaces, and facilities which would generate non-box office income, such as a new café and hospitality/conference area.[14] New foyers would connect everything together, removing the need to exit the building or to navigate staircases and multiple changes of level. For Judith Kilvington, appointed as the Citizens' executive director in 2013, a highly accessible building was essential.[15] Kilvington had previously overseen a major capital project for Graeae Theatre Company, whose members have physical and sensory disabilities, and sought to apply ideas from that project to the Citizens. Finally, for Glasgow City Council and the Gorbals Regeneration Group (a forum bringing together local representatives including members of the Community Council), the redevelopment of the Citizens was intended to make a significant contribution to the ongoing regeneration of the local area. The city council summarised its aspirations in this regard in 2018:

> The Citizens already contributes to individual and community confidence and sense of place. It is a source of great pride and a locally valued asset, the worth of which will increase even further with the culmination of the redevelopment project as proposed. A redeveloped Citizens Theatre is essential if the Gorbals is to become a genuine visitor destination because it will be a catalyst for further commercial and cultural development in its immediate environs.[16]

As of RIBA Stage 3 ('developed design'), the 'vision' had been formalised as follows:

1. To build our reputation for innovation and excellence as makers of theatre.
2. To protect and promote our heritage and make the Theatre much more accessible to audiences and visitors.
3. To develop and consolidate the activities of Citizens Learning as an integral part of our activities.
4. To develop the Theatre's role as a cultural hub and centre for talent development.
5. To develop and implement a strategy which places equality and access at the heart of the theatre's activities.
6. To grow and sustain our audiences.
7. To diversify our funding sources and increase our income.
8. To create a more energy efficient and environmentally sustainable building.[17]

The estimated cost of the project gradually rose from a notional £12 million in 2012 to c. £15 million during initial design work, and then to £21.5 million by 2019. The increase can be explained in several ways. The greater detail of the developing designs allowed accurate costings to be made, while the risks and challenges of the existing building came increasingly into focus; later, the nature of the construction market in which the project was to be delivered inevitably impacted on costs. Glasgow City Council promised funding from an early stage, while Creative Scotland offered £1.5 million. An early approach was also made to the Heritage Lottery Fund (HLF). At that stage, the project was planned in two phases, but the HLF felt that the initial phase lacked sufficient 'heritage' to justify their involvement.[18] Rather than proceed with two phases of c. £6 million each, it was therefore decided to reconfigure the project in a single phase, and a promise of HLF support to the tune of £4.8 million was accordingly secured in June 2014 (and confirmed in late 2017).[19] Graham Sutherland, the Citizens' client representative with oversight of the project, later commented that this change led to a better, more integrated scheme.[20] A sum of £500,000 for conservation and archaeological work was also promised by Historic Environment Scotland. Finally, the Citizens set out to raise £3 million itself.

As projected costs rose, 'value engineering' at intervals during the design period delivered some savings, but additional funding was also sought. For example, an approach was made to the Scottish Government's Regeneration Capital Grant Fund. Initially £4 million was requested; a subsequent application for £2.5 million was successful in March 2017.[21] Additional money was also sought from the Scottish Government: a direct approach won £1.5 million.[22] However, as of spring 2017, the project was still over budget. The funders met and confirmed their commitment to the Citizens, but their support came with a request to reduce costs by £2.5 million. As will be discussed in more detail shortly, the scheme was partly redesigned as a result. Nonetheless, in March 2018, Glasgow City Council increased its contribution from £4 million to £5 million.[23] The city authorities also promised a loan, if necessary. A year later, a slight shortfall remained following the receipt of construction tenders, and so, with the design being felt to be robust and no further cuts seeming possible, additional sums were awarded by Glasgow City Council, Historic Environment Scotland, and the Scottish Government.[24] Applying for money was a significant undertaking for the theatre management. Judith Kilvington later commented that at times 80 per cent of her week had been spent working on the logistics of developing and delivering the capital project, in addition to her actual 'day job' running the theatre.[25]

## The Design Proposals

The themes which shaped Bennetts Associates' approach to the Citizens Theatre were first elaborated in 2012 in their response to the Invitation to Tender.[26] The first comprised revealing and enhancing the theatre's heritage, not least through repairs and improvements in the auditorium and on stage (for which the architects worked with the theatre consultant Charcoalblue). Second, the architects sought to link the various parts of the theatre with 'inspirational spaces'. Finally, the theatre would be reorganised to work better for performers, staff, visitors, and audiences. These themes were worked out in a sequence of designs produced between 2012 and 2017.

The key move made by Bennetts Associates was to propose the replacement of the southern and western parts of the theatre building, including

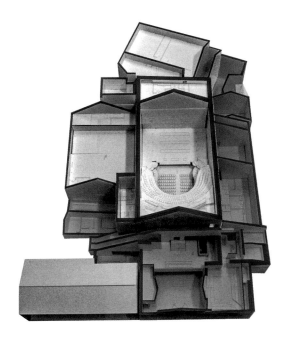

C8.4   Diagram showing the areas to be demolished (shaded)

the main street frontage. In their place will come new buildings and more flexible facilities, including significant new foyer space adjacent to the street. In developing this layout, the architects were inspired by the way in which the theatre was accessed before 1977. As we have noted, its entrance was through a narrow 'close' which led to a spacious 'court' with views of the stone-faced gable end of the auditorium. Bennetts Associates' designs are united by a desire to contrast similar moments of spatial compression (the 'close' reinterpreted) with more open areas in which the auditorium gable is clearly revealed (the 'court').

In the 2012 concept design, the central part of the street elevation is glazed, giving views from the pavement into the foyer and towards the rear wall of the auditorium, in front of which new stairs are inserted. To one side is a linear structure containing rehearsal, teaching, and performance spaces. It projects forward over the pavement in a way that suggests it would be visible in long views along Gorbals Street. Entry into the foyer

C8.5   The architects' original concept model, showing a linear building alongside the auditorium and a glass-fronted foyer

is shown below the projecting wing, recalling the compression of the pre-1977 entrance. The drawings show the studio theatre to the east of the main auditorium and stage, while technical facilities and administration were to be located to the north, partly repurposing existing spaces. These proposals were thought to be particularly strong by the client team.[27] They established much of the basic layout of the scheme as built.

Consultation took place with bodies including Glasgow City Council and Historic Environment Scotland.[28] Feedback revealed that the public especially liked the new studio theatre, the new entrance and foyer, the areas for community activities, the provision of improved access to the building, as well as such things as an increased number of toilets, comfortable seating in the foyer, an improved café, and better heating and lighting. A systematic programme of consultation with theatre staff was also carried out by Graham Sutherland.[29] Comments, suggestions and criticisms were recorded in a spreadsheet which ultimately contained over 500 entries, and specific responses were provided by the design team for circulation to all staff. This exercise, which was felt to be useful in building consensus and giving staff a sense of involvement, highlighted concerns including a lack of storage space in the proposals, the merits of open-plan working, and questions relating to security and access.[30] A Building Redevelopment Staff Advisory Group open to all staff was convened. The development of the design was also informed by a detailed condition survey and by client/design team visits to other theatres. (During this period, the lower levels of the auditorium were re-seated in a separate project.)

Drawings of 2014–15 show how the architects' initial ideas were developed into a revised proposal. The concept of a long extension to the south of the original building was retained, but the studio auditorium moved from the back of the theatre into the southern extension at ground (stalls) floor level, positioned off a compact main foyer. The area previously proposed for the studio is shown in the drawings as being given over to a rehearsal room, dressing rooms, and space for 'cultural tenants'. A learning/event space is shown adjacent to the street entrance. The new circle level foyer, meanwhile, leads to a further learning/event space, the studio theatre gallery, and a further studio dedicated to learning and outreach. Externally, the central part of the street elevation retains the glazing of the earlier proposal, with the Palace Theatre statues appearing at the level of the circle foyer. The rest of the extension is shown with a layered mesh cladding, a little like that used by Haworth Tompkins on the Young Vic in London in 2006.

Planning approval was sought in November 2015.[31] By now, the elevations had been further developed, with greater use of brick on the Gorbals Street front, which was partly angled to funnel visitors towards the entrance and to create a small balcony overlooking the street. However,

design work slowed during 2016, as the theatre assembled its funding package. As noted above, the funders met in spring 2017 and asked for a £2.5 million reduction in costs. Kilvington recalled the challenge that had been laid down: the design had planning consent and had already been through 'value engineering'.[32] The design team was essentially forced to go 'back to basics' and to test every element of the scheme. In October 2017, a revised proposal was submitted for a 'Section 42' amendment to the 2015–16 planning consent. Compared to the 2015 design, the floor area was reduced slightly, the learning studio was removed, and one level was culled entirely, leading to a slightly lowered parapet height.[33] Kilvington and Sutherland both credited the architects' creativity during this process, and noted the extent to which this version of the design was shaped by a real desire to achieve efficiencies in planning and use.[34] In other words, 'value engineering' offered positive, creative opportunities to think about how to co-locate facilities and make spaces work harder.

The 2017 design feels tougher than its 2015 predecessor. At street level, the frontage is slightly recessed, with the elevation to the foyer being glazed. To one side, a learning/event space is screened by a colonnade-like wall which can accommodate posters and which continues beyond the building, stretching out in front of the adjacent car park. Above, the upper foyer projects over the pavement, being largely clad in dark brick. The building has a definite, strong presence, evoking the scale and character of Glasgow's tenement architecture, which often features long terraces hard against the street line. Just below the parapet to one side of the elevation are the six preserved statues from the old Palace Theatre. The wing to the south has matching brick walls at ground-floor level, but adopts translucent polycarbonate cladding above, which will be lit after dark.

The foyer will form a single, accessible space connecting all the public areas. The contrast between open 'court' and compressed 'close' has been retained. The main stair will be a focal point in the foyer 'court', where finishes will be rugged and robust.[35] The planned aesthetic balances theatricality (for example, bold colour on the stair) with the warmth of natural materials such as dark timber and a sense that the foyer is also a technical

C8.6    The Citizens Theatre street elevation as proposed, 2018

space. There is to be provision for performance throughout, the servicing for which is not hidden.[36] The studio theatre will offer flexible seating for 140, with a combination of retractable seating units and loose seating that can be formed into rows on manually positioned rostra. The aim is a space that is flexible, but has character.[37] At ceiling level, a tension wire grid is proposed for ease of use and flexibility. Walls are to be lined in dark plywood with a Unistrut grid, while a window can be screened when daylight is not wanted.

History is important, too. There are to be views into backstage areas, including the theatre's historic paint frame (where scenery can be made in traditional fashion). Within the stage house, historic stage machinery will be restored to working order (although it is not intended for use in modern productions); the flytower will be increased in size and volume. Historic equipment below the stage will also be restored. The sub-stage area will be waterproofed with stair and partial lift

access to allow the public to visit. Meanwhile the final proposals for the historic auditorium were developed in collaboration with David Wilmore of Theatresearch, and in consultation with Glasgow City Council's Conservation Department and Historic Environment Scotland. The upper circle will be re-seated. Level access will be created, with new positions for wheelchair users, not least in new boxes at the rear of the stalls. Improvements are to be made to the ventilation and heating. The raked stage floor will be retained but returned from 1:17 to its original rake of 1:24 in order to be compatible with other Victorian theatres and so to facilitate co-productions. Re-raking will also provide level access to the stage for actors. Demountable panels will give flexibility for traps.

With consent secured, detailed design work continued during the first half of 2018. A two-stage contractor appointment was made, with Kier joining the team in April 2018. As in several other projects discussed in this book, the aim was that the

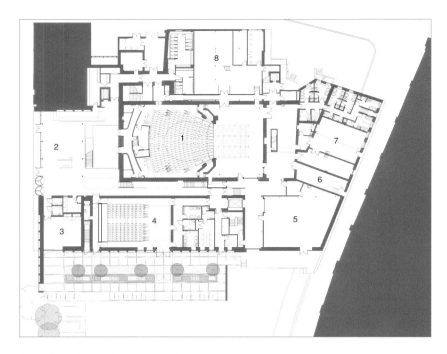

Key:
1 Historic auditorium
2 Foyer
3 Learning and events space
4 Studio theatre
5 Construction workshop
6 Paint frame
7 Metal workshop
8 LX workshop

C8.7　Ground floor plan as proposed

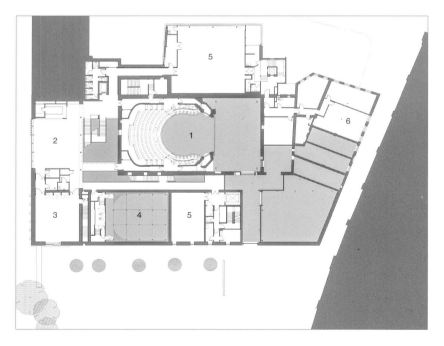

Key:
1 Historic auditorium
2 Foyer bar/events
3 Learning and events space
4 Studio theatre (upper part)
5 Rehearsal rooms
6 Wardrobe

C8.8　First floor plan as proposed

contractor's advice on buildability and cost would improve the efficiency and costs of the scheme. Work began on site in late 2018.

## Conclusions

The Citizens Theatre redevelopment will transform the image and usability of the building. For the client, the story has been one of the sheer effort needed to launch, develop, and fund a major capital project, and in particular the time needed to apply for money, the need to produce paperwork for each funder which specifically addresses their areas of interest, and the extent to which funding deadlines and opportunities can inform the process.[38] As at Perth Theatre, several complete proposals have been prepared. The initial 'vision' has survived largely intact, despite the impact of 'value engineering' on aspects of the design. In some ways, the challenges of funding have forced a more efficient approach. The external design of the Gorbals Street front has also matured, resulting in proposals which have real civic presence. In reaching this point, commitment and team-work have been important in navigating a sometimes tricky process. Of what is now being built, one might conclude that it embodies the Citizens' history of collaborative working, its belief in community engagement, and its pursuit of artistic excellence, and that this project therefore encapsulates the theatre's long-held core values.

# Leeds Playhouse

Architect: Page\Park

Client: Leeds City Council

Contractor: BAM

Structural engineer: Arup

M&E engineer: Max Fordham

Project manager: Turner & Townsend

Cost consultant: Rex Procter and Partners

CDM co-ordinator: CDM Scotland

Theatre consultant: Charcoalblue

Lighting consultant: Max Fordham

Leeds Playhouse is the only major producing theatre in West Yorkshire. Its roots lie in the mid-1960s, when a local campaigner, Doreen Newlyn, mobilised support for a new repertory theatre in the city. Leeds Theatre Trust was founded in 1968; two years later, a temporary theatre was squeezed into a converted university sports hall. In 1984, a design competition was held to find an architect for a more permanent building, which opened in 1990 with the name 'West Yorkshire Playhouse'. Designed by Ian and Marjorie Appleton, it was the last major theatre of the 'Housing the Arts' era. In 2018, fifty years after Newlyn had begun her campaign in earnest, the West Yorkshire Playhouse was re-named the Leeds Playhouse, in order better to reflect its heritage and the extent to which the theatre sees its work being rooted specifically in Leeds. James Brining, artistic director since 2012, commented at the time of the change: 'One of the most frequently asked questions we get is, "where are you?" [...] We're in Leeds.'[1]

Strengthening the theatre's connections with the city and its people was also one of the factors motivating the £16 million capital project which the theatre first conceived in 2013. A substantial extension 'turns the theatre around', giving it a new entrance facing the city centre, while a route cut through the building creates a new sequence of foyers and better access to its auditoria. The work also includes alterations to the auditoria, the creation of an atmospheric performance space in the basement, and technical upgrades. The intended result is a theatre which is even better connected to its locality, which offers an improved visitor experience, and which is financially resilient in an age of reducing subsidy. With new developments on the doorstep, including a new building for Leeds City College, there is real potential for the theatre's new cafés and restaurant to generate substantial income from daytime visitors.

## The Vision

Quarry Hill, just to the east of Leeds city centre, was condemned in the early 1930s as an area of slum housing, and a new Quarry Hill Estate was constructed later that decade. Inspired by

C9.1   West Yorkshire Playhouse, 1990

contemporaneous developments in Vienna, it comprised 938 flats in a series of steel-framed blocks of up to seven storeys.[2] By the 1970s, however, the estate seemed to be in decline. The area was cleared once again, creating space for the West Yorkshire Playhouse of 1990. As we have noted already, the theatre was planned as a permanent replacement for the temporary Leeds Playhouse of 1970, which had enjoyed great success despite its slightly makeshift premises.[3] There were plans for the area around the new theatre to be redeveloped, but only part of the intended scheme was ever built. At the eastern end of Quarry Hill, a large block of offices – Quarry House – was constructed to postmodern designs by Terry Farrell. This block was aligned so that it would close the key Headrow/Eastgate axis which cuts across central Leeds and continues up a broad flight of steps adjacent to the Playhouse. Much of the rest of the land between Quarry House and the new theatre was left empty.

As originally designed by the Appleton Partnership, the Playhouse was efficiently accommodated in a building essentially hexagonal in plan. It is set into Quarry Hill itself, which rises up from St Peter's Street. The result is that the theatre has a consistent roofline but 'loses' floors as the ground level rises up. At St Peter's Street level the building has, in effect, four storeys; on the hilltop there are two. Externally, the building has elevations of polychromatic brickwork below a pitched slate roof, responding to the wish of the city's planners in the 1980s for new buildings to demonstrate the 'Leeds look', that is, a contextual approach sympathetic to Leeds' heritage of Victorian brick industrial architecture. Some critics were unimpressed when the Playhouse opened in 1990, feeling that it looked more like a neo-vernacular supermarket than a major public building, although then director Jude Kelly was more positive, suggesting that its perhaps familiar appearance might make the theatre seem more approachable.[4]

In plan, the theatre originally turned its back on busy St Peter's Street, which forms part of an inner 'loop' road system. This side of the theatre comprised a largely blank elevation with a loading bay, next to a small staff car park. In view of the 1980s plans for development on Quarry Hill as well as the location of audience car parking, the sole public entrance to the theatre was located on the hilltop itself, meaning that anyone approaching on foot from the city had to climb the steps adjacent to the theatre. Patrons entered the building at an intermediate level, with an upper foyer giving access to the larger Quarry Theatre auditorium and the café, while a lower area led to the toilets and the smaller Courtyard Theatre. The Quarry Theatre is a 750-seat amphitheatre with an invisible proscenium arch and a flytower; the layout of the auditorium was closely related to the original Leeds Playhouse. The Courtyard Theatre, meanwhile, was designed to seat 350 in a more flexible arrangement. Like the National Theatre's Dorfman (Cottesloe) auditorium and the many other 'courtyard'-type auditoria which have been built since the late 1970s, it has fixed narrow seating galleries around the perimeter of the space

and a flexible floor area which can be divided between performance space and stalls seating as required.

## The 'Vision'

The first ambition for the Playhouse redevelopment was to take account of the theatre's changing setting. For example, the new Victoria Gate shopping centre created a major retail focus just to the west of the theatre, but the location of the Playhouse's original public entrance – facing away from the city centre – meant that it was not well connected to this or other nearby developments. Quarry Hill itself is also changing. A number of arts-related buildings have been constructed, including premises for the BBC, Leeds College of Music, and Northern Ballet. Leeds City College is moving to a site alongside the Playhouse, while a new masterplan for a mixed-use development on the land between the Playhouse and Quarry House has been prepared.

Furthermore, the Playhouse building itself was deemed to be problematic. Its various levels and

C9.2   Quarry Theatre auditorium, West Yorkshire Playhouse, 1990

half-levels were seen as an 'obstacle course' for visitors with mobility problems: there was, for example, a requirement to go up or down from the main entrance just to reach the auditoria.[5] The downstairs location of the Courtyard Theatre was felt to be especially unfortunate: it offered 'a slight feeling of entering the bowels of the earth'.[6] Although the theatre building itself was in fairly good condition structurally, some of the interiors were considered to be dated, while some of the technical plant was nearing the end of its working life.[7]

The theatre's operational requirements were also changing. The 1990 building had been designed with the expectation that much of the Playhouse's work would be produced in-house and would only be shown there. By 2015, a significant number of shows were co-productions with other theatres, while the Playhouse also presented a growing amount of touring work.[8] In addition, although the Playhouse continued to enjoy a significant level of support from the local authority and Arts Council England, in real terms its subsidy had fallen significantly from over 50 per cent of income to below 25 per cent, and for this reason the theatre management was keen to diversify its income streams by placing more emphasis on catering, hospitality, and external hires.[9]

By RIBA Stage 2 (concept design), these aspirations had been distilled into a series of 'headline' themes. They comprised: greater presence in Leeds; more visitors and improved access; the offer of new artistic opportunities; replacement of outdated plant; increased financial resilience for the organisation, through, for example, the provision of more hospitality space.[10] A feasibility study was produced by DLG Architects, who were already involved in other projects at Quarry Hill.[11] The architects proposed the construction of an addition to the theatre, largely on the site of its staff car park but also extending along the northern side of the building, adjacent to the Quarry Hill steps. The extension, shown in outline form as a large glass box, would give the theatre a new city-facing entrance and would be connected to the existing foyers by a sequence of escalators and lifts. Elsewhere, the building would be refurbished, while a new performance space was proposed for the so-called

'rock void', an unused area at basement level left over from when the theatre was built.[12] An initial approach to ACE for capital project funding was, however, rejected. Among other reasons, there was apparently some doubt as to how committed the local authority was to the project.[13]

Further work on the proposals followed, and firm assurances of support from the local authority were received. In 2013, David Beidas was appointed as a specialist client advisor, bringing experience of twentieth-century theatre building refurbishment. He had been the executive director of the Belgrade Theatre, Coventry, during its restoration and extension, and had later been client representative for projects including the refurbishment of Birmingham Repertory Theatre (1971). The formal client at the Playhouse was Leeds City Council, which owns the building (and which also offered a substantial amount of funding). The scheme would thus benefit from the council's expertise in delivering capital projects, not least its good track record of arts projects including Northern Ballet and the refurbishment of the Grand Theatre. An experienced officer, Chris Coulson, oversaw the project on behalf of the council, while a project board was created, chaired by Martin Farrington, Leeds' Director of City Development.

In 2015, a new Stage 1 application for ACE funding was made, with the theatre in the meantime having welcomed a new administrative director, Robin Hawkes. Hawkes later recalled that he had some doubts about aspects of the scheme, but there seemed little prospect of a further ACE capital funding round and so, rather than re-start the feasibility process and lose time (and miss the application deadline) there was little option but to be pragmatic and press on with the study's assumptions and costings.[14]

## Developing the Design and the 'Vision'

In January 2016, the Playhouse received the news that ACE had approved its Stage 1 application and that a Development Grant of £300,000 was to be provided.[15] The theatre was invited to make a Stage 2 application. Further development funding was contributed by the theatre itself (£152,000), and by the city council (£333,000). By this date, Leeds City Council had allocated £4.9 million to the project, the anticipated total cost of which was now £13.6 million.[16] It was now time to appoint the design team for the main part of the project. This process was managed by Leeds City Council and followed *OJEU* procedures. More than twenty expressions of interest were received, with five teams being invited to present their ideas.[17] The Glasgow-based architectural practice Page\Park was selected. Both Beidas and Hawkes remember feeling that Page\Park understood the brief as well as the Playhouse as an organisation.[18] Their work appealed aesthetically and included several well-regarded arts projects, including the extension of the Theatre Royal, Glasgow, and the refurbishment and extension of Eden Court, Inverness. The client team was also impressed with the effort that Page\Park had put into their proposal. Project architect Nicola Walls had been on a backstage tour and had seen a show.

RIBA Stage 2 was reached at the end of 2016. By this date, the 'vision' had developed in two key respects:

During the course of conversations with the Playhouse organisation and the city planners what has become apparent is that the original intention to reorientate the building to address the city centre, thus effectively turning its back onto Quarry Hill, is not necessarily the best way forward. The developed concept is now for a much more porous and permeable building, with entrances both from Quarry Hill and the terraced landscaped area, in addition to the new entrance addressing the city centre. This better reflects the ethos of the Playhouse organisation to be welcoming to all sections of society, and to offer as many opportunities to enter the building and encounter theatre as possible. This is a clear development of the original brief which focused more solely on the new public face to the city centre. The second aspect of the original brief that has developed during the course of Stage 2 is the thinking behind the scope of the proposed works within the exiting theatre spaces, particularly with regard to the seating capacity of the Courtyard Theatre. The Playhouse has identified a need to increase seat

numbers in the Courtyard and this has taken precedence over the early desire to increase the flexibility of format of this space (although the preferred shallow rake option does still offer some flexibility). The capacity increase has been driven by both the need to increase revenue and hence financial resilience, improving opportunities to programme a wider range of visiting productions, but also a recognition that, with the development of the Rock Void space and the continuing use of the Barber Studio, differing formats and scales of work can be accommodated elsewhere in the building.[19]

This revised brief in part developed from consultation sessions with Playhouse staff, and in particular a 'Visioning Session' in July 2016.[20] A detailed review of the theatre technical proposals was also carried out, testing them against criteria including safety improvements, income generation potential, potential to achieve efficiencies, support for new opportunities, sustainability, visitor experience enhancement, and aesthetic improvement.[21]

Page\Park's RIBA Stage 2 proposal established the three key moves of the executed scheme. The first of these moves was the creation of a route through the building, linking the proposed new entrance in the extension with the original theatre entrance as well as a new intermediate entrance from the adjacent steps, which are scheduled for re-landscaping under the name 'Gateway Court'. The internal route is, in effect, 'carved' through what had previously been back-of-house space. It improves access and connections through the building; it also renders the theatre more porous to its surroundings.

Page\Park's second (related) move affects the Quarry Theatre. The original entrance to the auditorium was at its rear, at the top of the seating rake. In its place, the architects proposed the creation of mid-tier entrances, accessed directly from the new route through the building. The position of these entrances recalls the layout of the original Leeds Playhouse and is also intended to improve the 'feel' of the auditorium, which could seem cavernous from the top of the steeply raked seating tier. The new entrances to the auditorium have other advantages, too. The old layout

C9.3    Page\Park's extension seeks not only to add new space but also to transform the image of the building, to address the city centre, and to respond to the vertical scale of nearby development

relegated wheelchair users to peripheral positions and resulted in queues at the end of performances as audience members waited, like passengers on a recently landed aeroplane, to leave the auditorium.[22] The new layout not only resolves these problems but also means that audience members wishing to use the toilets during the interval will no longer have to climb to the back of the auditorium only then to go down stairs again to the toilets. Accommodating all this has required alterations to parts of the auditorium rake.

Visually, Page\Park sought to contrast the extension with the horizontality of the 1990 building. The extension is thus conceived as something stridently vertical. It responds to the height and scale of the new buildings being built on Quarry Hill, giving the theatre its desired city-facing entrance and acting as a prominent statement of the Playhouse's presence in an increasingly vertical townscape. The upper part of the elevation is made up of eight 'bays', alternately glazed and solid,

which are divided by slender stone-clad piers. Some of the stone piers continue to ground level, but otherwise the upper elevation seems almost to float above the ground. The solid bays are decorated with colourful patterns in an echo of the locally made polychromatic tiles that are typical of Leeds' nineteenth-century architecture. They also recall the exuberant finishes of the nearby Victoria Gate development. The specifically geometric form of the tiles used at the Playhouse echoes the hexagonal plan of the 1990 building.

The new street-level entrance will lead into an area containing a café. Triple-height in part and largely glazed to the street, it is to be overlooked by galleries accommodating parts of the foyer bar and café. Access will be provided directly to the Barber studio, while the rest of the building will be accessible via stairs and a lift. The new stepped foyer route is planned to feature extensive wooden panelling in order to generate a distinct, warm aesthetic. The next level up in the extension

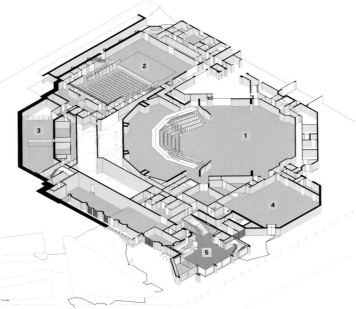

Key:
1  Quarry Theatre
2  Courtyard Theatre
3  Rock Void
4  Barber Studio
5  St Peter's Street entrance foyer

C9.4   Leeds Playhouse, proposed plan at Level 30 (St Peter's Street)

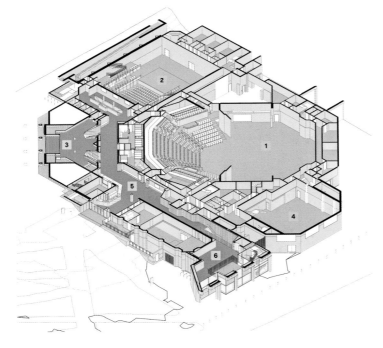

Key:
1  Quarry Theatre
2  Courtyard Theatre
3  Playhouse Square entrance
4  Barber Studio
5  Link route
6  St Peter's Street extension foyer

C9.5   Leeds Playhouse, proposed plan at Level 33

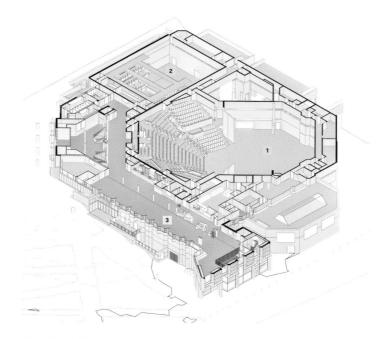

Key:
1 Quarry Theatre
2 Courtyard Theatre
3 Restaurant

C9.6    Leeds Playhouse, proposed plan at Level 36

will have further café seating. Above that is an extension to the restaurant, with good views back towards the city centre and the key Eastgate/Headrow axis. This space in turn is overlooked by the hospitality room. Where the new foyer route meets the original entrance onto Quarry Hill, the space is to be opened up to provide views through the building.

As defined at RIBA Stage 2, the scope of works within the Quarry Theatre included new seating and redecoration, in addition to technical enhancements and alterations to the seating rake needed to accommodate the new mid-level entrances. More fundamental alterations were proposed for Courtyard Theatre, not least an increase in capacity from 350 to 420 achieved by re-raking the stalls level. The Rock Void, the former unused basement, was defined as a flexible performance space for c. 100. As 'found', it comprised a cavernous series of spaces with unpainted brick walls and a sandy floor. Although it was always thought necessary to add acoustic panelling to some of the wall and ceiling surfaces, and to provide a flat floor for seating and staging, it was noted that it would nonetheless be desirable to preserve as much of the 'found' character of the space as possible, not least in the interests of creating an experience very different from the theatre's more formal auditoria. Part of the original dirt floor was to be left visible, for example, although in practice this aspiration proved difficult to realise.

Page\Park's scheme was developed through 2016/17, taking into account specialist input in areas including catering design as well as the results of consultation with external stakeholders. The project reached RIBA Stage 3 (developed design) in June 2017.[23] A planning submission was made in July 2017 and consent was secured in December 2017. That same month, ACE made a Stage 2 capital award to the project of £6.3 million.[24] By this point the Playhouse itself had committed £3.03 million and Leeds City Council £4.3 million. The Rock Void has been named to mark a donation from the Liz and Terry Bramall Foundation, while further funds have been secured from other trusts and foundations, and from local businesses and individuals.

C9.7 Quarry Theatre as proposed

C9.8 Courtyard Theatre as proposed

## Towards Construction

'Value engineering' took place during RIBA Stage 2 and Stage 3. Cost-cutting was needed in part because the original budget and funding applications had been based on the feasibility study scheme. Though slightly more extensive in terms of the extensions proposed for the Playhouse, the feasibility study proposed fewer alterations to the 1990 building.[25] The revised scope of works also required a longer construction time: around 55 weeks, rather than the 26 weeks of the feasibility study.[26] As we have seen elsewhere, this kind of mis-match between the cost of the 'final' scheme versus an earlier study is not unusual in theatre-building projects. Frequently the projected cost of a feasibility study is used as the basis for fundraising but becomes out-of-date when a new design team is appointed for the job 'proper' and/or when the client team changes during the briefing and design process.[27] These changes can productively bring new ideas – but also increased costs as the possibilities of a scheme become more apparent, or as new staff seek something different from their predecessors.

David Beidas reported that £3.5 million had to be taken out of the project at the end of RIBA Stage 2, including a saving of £900,000 on the St Peter's Street entrance and £400,000 on the Playhouse Square entrance, while the Rock Void plans were simplified and £1 million of theatre technical works were omitted on the basis that they could be added back later or done independently if more money was found.[28] The proposed refurbishment of staff offices was abandoned, as were plans to re-clad the theatre's flytower. Additional savings were made by opting not to renew the roof. The theatre's survey showed that it was in better condition than had been anticipated, and that targeted repairs would extend its life by twenty years.[29] Further value engineering during RIBA Stage 3, meanwhile, aimed to save £1.4 million through a slight reduction in the scope of numerous parts of the project, although additional funding was secured from Leeds City Council to cover upgrades to the Quarry Theatre lighting.[30]

A 'design and build' approach was selected, and the project went to tender in summer 2017.[31] The preferred contractor was BAM, to whom the design team was novated. For Page\Park's Nicola Walls, it was the first time she had experienced this form of contract and its requirement that all designer/client communication be passed formally through the contractor.[32] Nonetheless, she and other members of the team appreciated the early involvement of the contractor and the opportunity to work with them to ensure the buildability and affordability of the design.

C9.9   Rock Void as proposed

During 2017–18, BAM and the novated design team worked on the detailed design, which was issued in packages for pricing. However, many of the packages were returned at a significantly higher value than had been anticipated by market testing.[33] The over-run was attributed in part by the contractors to the complexity of the project and the risks of working with an existing building. At the same time, as the detail of the scheme was clarified during RIBA Stage 4 (technical design), its likely costs were firmed up.[34] Particular increases were noted in the anticipated costs of the mechanical and electrical works, the fire and smoke strategy, groundworks, specialist joinery, and demolition. A further round of 'value engineering' therefore took place.[35] The client team considered dropping the proposed change to the Courtyard Theatre seating rake or the reconfiguration of the Playhouse Square entrance, but eventually opted to keep these elements.[36] Around £1 million was saved through cuts to finishes, redecoration, ventilation plant, and theatre technical systems.[37] The proposed improvements to the Quarry Theatre lighting were dropped, although this work will ultimately

need to be done at some stage. Nonetheless, the project costs still exceeded the budget by £1.8 million in June 2018. Leeds City Council was asked to approve an increased grant of £1.3 million and to approve further spending by the Playhouse of £550,000, meaning that the overall budget was now £15.8 million.[38] Approval came through just in time for BAM to take possession of the site in July 2018.

## Conclusions

As a case study, Leeds Playhouse demonstrates the all-too-frequent conundrum in theatre-building projects when the scope and budget of a feasibility study proposal become established as the basis for fundraising but where costs later increase as the project scope is refined. This problem has been encountered elsewhere in *Play On*. Of course, additional fundraising would bridge the gap, but such fundraising may not always be feasible, leading to 'value engineering' and the need to evaluate which aspects of a project are critical. In Leeds, the decision was taken to

C9.10   Visualisation showing the extended Playhouse in its planned context

maintain those elements of the capital project which re-shape the audience experience, which enhance the theatre's prominence in the city, and which add to the financial sustainability of the building and organisation. Some of the originally proposed technical improvements to the building have been set aside for the time being. The order of priorities might seem odd, but technical improvements omitted from this capital project can always be carried out in the future; it is easier to manage such improvements as discrete projects. At the time of writing in autumn 2018, building work is in full swing. A temporary 'pop up' auditorium has been created in the theatre's dock area. Despite a slight delay caused by the discovery of a historic graveyard on site, the plan is to re-open in 2019, just under fifty years since the original theatre first welcomed its audiences.

C10.1   Bridge Theatre, entrance

# Bridge Theatre, London

Architect: Haworth Tompkins

Client: London Theatre Company

Main contractor: Rise Contracts

Auditorium contractor: Tait Stage Technologies

Structural engineer: Momentum

Services engineer: Skelly and Couch

Project director: Plann

Quantity surveyor: Bristow Johnson

There has been a significant shift in London's centre of gravity since the start of the twenty-first century. The redevelopment of the East End's former dock and industrial areas, begun in the 1980s, was catalysed by the construction of new transport links during the 1990s and 2000s. The 2012 London Olympics, held in Stratford, and its associated 'legacy' developments accelerated the process yet further. By 2017, more than half of London's population lived east of Tower Bridge.[1] Not quite east of Tower Bridge, but certainly emblematic of this eastwards shift, is the Bridge Theatre, which opened in 2017. The theatre is the creation of Sir Nicholas Hytner and Nick Starr, the former artistic and executive directors of the National Theatre sometimes known collectively as 'the two Nicks'. It exists within a bigger development including flats and restaurants on the former Potters Fields coach park, between Tower Bridge and London Bridge railway station. The developers had earmarked a space for 'cultural use'. It turned out to be just the right size for a 900-seat courtyard theatre auditorium, which has been designed by Haworth Tompkins. For the architects, the project offered the opportunity to develop an idea on which they had already been working but which until then had remained an abstract proposition, namely a densely-packed courtyard auditorium in which services and structure would be integrated. The result, developed in collaboration with the firm which manufactured it, is clever and efficient: it is essentially a replicable prototype. For Hytner and Starr, meanwhile, the Bridge aims to offer a new model for commercial theatre in Britain, one which brings to the sector some of the innovation associated since the 1960s with the subsidised sector.

## The 'Vision'

In 2013, Nicholas Hytner and Nick Starr announced their departure from the National Theatre after a decade at the helm, with Starr leaving in June 2014 and Hytner in April 2015. The pair decided nonetheless to continue working together, and in spring 2014 created the London Theatre Company as a vehicle for their ongoing partnership.[2] When the Bridge was completed in 2017, Hytner told *The Stage* that

> This all starts from us being theatre producers. We want to produce theatre. The best way of producing shows is to be in control of the places we produce in. The shows we want to produce are many and various. The people we want to work with work in many and various ways.[3]

The aim was to bring something of the ethos of subsidised theatres (such as the National) to the commercial sector: 'The mad thing to do would be to shift into a whole different mindset', reflected Starr.[4] Hytner noted that, before the rise of the subsidised sector in the 1950s and 1960s, new work had typically been commissioned for the West End.[5] Could that model be revived? He and Starr envisaged a theatre presenting new work 'with the occasional classic thrown in'. Nonetheless, 'this is not the National by other means', cautioned Starr.[6] Productions have to make a return on their investment, while the infrastructure in which they are created is rather less expansive than might be the case in many subsidised venues: 'all the amazing things you take for granted – rehearsal rooms, costume store, prop store – don't exist in the private sector [...] I can't pretend I don't miss that [...]'.[7] And yet, the project offered a sense of liberation. Whereas, Hytner suggested, 'everybody has a stake in the National', at the Bridge he feels free to say 'if you don't like it, don't come'.[8]

Starr and Hytner initially considered buying an existing theatre and refurbishing it.[9] Options were explored with Haworth Tompkins, with whom Starr and Hytner had worked on the National Theatre's 2008–15 transformation, 'NT Future'. There was, however, a sense that an existing West End theatre might be too limiting. Making a conscious break with the idea that commercial theatre could only take place in the West End, the pair started to look further afield.[10] Starr was pointed towards Potters Fields by Robert Wolstenholme, a property developer with whom he had been on the board of the Bush Theatre.[11] Wolstenholme gave the pair a crash course in the economics of property, advising them not to take more space than they needed as they would nonetheless have to pay for

it.[12] Hytner and Starr made a bid for the 'cultural space' at Potters Fields, which had been intended as a gallery,[13] and were successful. They were drawn by its riverside location, by the excellent transport links, and by the buzz of the area, as well as the specific qualities of the 6,873m² space itself. In spring 2015, they concluded an agreement to take the space.

As was discussed in the opening chapters, theatres in commercial developments are not new, having been found not only in nineteenth-century Britain but also among some of the new subsidised theatres of the 1960s and 1970s. However, the results (though often functionally good) were sometimes less than inspired architecturally. How would 'the two Nicks' and their designers respond to the challenge of working within a pre-determined shell, and in a commercial context?

## The Design

At first glance, only the Bridge's oversized illuminated red signage sets the theatre apart from the commercial units either side of it. Facing a small park (and beyond that the River Thames), it is found at the base of a building containing luxury flats, whose balconies and terraces dominate the upper part of the riverfront elevation. Glass doors at pavement level offer glimpses into the theatre's single-level foyer, which during the day works as a busy café. It is simply but stylishly finished. Warm, earthy tones dominate the walls and are juxtaposed with pale timber floors and unpainted concrete columns. In the central part of the foyer, which is naturally top-lit, pale drapes act as solar shading on sunny days. Elsewhere, darker felt is hung at right angles to the ceiling in playfully wavy lines in order to control the acoustic of the foyer and to ensure good speech intelligibility even with a capacity audience. Hundreds of lightbulbs hang from the ceiling in an apparently random pattern. With scrunched shades, they positively glow. There is the sense of a constellation of stars, or, perhaps, giant fireflies floating through the foyer. The result is quirky and characterful. It could easily have felt like a generic contemporary café/restaurant, with all the architectural clichés of those spaces. Instead it has a distinctive ambience.

C10.2    The foyer includes an extensive café/bar

From the middle of the foyer, stairs lead down towards the auditorium's lower levels. This has been created within the largest part of the space, a vast, cavern-like shell left by the developers. The insertion of a theatre into a pre-existing space recalls the creation of the Cottesloe Theatre at the National in the 1970s, where, as has been noted already, a concept by Iain Mackintosh and Theatre Projects Consultants was realised within a space allocated by the architect, Denys Lasdun. The Bridge's courtyard auditorium is not unlike a scaled up version of the Cottesloe – now the Dorfman – in form, either. Three tiers of narrow galleries, just three rows deep, are arranged around three sides of a flexible stalls/stage area. A fourth wall of galleries can be added to encircle the floor area completely when required.

The origins of the auditorium design lie in what architect Steve Tompkins has described as an 'intellectual research and development exercise'.[14] Tompkins, fresh from working on the National

Theatre's temporary Shed venue as well as the new auditorium at the Everyman, Liverpool, was along with his colleague Roger Watts exploring ideas for a closely packed courtyard-type auditorium.[15] Their work was very much in the abstract: it was not conceived with any particular building in mind. Its basis was the auditorium of the Young Vic, designed by Howell Killick Partridge and Amis in 1969–70 and reworked by Haworth Tompkins in 2005–07.[16] Described by Tompkins as his and Watts' 'personal favourite',[17] the Young Vic auditorium is a square with chamfered corners, 16 metres by 16 metres in plan. As designed, the theatre had a thrust stage, surrounded on three sides by the audience, who were seated predominantly in raked stalls although a single narrow gallery also encircled the auditorium.[18] The space was deliberately present, architecturally speaking. Architect Bill Howell initially assumed that the director, Frank Dunlop, would want a flexible, 'black box' kind of space.[19] Dunlop had other ideas, however. In his

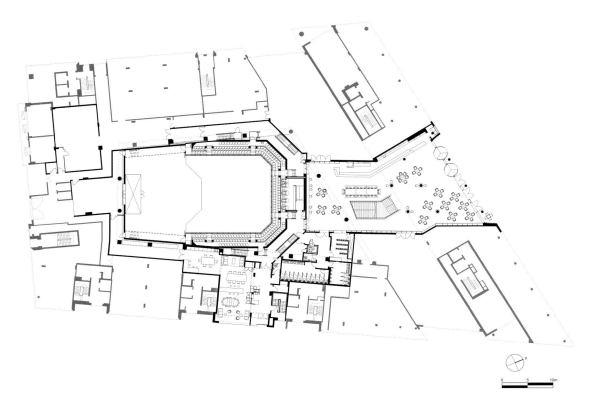

C10.3   Bridge Theatre, plan at foyer level

view, theatre comprised 'acting in architecture'.[20] Tompkins and Watts liked the resulting balance between flexibility and character:

> It's a democratic, relatively square format that can do everything. It's the space we've worked on that feels like it has the most capacity for transformation. […] But on the other hand too much flexibility can result in a space with no personality.[21]

Tompkins also noted the extent to which the Young Vic, despite its flexibility, 'remains a room in which everyone feels connected to one another'.[22] He and Watts therefore took the Young Vic's basic dimensions in plan, but added extra galleries to increase the capacity from c. 420 to around 900, similar to the Lyttelton auditorium at the National.[23]

To achieve this capacity without compromising sightline angles, the architects found that they needed to compress the height of each tier, bringing the galleries closer to each other and to the stage. They designed galleries three rows deep, to be made of laser-cut steel in order to minimise weight and structural depth, while torsion beams and cantilevering reduced the number of columns that would be needed. Around three sides of the space, the galleries would be fixed, with a manually demountable stalls/stage area allowing thrust, end-on, flat-floor and transverse stage layouts. A fourth wall of galleries could be inserted to create an in-the-round arrangement, something which, incidentally, recalls Howell's own development of the Young Vic in HKPA's theatre at Christ's Hospital, Horsham, in 1974.[24] Tompkins and Watts incorporated the technical infrastructure into their

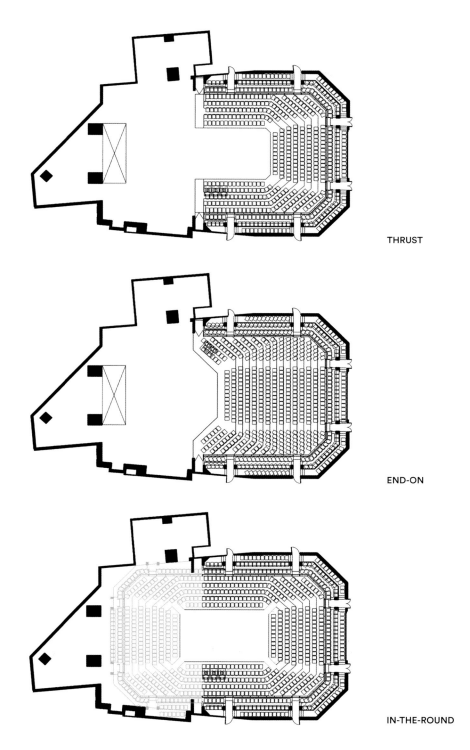

THRUST

END-ON

IN-THE-ROUND

C10.4   Bridge Theatre, auditorium configurations

C10.5   Bridge Theatre, auditorium

proposal, creating a single, co-ordinated 'object' which could be fabricated and installed in a suitable space.

When it came to the theatre that he and Hytner wanted to create, Starr summarised the brief as a requirement for as many seats as possible (given the unsubsidised nature of the operation), good levels of comfort, and for the space not to feel like a workshop; it was to be 'more refined than the Cottesloe'.[25] The experience of NT Future meant that he and Hytner had a good working relationship with Tompkins, likening it to the collaboration between theatre director and designer: 'good producers are precise about their role – they find the best person and engage them, and trust them to get it right'.[26] Tompkins

and Watts presented their courtyard concept, which appealed to Starr and Hytner. It was agreed to develop the design as a 'working prototype', with input from the Bridge's technical team.[27] Conveniently, in what Tompkins described as a 'fluke', the concept was just about the same size as the space available at Potters Fields.[28] The 10-metre height of the auditorium-to-be was tight, but strengthened the case for the close-packed galleries that Tompkins and Watts felt were critical for participation and theatrical atmosphere.[29] The wish for an intense auditorium was shared with the client team. As Tompkins later recalled, 'the Nicks weren't interested in perfect equal sight lines, they wanted the sense of chemistry, all the things old theatres excelled at'.[30]

The concept was developed in collaboration with a specialist manufacturer based in the United States, Tait Towers.[31] An 'extraordinarily detailed' three-dimensional virtual model was made in collaboration with the design engineers, Ewart Richardson, which allowed the view from every seat to be 'experienced', and for the engineering requirements of the design to be worked out in detail.[32] It also allowed the team to 'stand' at every point on all of the stage configurations in order to work out the point of command geometries. Haworth Tompkins' regular collaborators Skelly and Couch (environmental engineers) and Gillieron Scott (acoustics) joined the team to design the various systems. A digital sound model of the space was created, allowing the acoustics of every seat to be tested. 'Hundreds' of adjustments and recalibrations were made to ensure good acoustics for speech.[33] Models were also made of the seats themselves, with the final version as used in the galleries being able to swivel for better sightlines. Particular attention was given to the idea that all of the technical kit should be built in to the seating/staging structure. Wiring, lighting, and sound were all co-ordinated with the design, with, for example, integrated duct routes at each level. Finally, a prototype section of auditorium was constructed in a hanger in Norfolk, allowing further tweaks to its geometry and ergonomics. An important ambition was that the auditorium should be easily and efficiently reconfigured, with minimal staff input (and thus minimal cost).

The digital model was used to fabricate the steel structure, which was then transported to the site and installed in the existing shell. It is formed from fifty-seven pieces, which split into towers and seating galleries. The pieces are sized so as to be easily transported by lorry and assembled by a small, skilled crew. As in the foyers, the auditorium's materials and colours give it a warm atmosphere. Steel is painted brown, gallery fronts are made of slatted oak, recycled black rubber flooring has been used, while the seat fabric is burnt orange wool with tan details. The textural contrast in these two fabrics is typical of Haworth Tompkins' interest in the sensory experience of buildings, something which had been very much to the fore at Liverpool's Everyman Theatre.

## The Bridge in Use

The construction cost of £12 million (excluding fees) was raised up front from a small group of investors on a venture-capital basis; the theatre was conceived as a start-up business, in effect, and in this respect it surely benefitted from the star power of 'the two Nicks'. They did not approach institutional investors, but instead sought funds from wealthy individuals, who have committed for the long term. As a result, the theatre is not working on a show-by-show basis, and does not have to produce a return for each one. As Hytner put it, 'This is about building a company that is viable in the long term.'[34]

The first three productions in the auditorium demonstrated three of its possible arrangements, with the first being end-on, the second in-the-round, and the third having a thrust stage. These initial productions were well-received; so too was the architecture. In 2018, the theatre won the RIBA London Award, plus The Stage's Theatre Building of the Year Award, as well as recognition from the Royal Institute of Chartered Surveyors for the innovative way in which 'creativity, integrated design and fabrication, along with collaborative working […] achieve[d] something that would have been impossible with traditional methods of procurement and construction'.[35] From initial conception to opening night took less than two years. Although smaller theatres have been realised in similar timeframes, such as the Tricycle, Kilburn (the courtyard theatre of 1980 by Tim Foster now known as the Kiln), this speed of execution is notable for a project of this size and technical complexity.

For The Stage, the project is a welcome demonstration of the changing cultural landscape of London, and the extent to which good theatre can increasingly be found across the city: 'the Bridge is still fairly centrally – and expensively – located, but could it be the first step in a new direction: outwards and upwards?'[36] In summer 2018, it was rumoured that Starr and Hytner were planning to open a second theatre at King's Cross, in a similar mixed-use development. If it comes to fruition, it will test the extent to which Haworth Tompkins' design is a replicable prototype, as was originally intended, with the potential theatre being slightly smaller than the Bridge.[37] Perhaps one day there might be a chain of Hytner/Starr theatres, akin to the commercial circuits of the first half of the twentieth century.

Ultimately, however, the real lesson of the Bridge is one which holds true for all theatres, and which has been clear in many of those discussed in *Play On*. A well-defined artistic and operational 'vision', the willingness to think creatively, and trust between client and design teams (and funders) are all essential for good theatre architecture, just as they are for good theatre.

# Appendix: Project Team Details

## Everyman Theatre, Liverpool

Architect: Haworth Tompkins
Client: Liverpool and Merseyside Theatres Trust
Contractor: Gilbert Ash
Structural engineer: Alan Baxter and Associates
M&E: Watermans Building Services
Project manager: GVA Acuity
CDM co-ordinator: Turner and Townsend
Acoustic engineer: Gillieron Scott Acoustic Design
Theatre consultant: Charcoalblue
Access consultant: Earnscliffe Davies Associates
Stage engineering: Stage Technologies
Artists: Antoni Malinowski, Dan Kenyon, Jake Tilson

## Cast, Doncaster

Architect: RHWL Arts Team
Client: MUSE Waterdale/Doncaster MBC
Structural engineer: Arup
M&E: Arup
Lighting consultant: Arup
Landscape architect: Grontmij
Acoustic engineer: Arup
Theatre consultant: Charcoalblue
Access consultant: Arcadis Vectra
Quantity surveyor: Gardiner and Theobald

## Storyhouse, Chester

Architect (lead): Bennetts Associates
Architect (delivery): Ellis Williams Architects
Client: Cheshire West and Chester Council
Project director: Graham Lister
Contractor: Kier Construction (Northern)
Structural engineer: WSP
M&E: Foreman Roberts
Strategic project manager: Buro Four
Acoustics: Sandy Brown Associates
Access consultant: David Bonnett Associates/ CW&C Access Team
Furnishings & fit out consultant: Demco Interiors

## Tara Theatre, London

Architect: Aedas Arts Team
Client: Tara Arts
Main contractor, QS, and CDM co-ordinator: HA Marks Ltd
Structural engineer: engineersHRW, incorporating Jane Wernick Associates
M&E: Atelier Ten (to RIBA Stage D); Clear Springs (from RIBA Stage E)
Project manager: Cragg Management Services
Acoustic consultant: Arup
Theatre equipment consultant: Theatreplan
BREEAM consultant: Sol Environmental
Sustainability consultant: Sam Hunt
Building control: Butler and Young
Fire consultant: Trenton Fire

## National Theatre, London

Architect: Haworth Tompkins
Client: National Theatre
Main contractor: Lend Lease and Rise Contracts
Structural engineer: Flint and Neill

Services engineer: Atelier Ten

Project manager: Buro Four

Quantity surveyor: Aecom and Bristow Johnson

Acoustic engineer: Arup

Theatre consultant: Charcoalblue

Signage consultant: Jake Tilson

### Theatre Royal, Glasgow

Architect: Page\Park

Client: Scottish Opera

Main contractor: Sir Robert McAlpine

Structural engineer: Arup Scotland

M&E consultant (including lighting design): Max Fordham

Quantity surveyor: Capita

Project manager: TX2

CDM co-ordinator: CDM Scotland

Acoustic consultant: Sandy Brown Acoustics

Theatre consultant: Charcoalblue

Fire engineer: Atelier 10

Graphics: Studio Arc

### Perth Theatre

Architect: Richard Murphy Architects

Client: Horsecross Arts

Main contractor: Robertson Construction

Structural engineer: Arup

M&E: Buro Happold (design); FES (build)

Quantity surveyor: Red Skye Consulting/Robertson Construction

Project manager: Robertson Construction

CDM co-ordinator: McLeod and Aitken/Robertson Construction

Acoustic consultant: Arup

Theatre consultant: Charcoalblue

Conservation: Simpson and Brown

### Citizens Theatre, Glasgow

Architect: Bennetts Associates

Client: Citizens Theatre

Quantity surveyor: Turner and Townsend

Structural engineer: Struer Consulting Engineers Ltd

Theatre consultant: Theatreplan

Services engineer: Max Fordham

### Leeds Playhouse

Architect: Page\Park

Client: Leeds City Council

Contractor: BAM

Structural engineer: Arup

M&E engineer: Max Fordham

Project manager: Turner & Townsend

Cost consultant: Rex Procter and Partners

CDM co-ordinator: CDM Scotland

Theatre consultant: Charcoalblue

Lighting consultant: Max Fordham

### Bridge Theatre, London

Architect: Haworth Tompkins

Client: London Theatre Company

Main contractor: Rise Contracts

Auditorium contractor: Tait Stage Technologies

Structural engineer: Momentum

Services engineer: Skelly and Couch

Project director: Plann

Quantity surveyor: Bristow Johnson

# Notes

## Introduction

1   E.g. on theatre: *The Golden Generation: New Light on Post-war British Theatre*, ed. Dominic Shellard (London, 2008); Claire Cochrane, *Twentieth-Century British Theatre: Industry, Art and Empire* (Cambridge, 2011), pp. 2–5; *The Glory of the Garden: English Regional Theatre and the Arts Council, 1984–2009*, ed. Kate Dorney and Ros Merkin (Newcastle-upon-Tyne, 2010); George Rowell and Anthony Jackson, *The Repertory Movement: A History of Regional Theatre in Britain* (Cambridge, 1984). For theatre architecture, see Elain Harwood, *Space, Hope and Brutalism: English Architecture 1945–1975* (New Haven, CT and London, 2015), pp. 484–508; Alistair Fair, *Modern Playhouses: An Architectural History of Britain's New Theatres, 1945–1985* (Oxford, 2018).

2   E.g. Iain Mackintosh, *Architecture, Actor and Audience* (London, 1993); *Making Space for Theatre: British Architecture and Theatre since 1958*, ed. Ronnie Mulryne and Margaret Shewring (Stratford-upon-Avon, 1995).

3   Liz Tomlin, *British Theatre Companies: 1995–2014* (London, 2015).

4   E.g. the excellent *Theatre Buildings: A Design Guide*, ed. Judith Strong (Abingdon, 2010), or, indeed, the older but still useful book by Roderick Ham, *Theatre Planning* (London, 1972).

5   The ABTT's *Sightline* magazine offers useful insights into contemporary theatre technology.

6   C. Alan Short, Peter Barrett and Alistair Fair, *Geometry and Atmosphere: Theatre Buildings from Vision to Reality* (Farnham, 2011).

7   E.g. 'Belgrade Theatre, Coventry', CABE Case Study, 2008, archived from the CABE website at <https://webarchive.nationalarchives.gov.uk/20110118130815/http://www.cabe.org.uk/case-studies/belgrade-theatre> (accessed on 25 November 2018).

## 1   Historical Context

1   For Matcham, see *Frank Matcham & Co.*, ed. David Wilmore (Dacre, 2008). Phipps is covered in Görel Garlick, *Charles James Phipps F.S.A., Architect to the Victorian Theatre* (London, 2016).

2   Andrew Saint, 'Frank Matcham in Perspective', in *Frank Matcham & Co.*, ed. David Wilmore (Dacre, 2008), pp. 10–29 (pp. 27–8).

3   For Stratford, see Marian J. Pringle, *The Theatres of Stratford-upon-Avon, 1875–1992: An Architectural History* (Stratford-upon-Avon, 1994).

4   George Rowell and Anthony Jackson, *The Repertory Movement: A History of Regional Theatre in Britain* (Cambridge, 1984), pp. 16–53.

5   Ibid., pp. 114–15.

6   'Renaissance in the Provincial Theatre', *Country Life*, 1 June 1963, pp. 57–9.

7   '"For once let's recognise that British theatre is out of its sickbed" [...]', *The Guardian*, 30 December 1977.

8   Dominic Shellard, *British Theatre Since the War* (New Haven, CT and London, 2000), p. 177.

9   Patricia Hollis, *Jennie Lee: A Life* (Oxford, 1997).

10   A history of 'Housing the Arts' is found in Alistair Fair, *Modern Playhouses: An Architectural History of Britain's New Theatres, 1945–1985* (Oxford, 2018), chapter 2.

11   Hollis, *Jennie Lee*, p. 249.

12   Ibid., p. 268; Lawrence Black, '"Making Britain a Gayer and More Cultivated Country": Jennie Lee, the Creative Economy, and the 1960s' "Cultural Revolution"', *Contemporary British History* 20, no. 3 (2006), pp. 323–42.

13   For more on this, see Fair, *Modern Playhouses*, chapter 6.

14   'Theatre for All', *The Stage*, 19 August 1965.

15   V&A, Theatre Collections Thorndike file, clipping from the *Illustrated London News*, 15 March 1969.

16    Braham Murray, *The Worst It Can Be Is A Disaster: The Life Story of Braham Murray and the Royal Exchange Theatre* (London, 2007), p. 53.

17    For more on Castle Terrace, see Alistair Fair, '"An Object Lesson in How Not To Get Things Done": Edinburgh's Unbuilt "Opera House", 1960–1975', *Architectural Heritage* 27, no. 1 (2017), pp. 91–117.

18    Iain Mackintosh, 'Rediscovering the Courtyard', *Architectural Review* 175 (April 1984), pp. 64–71. The Cottesloe has since been renamed the Dorfman Theatre.

19    The Tricycle has since been altered and renamed the 'Kiln', with the auditorium structure being dismantled and moved to Valley Park School, Maidstone. For more on courtyard auditoria, see Fair, *Modern Playhouses*, pp. 199–201.

20    RIBA Archives, LaD/167/4, National Theatre Building Committee Minutes, 4 March 1964.

21    Andrew Todd and Jean-Guy Lecat, *The Open Circle: Peter Brook's Theatre Environments* (London, 2003).

22    Alan Bennett, *Untold Stories* (London, 2005), p. 385.

23    Subsequently published as 'On Not Building for Posterity', *Tabs* 31, no. 2 (1973), pp. 41–4, and reprinted in *Making Space for Theatre: British Architecture and Theatre Since 1958*, ed. Ronnie Mulryne and Margaret Shewring (Stratford-upon-Avon, 1995), pp. 16–20.

24    E.g. Iain Mackintosh and Michael Sell (eds), *Curtains!!! Or, a New Life for Old Theatres* (Eastbourne, 1982). Several late-Victorian theatres were listed in the early 1970s.

25    Iain Mackintosh, 'A Royal Return', *Tabs* 36, no. 2 (1978), pp. 3–6.

26    John Earl, 'Before I Forget', *Theatres Magazine* 49 (Autumn 2016), pp. 21–4 (p. 23).

27    For a detailed overview of the Lottery, see Prue Skene, *Capital Gains: How the National Lottery Transformed England's Arts* (London, 2017).

28    Rowan Moore, 'The Buildings that Won the National Lottery Jackpot – the Hits and Misses', *The Observer*, 2 November 2014, online at <https://www.theguardian.com/artanddesign/2014/nov/02/national-lottery-funding-buildings-won-jackpot-architecture-hits-and-misses> (accessed on 11 November 2018).

29    National Audit Office, 'Arts Council of England: Monitoring Major Projects Funded by the National Lottery', 1999, p. 1, online at <https://www.nao.org.uk/report/arts-council-of-england-monitoring-major-capital-projects-funded-by-the-national-lottery/> (accessed on 11 November 2018).

30    David Beidas, quoted in C. Alan Short, Peter Barrett and Alistair Fair, *Geometry and Atmosphere: Theatre Buildings from Vision to Reality* (Farnham, 2011), p. 110.

31    Skene, *Capital Gains*, pp. 58–9.

32    National Audit Office, 'Arts Council of England', p. 1.

33    Skene, *Capital Gains*, pp. 128–30.

34    Ibid., p. 254.

35    Ibid., pp. 254–5.

36    E.g. Miles Glendinning, *Architecture's Evil Empire: The Triumph and Tragedy of Global Modernism* (London, 2010).

37    E.g. 'How we rebuilt the Royal Opera House', *Daily Express*, 21 January 2010, online at <https://www.express.co.uk/expressyourself/153057/How-we-rebuilt-the-Royal-Opera-House> (accessed on 17 December 2018). A full account is provided in Skene, *Capital Gains*.

38    'Thousands of Lottery works miss deadlines and budget', *The Times*, 16 March 2007.

39    Culture, Media and Sport Select Committee, 'Funding of the Arts and Heritage', 2011, paras. 60–63, online at <https://publications.parliament.uk/pa/cm201011/cmselect/cmcumeds/464/46405.htm#a7> (accessed on 14 November 2018).

40    Ibid.

41    For The Lowry's impact, see [Manchester's Commission on the New Economy], 'Beyond the Arts: Economic and Wider Impacts of The Lowry and its Programmes', 2013, online at <http://www.thelowry.com/Downloads/reports/The_Lowry_Beyond_the_Arts.pdf> (accessed on 9 January 2017).

42    Keith Williams, *Keith Williams: Architecture of the Specific* (Mulgrave, 2010), pp. 83–97.

43    Kate Dorney and Ros Merkin, 'Introduction', in *The Glory of the Garden: English Regional Theatre and the Arts Council, 1984–2009*, ed. Kate Dorney and Ros Merkin (Newcastle-upon-Tyne, 2010), pp. 1–14 (p. 1).

44    Arts Council of Great Britain, 'The Glory of the Garden: The Development of the Arts in England. A Strategy for a Decade', 1984.

45  Olivia Turnbull, 'Bringing Down the House: The Inevitable Crisis in Britain's Regional Theatres, 1979–1997' (PhD thesis, Tufts University, 2004), p. 142, p. 160; Dorney and Merkin, 'Introduction', pp. 5–8.

46  Turnbull, 'Bringing Down the House', pp. 164–8.

47  Ibid., p. 142; Liz Tomlin, *British Theatre Companies: 1995–2014* (London, 2015), pp. 1–54 (p. 26).

48  Dorney and Merkin, 'Introduction', p. 9.

49  Ibid., p. 10.

50  Ros Merkin, 'Devolve and/or Die: The Vexed Relationship Between the Centre and the Regions, 1980–2006', in *The Glory of the Garden: English Regional Theatre and the Arts Council, 1984–2009*, ed. Kate Dorney and Ros Merkin (Newcastle-upon-Tyne, 2010), pp. 69–102 (p. 91).

51  Turnbull, 'Bringing Down the House', p. 111.

52  Olivia Turnbull, 'Salisbury Playhouse: Anatomy of a Theatre in Crisis', in *The Glory of the Garden: English Regional Theatre and the Arts Council, 1984–2009*, ed. Kate Dorney and Ros Merkin (Newcastle-upon-Tyne, 2010), pp. 151–71 (p. 151).

53  Tomlin, *British Theatre Companies*, p. 27.

54  Ibid., pp. 7–10.

55  Merkin, 'Devolve', pp. 93–5. Olivia Turnbull ('Bringing Down the House', p. 373) notes that some organisations nonetheless lost their funding, and that there were additional caveats to the new funding arrangements.

56  Tomlin, *British Theatre Companies*, p. 124.

57  Ibid., p. 43.

58  Kate Dorney, 'What's Possible and Who Cares? The Future of Regional Theatre', in *The Glory of the Garden: English Regional Theatre and the Arts Council, 1984–2009*, ed. Kate Dorney and Ros Merkin (Newcastle-upon-Tyne, 2010), pp. 197–207 (p. 207).

59  Ibid.

60  Ibid.

61  'The bold, the old and the obsolete', *The Guardian*, 27 April 2009, online at <https://www.theguardian.com/stage/2009/apr/27/regional-theatre-bristol-old-vic> (accessed on 11 November 2018).

62  Ibid.

63  'Bricks and Mortifying', *The Guardian*, 26 May 1972.

## 2  Theatre in an Age of Austerity

1  ACE, Annual Report 2008–09, p. 5.

2  Ibid., p. 2.

3  ACE, Annual Report 2010–11, pp. 4–5.

4  DCMS, 'The Culture White Paper', 2016, online at <https://assets.publishing.service.gov.uk/government/uploads/system/uploads/attachment_data/file/510798/DCMS_The_Culture_White_Paper__3_.pdf> (accessed on 14 November 2018).

5  A useful discussion of the financial context is provided in Liz Tomlin, *British Theatre Companies: 1995–2014* (London, 2015), pp. 16–18.

6  Creative Scotland, 'Regular Funding Network 2018–21', online at <https://www.creativescotland.com/funding/latest-information/funded-organisations/regular-funding-2018-21/regular-funding-2018-21-info-sheet> (accessed on 14 November 2018).

7  E.g. 'St Peter's Seminary rescue arts group to close', BBC News, 5 June 2018, online at <https://www.bbc.co.uk/news/uk-scotland-44373883> (accessed on 16 November 2018).

8  HM Treasury, 'Spending Review 2010', online at <https://www.gov.uk/government/publications/spending-review-2010> (accessed on 14 November 2018).

9  Culture, Media and Sport Select Committee, 'Funding of the Arts and Heritage', 2011, para. 18, online at <https://publications.parliament.uk/pa/cm201011/cmselect/cmcumeds/464/46405.htm#a7> (accessed on 14 November 2018).

10  Ibid., paras. 20–23.

11  ACE, Annual Report 2010–11, p. 6.

12  'Theatres Round Up', *Theatres Magazine* 28 (Summer 2011), p. 22.

13  Culture, Media and Sport Select Committee, 'Work of the Arts Council', 2014, para. 19, online at <https://publications.parliament.uk/pa/cm201415/cmselect/cmcumeds/279/27902.htm> (accessed on 14 November 2018).

14  Ibid., paras 33–4.

15  'Good causes squeezed as Lottery ticket sales fall', *Financial Times*, 2 September 2017.

16  Welsh Arts Council, Annual Report and Financial Statements 2016–17, p. 6, online at <http://www.arts.wales/c_annual-reports/report-and-financial-statements-2016-17> (accessed on 9 December 2018).

17    Tomlin, *British Theatre Companies*, p. 51.

18    'Welsh Assembly Opens Inquiry into Alternative Income for the Arts', *The Stage*, 25 August 2017, online at <https://www.thestage. co.uk/news/2017/welsh-assembly-opens-inquiry-alternative-income-arts/> (accessed on 16 November 2018).

19    Ibid.

20    Tomlin, *British Theatre Companies*, p. 49; also Joyce McMillan, 'Three Deadly Sins of Scotland's Bad Funding Review', 25 May 2012, online at <https://joycemcmillan.wordpress. com/2012/05/25/three-deadly-sins-of-creative-scotlands-bad-funding-review-column-25-5-12/> (accessed on 14 November 2018).

21    'No Stooshie – but is the Scottish funding fall-out really over?', *The Stage*, 20 November 2014.

22    Tomlin, *British Theatre Companies*, p. 52.

23    Ibid.

24    Creative Scotland, 'Regular Funding Network 2018–21', online at <https://www. creativescotland.com/funding/latest-information/ funded-organisations/regular-funding-2018-21/ regular-funding-2018-21-info-sheet> (accessed on 14 November 2018).

25    'Creative Scotland reverses funding decisions following outcry', *The Stage*, 6 February 2018, online at <https://www.thestage.co.uk/ news/2018/creative-scotland/> (accessed on 14 November 2018); 'Big Losers but Arts funding avoids 'cultural carnage', BBC News, 25 January 2018, <https://www.bbc.co.uk/news/uk-scotland-42816509> (accessed on 14 November 2018).

26    'Arts Council calls halt to new English galleries', *The Guardian*, 1 November 2011, online at <https://www.theguardian.com/culture/2011/ nov/01/arts-council-england-galleries> (accessed on 7 December 2018).

27    'Arts Council England limits access to capital grants', *ArtsProfessional*, 6 April 2018, online at <https://www.artsprofessional.co.uk/news/arts-council-england-limits-access-capital-grants-0> (accessed on 7 December 2018).

28    Culture, Media and Sport Select Committee, 'Funding of the Arts and Heritage', 2011, para. 74, online at <https://publications.parliament. uk/pa/cm201011/cmselect/cmcumeds/464/46405. htm#a7> (accessed on 14 November 2018).

29    Ibid., para. 75.

30    Ibid.

31    Culture, Media and Sport Select Committee, 'Work of the Arts Council', 2014, Audience Agency submission, para. 5.3, online at <http://data. parliament.uk/writtenevidence/committeeevidence. svc/evidencedocument/culture-media-and-sport-committee/work-of-the-arts-council-england/ written/6424.pdf> (accessed on 14 November 2018).

32    Mhora Samuel, 'Looking Ahead to Thriving Theatres', *Theatres Magazine* 35 (Spring 2013), pp. 7–8 (p. 8).

33    ACE, 'Funding Arts and Culture in a Time of Austerity', 2016, p. 9, online at <https://www. artscouncil.org.uk/publication/funding-arts-and-culture-time-austerity> (accessed on 14 November 2018).

34    Ibid., p. 12.

35    Scottish Cultural Enterprise, 'Creative Scotland Theatre Review Digest of Statistics', p. 5, online at <https://www.creativescotland.com/__ data/assets/pdf_file/0004/21469/Theatre-Review-Digest-of-Statistics.pdf> (accessed on 7 December 2018).

36    'Local authority arts funding – what should be done?', *ArtsProfessional*, 2017, online at <https:// www.artsprofessional.co.uk/pulse/survey-report/ pulse-report-local-authority-arts-funding-what-should-be-done> (accessed on 14 November 2018).

37    E.g. 'Statement on Cardiff Council's proposed budget cut to the arts', Chapter Arts, online at <https://www.chapter.org/news-noise/ news/statement-cardiff-councils-proposed-budget-cut-arts> (accessed on 16 November 2018).

38    ACE, 'Funding Arts and Culture in a Time of Austerity', p. 16.

39    'Wrexham Theatre turns to £50k crowdfunding campaign in face of funding cuts', *The Stage*, 4 September 2015, online at <http:// www.thestage.co.uk/news/2015/wrexham-theatre-turns-50k-crowdfunding-campaign-face-funding-cuts> (accessed on 16 November 2018).

40    'In the news', *Theatres Magazine* 54 (Spring 2018), p. 28.

41    The Theatres Trust, written evidence to the Culture, Media and Sport Select Committee, 2014, para. 33, online at <http://data.parliament. uk/writtenevidence/committeeevidence.svc/ evidencedocument/culture-media-and-sport-

committee/work-of-the-arts-council-england/ written/6490.pdf.> (accessed on 9 December 2018).

42    'Why a Council pulled the plug on a £17m Arts Centre', *ArtsProfessional*, 26 October 2017, online at <https://www.artsprofessional.co.uk/ magazine/article/why-council-pulled-plug-ps17m-arts-centre> (accessed on 13 November 2018).

43    Claire Appleby, 'Theatres of Opportunity', *Theatres Magazine* 54 (Winter/Spring 2018), pp. 1–3 (p. 2).

44    Ibid.

45    'Local authority arts funding', *ArtsProfessional*, online.

46    Graham Lister, 'Doing a Chester', *Theatres Magazine* 36 (Summer 2013), pp. 21–2 (p. 22).

47    'Q&A with Cultural Champions Waltham Forest Council', *Theatres Magazine* 55 (Summer 2018), pp. 20–21 (p. 20).

48    The Theatres Trust, 'Thriving Theatres', 2013 conference report, p. 11; Colin Marr, 'Eden Court', *Theatres Magazine* 16 (Summer 2008), pp. 11–12 (p. 12).

49    National Planning Policy Framework, 2012, para. 7, online at <https://www.gov.uk/guidance/ national-planning-policy-framework/achieving-sustainable-development> (accessed on 25 November 2018).

### 3    Ten Years of Theatre Architecture

1    OMA, Factory Design and Access Statement, October 2016, p. 10.

2    Ibid., p. 7.

3    Ibid., p. 11.

4    'The Factory Manchester: Cost of arts venue rises £20m', BBC News, online at <https://www.bbc. co.uk/news/uk-england-manchester-46076539> (accessed on 7 December 2018).

5    Piccadilly Liberal Democrats, online at <https://twitter.com/PiccLibDems/ status/1067747199130300417> (accessed on 28 November 2018); '"Embarrassed" council leader admits he has considered scrapping Factory arts centre project as costs surge to £130m', *Manchester Evening News*, 9 November 2018.

6    Iain Mackintosh, *Architecture, Actor and Audience* (London, 1993), pp. 95–6.

7    Ian Timms, interviewed on 16 March 2018; Vanessa Lefrancois, interviewed on 26 April 2018.

8    Hawkins\Brown Architects website, 'Corby Cube\A Town Hall for the 21st Century', online at <https://www.hawkinsbrown.com/projects/corby-cube> (accessed on 27 November 2018).

9    Mark Foley, 'Marlowe Theatre, Canterbury', *Theatres Magazine* 30 (Winter 2011), pp. 13–16.

10    Ibid.; Keith Williams, *Keith Williams: Architecture of the Specific* (Mulgrave, 2010), pp. 167–73.

11    Aedas Arts Team, online at <https://www. aedas.com/en/what-we-do/architecture/art-and-leisure/aylesbury-waterside-theatre> (accessed on 3 November 2018).

12    Wright and Wright Architects, 'Hull Truck Theatre', online at <http://www.wrightandwright. co.uk/projects/culture/hull-truck-theatre> (accessed on 26 November 2018).

13    John Godber, 'Hull's New Truck', *Theatres Magazine* 21 (Autumn 2009), pp. 14–17.

14    Stephen Kennett, 'How Cool is That? Hull Truck's Passive-Ventilated Venue', *Building*, 9 April 2009, online at <http://www.building.co.uk> (accessed on 26 November 2018).

15    Thom Dibdin, 'Scotland – a Nation of Theatres', *Theatres Magazine* 38 (Winter 2013), pp. 2–5.

16    RIAS Awards 2013, online at <http://www. rias.org.uk/awards/rias-awards-2013/> (accessed on 28 November 2018).

17    'Theatres Round Up', *Theatres Magazine* 24 (Summer 2010), p. 22; 'Lyric Theatre, Belfast', *Theatres Magazine* 29 (Autumn 2011), pp. 13–16.

18    'The MAC, Belfast', *Theatres Magazine* 32 (Summer 2012), pp. 13–16.

19    'Manchester's £25m Home is a sorely missed opportunity', *The Guardian*, 15 May 2015, online at <https://www.theguardian.com/artanddesign/2015/ may/15/manchesters-25m-home-sorely-missed-architectural-opportunity> (accessed on 5 December 2018).

20    Ibid.

21    Tim Foster, interviewed on 18 April 2018.

22    'Step inside NST City, Southampton's flexible new venue for performing arts', *The Stage*, 13 February 2018, online at <https://www. thestage.co.uk/features/2018/step-inside-nst-city-

southamptons-flexible-new-venue-for-performing-arts/> (accessed on 7 December 2018).

23   'Studio 144: why has Southampton hidden its £30m culture palace behind a Nando's?' *The Guardian*, 22 February 2018, online at <https://www.theguardian.com/artanddesign/2018/feb/22/studio-144-southampton-new-arts-venue> (accessed on 3 December 2018).

24   Ibid.

25   'Step inside NST City', *The Stage*, online.

26   'Studio 144', *The Guardian*, online.

27   'The Shadow Factory review – Howard Brenton's bolshy drama declares war', *The Guardian*, 16 February 2018, online at <https://www.theguardian.com/stage/2018/feb/16/shadow-factory-review-nst-city-southampton-howard-brenton> (accessed on 3 December 2018).

28   Theatres Trust database, online at <https://database.theatrestrust.org.uk/resources/theatres/show/3093-peacock-theatre-royalty> (accessed on 28 November 2018).

29   Theatres Trust, 'Thriving Theatres', 2013 conference report, p. 16.

30   Foster, interviewed on 18 April 2018.

31   'More than £550m needed over the next five years for capital projects', Theatres Trust, online at <http://www.theatrestrust.org.uk/latest/news/730-more-than-550m-needed-over-the-next-five-years-for-capital-projects> (accessed on 28 November 2018).

32   'Investing in our Theatres', *Theatres Magazine* 38 (Winter 2013), p. 1.

33   'Maintaining and Modernizing Historic Theatres', *Theatres Magazine* 40 (Summer 2014), pp. 3–5.

34   'Bringing the West End up to Scratch', *Theatres Magazine* 19 (Spring 2009), pp. 2–5; 'Victoria Palace Theatre Reimagination', *Theatres Magazine* 56 (Autumn 2018), pp. 11–16; 'Shaftesbury Theatre, London', *Theatres Magazine* 47 (Spring 2016), pp. 13–18.

35   Tim Ronalds Architects, Wilton's Music Hall, online at <http://www.timronalds.co.uk/projects-wiltons.html> (accessed on 30 November 2018).

36   Rory Olcayto, 'Chapter Arts Centre', *Architects' Journal*, 11 March 2010, online at <https://www.architectsjournal.co.uk/home/chapter-arts-centre-cardiff-by-ash-sakula-architects/5215220.article> (accessed on 28 November 2018).

37   'Royal Shakespeare Theatre: All's well …', *The Guardian*, 23 November 2011, online at <https://www.theguardian.com/artanddesign/2010/nov/23/royal-shakespeare-theatre-revamp> (accessed on 2 September 2018).

38   For an overview, see Alistair Fair, 'Stage Set', *Architecture Today* 292 (October 2018), pp. 36–45.

39   National Heritage List for England, online at <http://historicengland.org.uk/listing/the-list> (accessed on 30 November 2018): Chichester Festival Theatre (Grade II*); Christ's Hospital Arts Centre (II*); Congress, Eastbourne (II*); Gardner Arts Centre, Brighton (II*); National Theatre (II*); Nottingham Playhouse (II*); Barbican Arts Centre, London (II); Belgrade, Coventry (II); Billingham Forum (II); Crucible, Sheffield (II); Gulbenkian Centre, Hull (II); Plymouth Theatre Royal (II); Thorndike Theatre, Leatherhead (II); and the Yvonne Arnaud Theatre, Guildford (II). The listing of York Theatre Royal (II*) includes the 1967 foyer extensions; Liverpool Playhouse is also listed (II*). In Wales, Theatr Ardudwy/Harlech is listed (II*); in Scotland, Eden Court is a Category 'A' listed building.

40   'Birmingham Rep reopens after revamp', BBC News, 3 September 2013, online at <https://www.bbc.co.uk/news/uk-england-birmingham-23946636> (accessed on 30 November 2018).

41   Ibid.

42   'Sherman Cymru', *Theatres Magazine* 31 (Spring 2012), pp. 13–16.

43   'Lyric Hammersmith', *Theatres Magazine* 45 (Autumn 2015), pp. 13–16.

44   'Haworth Tompkins completes Chichester Theatre revamp', *Architects' Journal*, 22 July 2014, online at <https://www.architectsjournal.co.uk/news/haworth-tompkins-completes-chichester-theatre-revamp/8665974.article> (accessed on 30 November 2018).

45   For a full description, see Alistair Fair, 'Light-hearted Pavilion', *C20 Magazine* 2016/3, pp. 16–17.

46   'Pitlochry Festival Theatre awarded £10m towards redevelopment', *The Stage*, 23 November 2018, online at <https://www.thestage.co.uk/news/2018/pitlochry-festival-theatre-10m-redevelopment/> (accessed on 30 November 2018).

47   Merlin Fulcher, 'Haworth Tompkins' Battersea Arts Centre overhaul plans revealed',

*Architects' Journal*, 20 June 2013, online at <https://www.architectsjournal.co.uk/home/haworth-tompkins-battersea-arts-centre-overhaul-plans-revealed/8649574.article> (accessed on 30 November 2018).

48  Steve Tompkins, 'Finding Space', *Theatres Magazine* 28 (Summer 2011) pp. 6–9.

49  The Theatres Trust, 'Converting Spaces – Creating Theatres', 2011 conference report, p. 16.

50  Ibid.

51  Merlin Fulcher, 'Immersive Architecture: Battersea Arts Centre by Haworth Tompkins', *Architects' Journal*, 21 November 2018, online at <https://www.architectsjournal.co.uk/story.aspx?storyCode=10037349> (accessed on 30 November 2018).

52  Ibid.

53  Ibid.

54  Kully Thiarai, 'Thinking Outside the Box', *Theatres Magazine* 12 (Summer 2007), pp. 6–7.

55  'Studio 144', *The Guardian*, online.

56  Alex Clifton, interviewed on 15 December 2017.

57  UK Theatre, 2017 Sales Data Report, online at <https://uktheatre.org/theatre-industry/guidance-reports-and-resources/sales-data-reports/> (accessed on 30 November 2018).

58  Ibid.

59  NT Live, online at <http://ntlive.nationaltheatre.org.uk/about-us> (accessed on 30 November 2018).

## Everyman Theatre, Liverpool

1  'Stirling Prize 2014: Liverpool Everyman Theatre – the architect', BBC News, online at <https://www.bbc.co.uk/news/av/magazine-29514594/stirling-prize-2014-liverpool-everyman-theatre-the-architect> (accessed on 7 October 2018).

2  'Steve Tompkins: A theatre should behave like a good host', *The Observer*, 16 October 2016, online at <https://www.theguardian.com/stage/2016/oct/16/steve-tompkins-architect-haworth-tompkins-q-and-a-national-theatre-liverpool-everyman> (accessed on 9 October 2018).

3  'Magical Mystery Tour', *RIBA Journal* 121, no. 4 (April 2014), pp. 19–25 (p. 22).

4  George Rowell and Anthony Jackson, *The Repertory Movement: A History of Regional Theatre in Britain* (Cambridge, 1984), p. 165.

5  John Elsom, *Theatre Outside London* (London, 1971), p. 206.

6  Rowell and Jackson, *Repertory Movement*, pp. 157–65.

7  'Liverpool Everyman', *Theatres Magazine* 40 (Summer 2014), pp. 13–16 (p. 13).

8  Elsom, *Theatre Outside London*, p. 206.

9  Rowell and Jackson, *Repertory Movement*, p. 163.

10  'Liverpool Everyman' [2014], p. 13.

11  For more on the Playhouse, see Alistair Fair, *Modern Playhouses: An Architectural History of Britain's New Theatres, 1945–1985* (Oxford, 2018), pp. 251–2.

12  Robert Longthorne, interviewed on 21 May 2018.

13  Ibid.; Deborah Aydon, interviewed on 9 July 2018.

14  'Liverpool Everyman' [2014], p. 13.

15  Longthorne, interviewed on 21 May 2018.

16  Ibid.

17  Aydon, interviewed on 9 July 2018.

18  Ibid.

19  Haworth Tompkins [hereafter 'HT'], Everyman Stage C report (2010), p. 16.

20  Steve Tompkins, interviewed on 19 April 2018.

21  'Liverpool Everyman' [2014], p. 14.

22  Aydon, interviewed on 9 July 2018.

23  HT, Stage C report, p. 15.

24  'Future Secured for Haworth Tompkins' Liverpool Everyman Theatre Revamp', *Building Design*, 5 April 2011, online at <https://www.bdonline.co.uk/news/future-secured-for-haworth-tompkins-liverpool-everyman-theatre-revamp-/5016220.article> (accessed on 8 October 2018).

25  HT, LMTT Feasibility Study Design Report, March 2008, p. 4.

26  Aydon, interviewed on 9 July 2018.

27  'Liverpool Everyman', *Theatres Magazine* 26 (Winter 2010), pp. 13–16 (p. 16).

28  HT, LMTT Feasibility Study Design Report, p. 4.

29  Ibid., p. 8.

30  Ibid., p. 8.

31   Ibid., p. 12.
32   HT, Stage C report, p. 8.
33   HT, LMTT Feasibility Study Design Report, p. 8.
34   'Tompkins on the Everyman Theatre', *Architects' Journal*, 10 October 2014, online at <https://search-proquest-com.ezproxy.is.ed.ac.uk/docview/1609632341> (accessed on 10 October 2018).
35   HT, Stage C report, p. 16.
36   Ibid., p. 6.
37   HT, LMTT Feasibility Study Design Report, p. 8
38   HT, Stage C report, p. 11.
39   'Liverpool Everyman' [2014], p. 14.
40   'Tompkins on the Everyman Theatre', *Architects' Journal*, online.
41   'Steve Tompkins […] good host', *The Observer*, online.
42   Juliet Rufford, 'Haworth Tompkins' Young Vic Theatre: Remembering the Blitz … and Beyond', *Contemporary Theatre Review* 18, no. 2 (2008), pp. 161–79.
43   '"Like something from Pompeii" – Battersea Arts Centre's scorching resurrection', *The Guardian*, 6 September 2018, online at <https://www.theguardian.com/artanddesign/2018/sep/06/like-something-from-pompeii-battersea-arts-centre-scorching-resurrection> (accessed on 10 October 2018).
44   Quoted in Rufford, 'Haworth Tompkins', p. 163.
45   Steve Tompkins and Andrew Todd, 'The Unfinished Theatre', *Architectural Review*, July 2007, online at <http://www.studioandrewtodd.com/repository/publications/pdf/The-Unfinished-The-d89ae0e8.pdf> (accessed on 23 November 2018).
46   Ibid.
47   Daniel Rosenthal, *The National Theatre Story* (London, 2013), pp. 156–65; Geraint Franklin, *HKPA* (Swindon, 2017), pp. 132–7.
48   Rufford, 'Haworth Tompkins' Young Vic', pp. 176–78.
49   See e.g. Allegra Galvin, 'Playgrounding: Developments in Contemporary Theatre Practice Informing the Design and Delivery of Capital Projects', MPhil dissertation, University of Cambridge, 2009.
50   Steve Tompkins and Roger Watts, interviewed on 19 April 2018.
51   Ibid.
52   Ibid.
53   'Tompkins on the Everyman', *Architects' Journal*, online.
54   Ibid.
55   HT, LMTT Feasibility Study Design Report, p. 36.
56   'Liverpool Everyman', p. 15.
57   'Stirling interview: "The Everyman Theatre is Quite Gobby"', *Architects' Journal*, 23 October 2014, online at <https://search-proquest-com.ezproxy.is.ed.ac.uk/docview/1615406939> (accessed on 10 October 2018).
58   'Steve Tompkins: […] good host', *The Observer*, online.
59   Ibid.
60   Longthorne, interviewed on 21 May 2018.
61   Ibid.
62   Tompkins and Watts, interviewed on 19 April 2018.
63   'Steve Tompkins: […] good host', *The Observer*, online.
64   Longthorne, interviewed on 21 May 2018.
65   Aydon, interviewed on 9 July 2018.
66   Ibid.
67   Roderick Ham, *Theatre Planning* (London, 1972), pp. 235–6.
68   'Magical Mystery Tour', p. 22.
69   This description of the system draws on Andy Pearson, 'Leading Man – the environmental strategy at Liverpool's Everyman Theatre', *CIBSE Journal*, February 2015, online at <https://www.cibsejournal.com/case-studies/leading-man/> (accessed on 10 October 2018).
70   E.g. C.A. Short, Malcolm Cook, and Kevin J. Lomas, 'Delivery and Performance of a Low-Energy Ventilation and Cooling Strategy', *Building Research and Information* 37, no. 1 (2009), pp. 1–30.
71   Longthorne, interviewed on 21 May 2018.
72   Liverpool and Merseyside Theatres Trust, Annual Report 2014–15, p. 8, online at <http://apps.charitycommission.gov.uk/Accounts/Ends29/0001081229_AC_20150331_E_C.PDF> (accessed on 10 October 2018).
73   Ibid., p. 4.
74   Liverpool and Merseyside Theatres Trust, Annual Report 2015–16, p. 10, online at <http://

apps.charitycommission.gov.uk/Accounts/
Ends29/0001081229_AC_20160331_E_C.PDF>
(accessed on 10 October 2018).

75   'Everyman Theatre Gets Resident Company
of Actors', BBC News, 20 April 2016, online at
<https://www.bbc.co.uk/news/entertainment-
arts-36090310> (accessed on 10 October 2018).

76   'Stirling interview: "The Everyman Theatre is
Quite Gobby"', Architects' Journal, online.

77   Ibid.

78   Ibid.

### Cast, Doncaster

1   'Doncaster Cast', Theatres 38 (Winter 2013),
pp. 13–16 (p. 13).

2   Ibid.

3   'Doncaster council to be stripped of
children's services', BBC News, 16 July 2013, online
at <https://www.bbc.co.uk/news/uk-england-south-
yorkshire-23324587> (accessed on 1 October 2018).

4   'Doncaster's new £22m venue Cast opens',
The Stage, 9 September 2013, online at <https://www.
thestage.co.uk/news/2013/doncasters-new-22m-
venue-cast-opens/> (accessed on 11 December 2018).

5   'Doncaster Civic Centre', Architectural
Review 120 (August 1956), pp. 121–2.

6   Johanna Roethe, '"A Pretty Toy" or "Purely
Functional"? Town, City, and County Halls in the
Interwar Period', in The Architecture of Public Service:
Twentieth Century Architecture 13, ed. Elain Harwood
and Alan Powers (London, 2018), pp. 25–40.

7   Christine Hui Lan Manley, Frederick Gibberd
(Swindon, 2017), pp. 131, 141.

8   'Law Courts Doncaster', Architectural Review
146 (December 1969), pp. 420–25.

9   'Those Were The Days', Doncaster Free
Press, 8 June 2015, online at <https://www.
doncasterfreepress.co.uk/lifestyle/nostalgia/
those-were-the-days-when-the-show-couldn-t-go-
on-1-7298461> (accessed on 11 August 2018).

10   Theatres Trust database, online at <https://
database.theatretrust.org.uk/resources/theatres/
show/1145-1145> (accessed on 11 August 2018).

11   E.g. Billingham: Alistair Fair, Modern
Playhouses: An Architectural History of Britain's New
Theatres, 1945–1985 (Oxford, 2018), pp. 26, 62.

12   Ibid., pp. 99, 174, 176.

13   News, Architects' Journal, 8 February 2001,
p. 12.

14   Doncaster Metropolitan Borough Council
[hereafter 'DMBC'], Cabinet Papers 20 February
2008, 'Doncaster's Civic and Cultural Quarter',
section 6.

15   Ibid., section 4.

16   Ibid., section 3.

17   Ibid., section 32.

18   Clare Clarkson, interviewed on 16 November
2017.

19   Arts Team, Design and Access Statement,
section 1.1.

20   Ibid., section 3.2.

21   DMBC, Cabinet Papers 20 February 2008,
'Doncaster's Civic and Cultural Quarter', section 3.

22   Arts Team, Design and Access Statement,
section 2.2.

23   DMBC, Cabinet Minutes, 16 June 2010,
Civic and Cultural Quarter Update, para. 10.

24   Arts Team, Design and Access Statement,
section 3.1.

25   'Mayor Reluctantly Starts Phase One of
£300 million Plan', Doncaster Free Press, 3 July
2009, online at <https://www.doncasterfreepress.
co.uk/news/mayor-reluctantly-starts-phase-one-
of-163-300-million-plan-1-524309> (accessed on 17
August 2018).

26   'This is an important milestone for
Doncaster's new venue which is changing the
skyline in Waterdale and helping to rejuvenate this
part of town. You can now visualise its performance
spaces which will make it another major attraction
for our residents and visitors to the town to enjoy.'
See 'Doncaster's New Venue is the Tops', October
2012, online at <https://www.musedevelopments.
com/news/doncaster's-new-venue-tops> (accessed
on 17 August 2018).

27   Clarkson, interviewed on 16 November 2017.

28   Arts Team, New Performance Venue Stage
B report, 2009, section 1.1.

29   Ibid.

30   Arts Team, New Performance Venue
Stage C report.

31   Arts Council England, Doncaster NPV
Architectural Assessment, 11 November 2009.

32   Arts Team, Design and Access Statement,
section 5.1.

33   Ibid., section 4.0.

34   Ibid.

35   'Busy Buildings', *ArtsProfessional*, <https://www.artsprofessional.co.uk/magazine/279/feature/busy-buildings> (accessed on 14 August 2018).

36   Arts Team, Design and Access Statement, section 3.3.

37   Sigfried Giedion, 'Social Imagination', in his *Architecture, You, and Me: The Diary of a Development* (Cambridge, MA, 1958), pp. 157–77 (p. 165).

38   Julian Middleton, interviewed on 12 December 2017.

39   'Doncaster Cast', p. 15.

40   Clarkson, interviewed on 16 November 2017.

41   Doncaster Performance Venue Ltd., Annual Report, 31 March 2013, p. 4, online at <https://apps.charitycommission.gov.uk> (accessed on 11 December 2018).

42   DMBC, Cabinet Minutes, 5 November 2008, 'Options for the Future Management of Leisure and Culture Facilities in Doncaster'.

43   Doncaster Performance Venue Ltd., Annual Report, 31 March 2014, p. 7, online at <https://apps.charitycommission.gov.uk> (accessed on 11 December 2018).

44   Kully Thiarai, interviewed on 1 October 2018.

45   Doncaster Performance Venue Ltd., Annual Report, 31 March 2014, pp. 6–7, online at <https://apps.charitycommission.gov.uk> (accessed on 11 December 2018).

46   Thiarai, interviewed on 1 October 2018.

47   Doncaster Performance Venue Ltd., Annual Report, 31 March 2014, p. 7, online at <https://apps.charitycommission.gov.uk> (accessed on 11 December 2018).

48   Ibid.

49   Ibid.

50   Clarkson, interviewed on 16 November 2017.

51   Thiarai, interviewed on 1 October 2018.

52   Ibid.

53   Ibid.

54   Ibid.; Clarkson, interviewed on 16 November 2017.

55   Thiarai, interviewed on 1 October 2018.

56   Ibid.

57   Doncaster Performance Venue Ltd., Annual Report, 31 March 2014, p. 7, online at <https://apps.charitycommission.gov.uk> (accessed on 11 December 2018).

58   Ibid.

59   Ibid.; Clarkson, interviewed on 16 November 2017.

60   Doncaster Performance Venue Ltd., Annual Report, 31 March 2015, p. 6, online at <https://apps.charitycommission.gov.uk> (accessed on 11 December 2018).

61   Doncaster Performance Venue Ltd., Annual Report, 31 March 2015, p. 4, online at <https://apps.charitycommission.gov.uk> (accessed on 11 December 2018).

62   Doncaster Performance Venue Ltd., Annual Report, 31 March 2017, p. 4, online at <https://apps.charitycommission.gov.uk> (accessed on 11 December 2018).

63   Thiarai, interviewed on 1 October 2018.

64   Mark Brown, 'Doncaster Stages Bold Revival of the Arts with Cultural "Living Room"', *The Guardian*, 1 January 2014, online at <https://www.theguardian.com/uk-news/2014/jan/01/doncaster-arts-revival-cast-theatre-venue> (accessed on 2 October 2018).

65   Ibid.

66   'Putting the Cast in Doncaster', *The Stage*, 9 September 2013, online at <https://www.thestage.co.uk/opinion/2013/putting-cast-doncaster/> (accessed on 11 December 2018).

67   Ibid.

## Storyhouse, Chester

1   Following an unsuccessful Heritage Lottery Fund bid, the local authority contribution increased from an initial £29.5 million to £32.5 million to make up the shortfall. Cheshire West and Chester Council [hereafter 'CW&C'], 'Internal Audit Report: Review of Governance and Project Management Arrangements for the Delivery of Storyhouse', 13 July 2018, p. 7 (copy supplied by Graham Lister).

2   'Chester Gateway: A creation for theatre and social life', *The Stage*, 28 November 1968, pp. 18–19.

3   Kate Dorney and Ros Merkin, 'Introduction', in *The Glory of the Garden: English Regional Theatre and the Arts Council, 1984–2009*, ed. Kate Dorney and Ros Merkin (Newcastle-upon-Tyne, 2010), pp. 1–14 (p. 10); Alex Clifton, interviewed on 15 December 2017.

4   Clifton, interviewed on 15 December 2017.

5   Gary Young, interviewed on 2 November 2017.

6   'Eyesore to be demolished for theatre work to begin', *Chester Chronicle*, 8 August 2013, online at <https://www.chesterchronicle.co.uk/news/chester-cheshire-news/commerce-house-demolished-make-room-5678340> (accessed on 2 September 2018).

7   Bennetts Associates, Chester Theatre and Library Stage B Design Report, 2012, p. 7.

8   Ibid., p. 2.

9   Graham Lister, 'Storyhouse', *Theatres Magazine* 51 (Spring 2017), pp. 11–16 (p. 12)

10   Grahame Morris, interviewed on 9 November 2018.

11   Ibid.

12   CW&C, 'Audit', p. 5.

13   Morris, interviewed on 9 November 2018.

14   Lister, 'Storyhouse', p. 16

15   CW&C, 'Audit', p. 5.

16   Morris, interviewed on 9 November 2018.

17   Louise Gittins, interviewed on 21 December 2017.

18   Ibid.

19   Lister, 'Storyhouse', p. 13.

20   'Chester Theatre and Library – Outline Brief', September 2013. Copy supplied by Graham Lister.

21   Ibid.

22   Ibid.

23   Lister, 'Storyhouse', p. 15.

24   Ibid., p. 12.

25   'Alex Clifton Becomes Chester Performs Artistic Director', *Cheshire Live*, 26 May 2015/1 June 2015, online at <http://www.cheshire-live.co.uk/whats-on/alex-clifton-becomes-chester-performs-9335559> (accessed on 7 November 2018).

26   Chester Performing Arts Centre annual report, 2015–16, p. 2, online at <http://apps.charitycommission.gov.uk/Accounts/Ends07/0001121007_AC_20160331_E_C.PDF> (accessed on 29 August 2018).

27   CW&C, 'One City Plan', online at <http://chester.westcheshiregrowth.co.uk/wp-content/uploads/sites/2/2015/12/Chester-One-City-Plan-2012-20127-PDF-8.1MB.pdf> (accessed on 27 August 2018).

28   Bennetts, Stage B report, p. 3.

29   Ibid., p. 13.

30   Simon Erridge, interviewed on 1 November 2017.

31   Bennetts, Stage B report, p. 3.

32   Ibid., p. 15.

33   Bennetts, Stage B report, p. 3.

34   Young, interviewed on 2 November 2017.

35   Ibid.

36   Bennetts, Stage B report, pp. 35–61.

37   CW&C, 'Audit', p. 6.

38   Bennetts Associates, 'RE:New, Chester's Cultural Centre', Stage C Design Summary, March 2014, p. iv.

39   'A New Chapter for Chester', *Architects' Journal*, 26 May 2017, online at <https://www.architectsjournal.co.uk/buildings/a-new-chapter-for-chester-bennetts-storyhouse/10020236.article> (accessed on 4 November 2018).

40   CW&C, 'Audit', p. 6.

41   Erridge, interviewed on 1 November 2017.

42   Denys Lasdun, 'Humanising the Institution', *Architectural Review* 161 (January 1977), pp. 25–6 (p. 25).

43   Iain Mackintosh, 'Rediscovering the Courtyard', *Architectural Review* 175 (April 1984), pp. 64–71.

44   Jane Hetherington, interviewed on 21 December 2017.

45   Ibid.

46   Young, interviewed on 2 November 2017.

47   Lister, pers. comm., 7 November 2018.

48   Erridge, interviewed on 1 November 2017.

49   Hetherington, interviewed on 21 December 2017.

50   Erridge, interviewed on 1 November 2017; Young, interviewed on 2 November 2017.

51   Lister, pers. comm., 7 November 2018.

52   Young, interviewed on 2 November 2017.

53   Ibid.

54   Hetherington, interviewed on 21 December 2017.

55   CW&C, 'Audit', p. 3.

56   Tripadvisor review: 'Library? What Library?', 29 May 2017, online at <https://www.tripadvisor.co.uk/ShowUserReviews-g186233-d12414981-r488754027-Storyhouse-Chester_Cheshire_England.html> (accessed on 1 September 2018)

57   'A New Chapter for Chester', *Architects' Journal*, online.

58   Tripadvisor review: 'Library? What Library?'
59   Morris, interviewed on 9 November 2018.
60   CW&C, 'Audit', p. 11.
61   Clifton, interviewed on 15 December 2017.
62   E.g. Young, interviewed on 2 November 2017.

**Tara Theatre, London**

1   'Tara for Now', *The Stage*, 18 May 2012, p. 44.
2   'How Tara Breathed New Life Into Its Home', *The Stage*, 27 October 2016, pp. 44–5.
3   Arts Team, Tara Theatre Stage D Design Report (2012), p. 72 (p. 60 on printed copy).
4   Arts Team, Tara Theatre Stage C Report (2012), p. 15.
5   Ibid.
6   Jatinder Verma and Claudia Mayer, interviewed on 16 August 2018.
7   Ibid.
8   Ibid.
9   Arts Team, Stage C Report, p. 14.
10   'Aedas Arts Team's "Endearingly Dotty" Transformation of the Tara Theatre', *Architects' Journal,* 14 September 2016, online at <http://www.architectsjournal.co.uk> (accessed on 16 October 2018).
11   Ibid.
12   Verma and Mayer, interviewed on 16 August 2018.
13   Arts Team, Stage C report.
14   Arts Team, Stage D Report, p. 36 (printed copy: p. 24).
15   '"Endearingly Dotty"', *Architects' Journal*, online.
16   Arts Team, Stage D Report, p. 20 (printed copy: p. 8).
17   Ibid.
18   Verma and Mayer, interviewed on 16 August 2018.
19   'How Tara Breathed New Life', pp. 44–5.
20   Ibid.
21   Ibid.
22   Ibid.
23   Ibid.
24   Ibid.
25   Verma and Mayer, interviewed on 16 August 2018.
26   Ibid.
27   Jatinder Verma, 'Tara Arts', *Theatres Magazine* 49 (Autumn 2016), pp. 9–14 (p. 12).
28   Ibid., p. 13.
29   Julian Middleton, interviewed on 24 October 2018.
30   Ibid.
31   Tara Theatre, Annual Report 2015–16, p. 4, online at <http://apps.charitycommission.gov.uk/Accounts/Ends47/0000295547_AC_20170331_E_C.PDF> (accessed on 17 October 2018).
32   Verma, 'Tara Arts', p. 13.
33   '"Endearingly Dotty"', *Architects' Journal*, online.
34   Verma and Mayer, interviewed on 16 August 2018.
35   Ibid.
36   Ibid.
37   Ibid.
38   Ibid.
39   Ibid.
40   Verma, 'Tara Arts', p. 14.
41   Verma and Mayer, interviewed on 16 August 2018.
42   Ibid.

**National Theatre, London: NT Future**

1   'A school without five minutes of arts can get a good Ofsted rating', *The Times*, 7 April 2018, online at <https://www.thetimes.co.uk/article/rufus-norris-interview-a-school-without-five-minutes-of-arts-can-get-a-good-ofsted-rating-sktrmxgnd> (accessed on 13 December 2018).
2   Denys Lasdun, 'Humanising the Institution', *Architectural Review* 161 (January 1977), pp. 25–6 (p. 25).
3   Quoted in William J.R. Curtis, *Denys Lasdun: Architecture, City, Landscape* (London, 1994), p. 154.
4   RIBA, LaD/167/1, Handwritten note by Denys Lasdun, n.d.
5   National Theatre, NT Future website, <http://ntfuture.nationaltheatre.org.uk/news/nt-future-–-story-so-far-0> (accessed on 28 September 2018).
6   Barnabas Calder, *Raw Concrete: The Beauty of Brutalism* (London, 2016), p. 278.

7 Elain Harwood, *Space, Hope and Brutalism: English Architecture 1945–1975* (New Haven, CT and London, 2015), p. 485.

8 Calder, *Raw Concrete*, pp. 280–83.

9 Harwood, *Space, Hope and Brutalism*, p. 491.

10 Ibid.; Barnabas Calder, 'Committees and Concrete: The Genesis and Architecture of Denys Lasdun's National Theatre' (PhD thesis, University of Cambridge, 2007), p. 24.

11 Calder, 'Committees and Concrete', pp. 41–62.

12 Calder, *Raw Concrete*, pp. 287–9; 294–6; Harwood, *Space, Hope and Brutalism*, p. 491.

13 Michael Elliott, 'On Not Building for Posterity', *Tabs* 31, no. 2 (1973), pp. 41–4.

14 Paddy Dillon, *Concrete Reality: Denys Lasdun and the National Theatre* (London, 2015), p. 77.

15 Calder, *Raw Concrete*, pp. 319–22.

16 Richard Eyre, *National Service: Diary of a Decade* (London, 2003), p. 53 (8 November 1988).

17 Dillon, *Concrete Reality*, p. 82.

18 E.g. Calder, 'Committees and Concrete', p. 9.

19 Nick Starr, interviewed on 18 April 2018.

20 Ibid.

21 Paddy Dillon, interviewed on 17 April 2018.

22 Starr, interviewed on 18 April 2018.

23 Dillon, interviewed on 17 April 2018; Anna Anderson and Paul Jozefowski, interviewed on 8 June 2018.

24 National Theatre, Annual Report and Financial Statements, 2013–14, p. 12, online at <https://www.nationaltheatre.org.uk/about-the-national-theatre/key-facts-and-figures/annual-reports> (accessed on 13 December 2018).

25 Ibid.

26 Starr, interviewed on 18 April 2018.

27 Quoted in Haworth Tompkins, National Theatre Conservation Management Plan (2007) [hereafter 'National Theatre CMP'], p. 60, online at <https://www.nationaltheatre.org.uk/sites/default/files/nt_conservation_plans_dec_08.pdf> (accessed on 13 December 2018).

28 Ibid., p. 61.

29 Ibid., p. 72.

30 Ibid., p. 262

31 National Theatre, Annual Review 2016–17, online at <https://review.nationaltheatre.org.uk/#2017/finance/31> (accessed on 5 November 2018).

32 National Theatre CMP, p. 82.

33 Ibid., p. 63.

34 Paddy Dillon, pers. comm., November 2018.

35 Starr, interviewed on 18 April 2018.

36 James Semple Kerr, *The Conservation Plan: A Guide to the Preparation of Conservation Plans for Places of European Cultural Significance* (Sydney, 1996).

37 'Jury is out on HLF's new conservation guidance', *Architects' Journal* 207 (2 April 1998), p. 24. The HLF required a Plan for projects of £500,000 in the late 1990s; by 2017, the threshold had risen to £2 million.

38 'National Theatre CMP', p. 10.

39 Ibid., p. 122.

40 Heritage Lottery Fund, 'Conservation Plan Guidance, September 2017', online at <http://www.hlf.org.uk> (accessed on 1 October 2018).

41 Dillon, interviewed on 17 April 2018; John Langley, interviewed on 18 June 2018.

42 Langley, interviewed on 18 June 2018.

43 Starr, interviewed on 18 April 2018.

44 Ibid.

45 Dillon, interviewed on 17 April 2018.

46 New London Architecture, 'Culture Triumphs: The National Theatre and BCA', 12 August 2015, online at <http://www.newlondonarchitecture.org/news/2015/august-2015/culture-triumphs-the-national-theatre-and-bca> (accessed on 4 November 2018).

47 Dillon, interviewed on 17 April 2018.

48 Calder, 'Committees and Concrete', p. 121.

49 'National Theatre CMP', p. 208.

50 'Creating the Dorfman', *Theatres Magazine* 42 (Winter 2014), pp. 2–4.

51 Ibid., p. 2.

52 Charcoalblue, Dorfman Theatre at the National Theatre, online at <http://www.charcoalblue.com> (accessed on 10 December 2018).

53 National Theatre, Annual Report and Financial Statements, 2013–14, p. 42, online at <http://d1wf8hd6ovssje.cloudfront.net/documents/National_Theatre_Annual_Report_and_Financial_Statements_2013-14_v2.pdf> (accessed on 14 December 2018).

54   Anderson and Jozefowski, interviewed on 8 June 2018.

55   Ibid.

56   Ibid.

57   Ibid.

58   Steve Tompkins and Andrew Todd, 'The Unfinished Theatre', *Architectural Review*, July 2007, online at <http://www.studioandrewtodd. com/repository/publications/pdf/The-Unfinished-The-d89ae0e8.pdf> (accessed on 23 November 2018).

59   'The Tortoise and the Hare', *Architects' Journal*, 20 June 2013, online at <https://www. architectsjournal.co.uk/buildings/the-tortoise-and-the-hare-the-shed-by-haworth-tompkins/8649497> (accessed on 22 November 2018).

60   'The Shed at the National Theatre Sheds its Name', BBC News, online at <http://www. bbc.co.uk/news/entertainment-arts-27339926> (accessed on 1 October 2018).

61   NT Future website, online at <http:// ntfuture.nationaltheatre.org.uk> (accessed on 1 October 2018).

62   Steve Tompkins and Roger Watts, interviewed on 19 April 2018; Dillon, interviewed on 16 April 2018.

63   Eyre, *National Service*, pp. 52–3.

64   National Theatre CMP, pp. 50–51.

65   Stephen Douglas, 'A Concrete Performance: Conservation at the National Theatre', *ICE Proceedings: Engineering History and Heritage* 169, no. 1 (2016), pp. 36–41.

66   Tompkins and Watts, interviewed on 19 April 2018.

67   Ibid.

68   Dillon, interviewed on 17 April 2018.

### Theatre Royal, Glasgow

1   Alex Reedijk, interviewed on 16 March 2018.

2   Page\Park, 'Scottish Opera Theatre Royal: A Feasibility Study', n.d., p. 24.

3   Theatres Trust database, online at <https:// database.theatrestrust.org.uk/resources/theatres/ show/2308-theatre-royal> (accessed on 19 October 2018).

4   For more on these projects, see Alistair Fair, '"An Object Lesson in How Not To Get Things Done": Edinburgh's Unbuilt "Opera House", 1960–75', *Architectural Heritage* 27, no. 1 (2017), pp. 91–117; Alistair Fair, *Modern Playhouses: An Architectural History of Britain's New Theatres, 1945–1985* (Oxford, 2018), pp. 118–22.

5   'Arup: Opera House', *Architectural Review* 159 (April 1976), pp. 202–207.

6   'From Conservation to Pastiche', *Architectural Review* 159 (April 1976), pp. 213–14.

7   Theatres Trust database, online at <https:// database.theatrestrust.org.uk/resources/theatres/ show/2308-theatre-royal> (accessed on 19 October 2018).

8   Page\Park, 'Theatre Royal: A Conservation Statement', March 2009, p. 5.

9   'From Conservation to Pastiche', p. 214.

10   Reedijk, interviewed on 16 March 2018.

11   Nicola Walls, interviewed on 16 March 2018.

12   'Scottish Opera Buys Land Next Door to Expand Front of House Facilities' *The Stage,* 15 October 2009, p. 5.

13   Reedijk, interviewed on 16 March 2018. A chimney was found, for example, in a place where a new door was to go.

14   Page\Park, Feasibility Study, p. 3.

15   Walls, interviewed on 16 March 2018.

16   Page\Park, Feasibility Study, p. 4.

17   Ibid.

18   Reedijk, interviewed on 16 March 2018; 'Theatre Royal, Glasgow', *Theatres Magazine* 43 (Summer 2015), pp. 13–16 (p. 13).

19   Page\Park, Feasibility Study, p. 5.

20   Ibid., p. 4.

21   Reedijk, interviewed on 16 March 2018.

22   Page\Park, Feasibility Study, p. 10.

23   Ibid., p. 4.

24   'Theatre Royal Glasgow by Page\Park Architects', *Architects' Journal*, 29 May 2015, online at <http://https://www.architectsjournal. co.uk/buildings/theatre-royal-by-page/park-architects/8683743.article> (accessed on 2 November 2018).

25   Page\Park, 'Scottish Opera Theatre Royal – Design Statement (Stage C)' (August 2011), p. 36.

26   Page\Park, Feasibility Study, p. 22.

27   Ibid.

28   Page\Park, 'A Weave of Exuberance and Sobriety', internal design document supplied by Nicola Walls.

29   Ibid.
30   Ibid.
31   Ibid., p. 5.
32   Ibid., pp. 23–5.
33   'Theatre Royal', p. 15.
34   Reedijk, interviewed on 16 March 2018.
35   Walls, interviewed on 16 March 2018.
36   Ibid.
37   'Theatre Royal', p. 16.
38   'Scottish Opera's £14m revamp of Theatre Royal is hit by new delay', *The Herald*, 26 September 2014, online at <https://www.heraldscotland.com/news/13181822.scottish-operas-14m-revamp-of-theatre-royal-is-hit-by-new-delay/> (accessed on 21 October 2018).
39   Ibid.
40   'Glasgow's Theatre Royal redevelopment suffers delays', *ArtsProfessional*, 7 March 2014, online at <https://www.artsprofessional.co.uk/news/newsreel/glasgows-theatre-royal-redevelopment-suffers-delays> (accessed on 21 October 2018).
41   Reedijk, interviewed on 16 March 2018.
42   'Theatre Royal by Page\Park', *Architects' Journal*, online; Ian Nairn, *Nairn's Towns*, intro. Owen Hatherley (London, 2013), p. 63.
43   Reedijk, interviewed on 16 March 2018.

**Perth Theatre**

1   'Richard Murphy's Perth Theatre Makes an Entrance', *Architects' Journal*, 9 May 2018, online at <www.architectsjournal.co.uk> (accessed on 24 October 2018).
2   For a comprehensive history of the building, see Simpson and Brown, 'Perth Theatre: Conservation Plan' (October 2008).
3   John Elsom, *Theatre Outside London* (London, 1971), p. 215.
4   Ibid.
5   Simpson and Brown, 'Perth Theatre: Conservation Plan', p. 62.
6   Ibid., pp. 62–9.
7   For more on 'Housing the Arts': Alistair Fair, *Modern Playhouses: An Architectural History of Britain's New Theatres, 1945–1985* (Oxford, 2018), pp. 27–44.
8   Bill Black, interviewed on 30 July 2018.
9   Ibid.
10   Peter Hood, interviewed on 20 July 2018.
11   Black, interviewed on 30 July 2018.
12   Ibid.
13   C. Alan Short, Peter Barrett, and Alistair Fair, *Geometry and Atmosphere: Theatre Building from Vision to Reality* (Farnham, 2011), p. 117.
14   Simpson and Brown, 'Perth Theatre: Conservation Plan'.
15   Hood, interviewed on 20 July 2018.
16   'Board members quit Perth as financial problems are revealed', *The Stage*, 7 November 2013, p. 4.
17   Richard Murphy Architects, 'Planning Application Design Statement: Transform Perth Theatre' (2015).
18   The following is based on the three Design Statements prepared by Richard Murphy Architects in 2010, 2013 and 2015, included in the applications to Perth and Kinross Council for planning consent.
19   Black, interviewed on 30 July 2018.
20   Ibid.; Richard Murphy Architects, 'Transform Perth Theatre: Planning Application Design Statement' (2013).
21   'Richard Murphy reworks Perth Theatre overhaul plans' *Architects' Journal*, 15 July 2013, online at <https://www.architectsjournal.co.uk/home/richard-murphy-reworks-perth-theatre-overhaul-plans/8650776.article> (accessed on 16 December 2018).
22   'Take three: Richard Murphy submits revised Perth Theatre plans', *Architects' Journal*, 7 August 2015, online at <https://www.architectsjournal.co.uk/home/richard-murphy-reworks-perth-theatre-overhaul-plans/8650776.article> (accessed on 16 December 2018).
23   Black, interviewed on 30 July 2018.
24   Ibid.
25   Hood, interviewed on 20 July 2018.
26   Black, interviewed on 30 July 2018.
27   'Richard Murphy's Perth Theatre', *Architects' Journal*, online.
28   Black, interviewed on 30 July 2018.
29   'Council agrees to foot bill for Perth Theatre after funding shortfall', *The Courier*, 4 December 2018, online at <https://www.thecourier.co.uk/fp/news/local/perth-kinross/556624/council-agrees-to-foot-bill-for-perth-theatre-after-funding-shortfall/> (accessed on 24 October 2018).

30    Black, interviewed on 30 July 2018.
31    Hood, interviewed on 20 July 2018.
32    Black, interviewed on 30 July 2018.


## Citizens Theatre, Glasgow

1    John R. Gold, *The Practice of Modernism: Modern Architects and Urban Transformation, 1954–1972* (Abingdon, 2007), p. 178.

2    Florian Urban, *The New Tenement: Residences in the Inner City since 1970* (Abingdon, 2017), pp. 124–30.

3    John Earl and Michael Sell (eds), *The Theatres Trust Guide to British Theatre 1750–1950: A Gazetteer* (London, 2000), pp. 66–7.

4    George Rowell and Anthony Jackson, *The Repertory Movement: A History of Regional Theatre in Britain* (Cambridge, 1984), pp. 139–46.

5    Ibid.

6    Ibid., p. 141.

7    Ibid., p. 142.

8    John Elsom, *Theatre Outside London* (London, 1971), pp. 196–7. For more on these projects, see Alistair Fair, *Modern Playhouses: An Architectural History of Britain's New Theatres, 1945–1985* (Oxford, 2018), pp. 118–22.

9    Earl and Sell (eds), *The Theatres Trust Guide*, p. 67.

10    Graham Sutherland, interviewed on 27 March 2018.

11    'Dominic Hill on Glasgow Citizens Theatre Redevelopment', *The Stage*, 8 May 2018, online at <https://www.thestage.co.uk/features/2018/dominic-hill-glasgow-citizens-theatre-redevelopment/> (accessed on 12 September 2018).

12    Ibid.

13    Sutherland, interviewed on 27 March 2018.

14    Ibid.

15    Judith Kilvington, interviewed on 27 March 2018.

16    Glasgow City Council, 'Support for the Citizens Theatre Redevelopment', report to the City Administration Committee, February 2018, online at <https://www.glasgow.gov.uk/councillorsandcommittees/submissiondocuments.asp?submissionid=87872> (accessed on 12 September 2018).

17    Bennetts Associates, Citizens Theatre Stage 3 report, p. 6.

18    Sutherland, interviewed on 27 March 2018.

19    HLF Press Releases: 'HLF helps lift the curtain on Citizens Theatre redevelopment', 11 June 2014, <https://www.hlf.org.uk/about-us/media-centre/press-releases/hlf-helps-lift-curtain-citizens-theatre-redevelopment>; 'Citizens Theatre Awarded £4.8million National Lottery support', 18 December 2017, <https://www.hlf.org.uk/about-us/media-centre/press-releases/citizens-theatre-awarded-£48million-national-lottery-support> (both accessed on 12 September 2018).

20    Sutherland, interviewed on 27 March 2018.

21    Ibid.; Scottish Government, 'Regeneration Capital Grant Fund', details of funded projects online at <https://beta.gov.scot/binaries/content/documents/govscot/publications/transparency-data/2017/05/regeneration-capital-grant-fund-supported-project-list/documents/26d38584-7eab-490b-9a6f-1ac14727119e/26d38584-7eab-490b-9a6f-1ac14727119e/govscot:document/> (accessed on 12 September 2018); '£20m Citizens Theatre revamp to get £2.5m cash boost', *Evening Times*, 20 March 2017, online at <https://www.eveningtimes.co.uk/news/15147180.20m-citizens-theatre-revamp-to-get-25m-cash-boost/> (accessed on 12 September 2018).

22    Kilvington, interviewed on 27 March 2018.

23    Glasgow City Council, 'Support for the Citizens Theatre Redevelopment', report to the City Administration Committee, February 2018, online at <https://www.glasgow.gov.uk/councillorsandcommittees/submissiondocuments.asp?submissionid=87872> (accessed on 12 September 2018).

24    'Glasgow Citizens secures an extra £1.8 million of funding as cost of redevelopment rises', *The Stage*, 8 March 2019, online at <https://www.thestage.co.uk/news/2019/glasgow-citizens-secures-1-8m-extra-funding-cost-redevelopment-rises/> (accessed on 8 March 2019).

25    Kilvington, interviewed on 27 March 2018.

26    Bennetts Associates, Response to Invitation to Tender, 2012; Citizens Theatre Design and Access Statement, 2017, p. 22; Phil Eccles and James Nelmes, interviewed on 7 March 2018.

27    Sutherland, interviewed on 27 March 2018.

28    Bennetts Associates, Citizens Theatre Stage 2 Report, pp. 9–12.

publishing.service.gov.uk/government/uploads/
system/uploads/attachment_data/file/510798/
DCMS_The_Culture_White_Paper__3_.pdf>
(accessed on 14 November 2018)

Doncaster Free Press, 'Those Were The Days',
8 June 2015, <https://www.doncasterfreepress.
co.uk/lifestyle/nostalgia/those-were-the-days-
when-the-show-couldn-t-go-on-1-7298461>
(accessed on 11 August 2018)

Glasgow City Council, committee papers, <https://
www.glasgow.gov.uk/councillorsand
committees/> (accessed on 16 December 2018)

Hawkins\Brown, 'Corby Cube\A Town Hall for the
21st Century' <https://www.hawkinsbrown.
com/projects/corby-cube> (accessed on 27
November 2018)

Haworth Tompkins, <http://www.haworthtompkins.
com/news/bridge-theatre-wins-two-awards>
(accessed on 13 October 2018)

Heritage Lottery Fund, 'Conservation Plan
Guidance, September 2017', <http://www.hlf.
org.uk> (accessed on 1 October 2018)

HM Treasury, 'Spending Review 2010', <https://www.
gov.uk/government/publications/spending-
review-2010> (accessed on 14 November 2018)

Leeds City Council, online committee papers,
<http://www.democracy.leeds.gov.uk>
(accessed on 10 March 2019)

[Manchester's Commission on the New Economy],
'Beyond the Arts: Economic and Wider Impacts
of The Lowry and its Programmes', 2013, <http://
www.thelowry.com/Downloads/reports/The_
Lowry_Beyond_the_Arts.pdf> (accessed on 9
January 2017)

McMillan, J., 'Three Deadly Sins of Scotland's
Bad Funding Review', 25 May 2012, <https://
joycemcmillan.wordpress.com/2012/05/25/
three-deadly-sins-of-creative-scotlands-bad-
funding-review-column-25-5-12/> (accessed on
14 November 2018)

MUSE, <https://www.musedevelopments.com/
news/doncaster's-new-venue-tops> (accessed
on 17 August 2018)

National Audit Office, <https://www.nao.org.uk/>
(accessed on 11 November 2018)

National Heritage List for England, <http://
historicengland.org.uk/listing/the-list>
(accessed on 30 November 2018)

National Planning Policy Framework, 2012, <https://
www.gov.uk/guidance/national-planning-policy-
framework/achieving-sustainable-development>
(accessed on 25 November 2018)

National Theatre, Annual Report and Financial
Statements, <https://www.nationaltheatre.
org.uk/about-the-national-theatre/key-facts-
and-figures/annual-reports> (accessed on 13
December 2018)

National Theatre, Conservation Management Plan,
<https://www.nationaltheatre.org.uk/sites/
default/files/nt_conservation_plans_dec_08.
pdf> (accessed on 13 December 2018)

New London Architecture, 'Culture Triumphs: The
National Theatre and BCA', 12 August 2015,
<http://www.newlondonarchitecture.org/
news/2015/august-2015/culture-triumphs-the-
national-theatre-and-bca> (accessed on
4 November 2018)

NT Future, <http://ntfuture.nationaltheatre.org.uk/
news/nt-future-–-story-so-far-0> (accessed on
28 September 2018)

NT Live, <http://ntlive.nationaltheatre.org.uk/about-
us> (accessed on 30 November 2018)

Royal Incorporation of Architects in Scotland,
<http://www.rias.org.uk/awards/rias-
awards-2013/> (accessed on 28 November 2018)

Scottish Cultural Enterprise, 'Creative Scotland
Theatre Review Digest of Statistics', <https://
www.creativescotland.com/__data/assets/
pdf_file/0004/21469/Theatre-Review-Digest-of-
Statistics.pdf> (accessed on 7 December 2018)

Scottish Government, 'Regeneration Capital Grant Fund', 2014/15, <https://beta.gov.scot/binaries/content/documents/govscot/publications/transparency-data/2017/05/regeneration-capital-grant-fund-supported-project-list/documents/26d38584-7eab-490b-9a6f-1ac14727119e/26d38584-7eab-490b-9a6f-1ac14727119e/govscot:document/> (accessed on 12 September 2018)

The Theatres Trust, <http://www.theatrestrust.org.uk> (accessed on 28 November 2018)

The Theatres Trust database, <https://database.theatrestrust.org.uk> (accessed on 28 November 2018)

Tim Ronalds Architects, Wilton's Music Hall, <http://www.timronalds.co.uk/projects-wiltons.html> (accessed on 30 November 2018)

Tripadvisor, 'Library? What Library', 29 May 2017, <https://www.tripadvisor.co.uk/ShowUserReviews-g186233-d12414981-r488754027-Storyhouse-Chester_Cheshire_England.html> (accessed on 1 September 2018)

Twitter, Piccadilly Liberal Democrats, <https://twitter.com/PiccLibDems/status/1067747199130300417> (accessed on 28 November 2018)

UK Theatre, 2017 Sales Data Report, <https://uktheatre.org/theatre-industry/guidance-reports-and-resources/sales-data-reports/> (accessed on 30 November 2018)

Welsh Arts Council, Annual Report and Financial Statements 2016–17, <http://www.arts.wales/c_annual-reports/report-and-financial-statements-2016-17> (accessed on 9 December 2018)

Wright and Wright Architects, 'Hull Truck Theatre', <http://www.wrightandwright.co.uk/projects/culture/hull-truck-theatre> (accessed on 26 November 2018)

# Index

References to black and white photographs and diagrams are in *italics*.

References to colour plates (pp. 49–64) are in **bold** and placed at the end of other references, preceded by the word '**Plate**'.